Francis L. M'Clintock

Fate of Sir John Franklin

The voyage of the 'Fox' in the Arctic seas in search of Franklin and his companions

Francis L. M'Clintock

Fate of Sir John Franklin

The voyage of the 'Fox' in the Arctic seas in search of Franklin and his companions

ISBN/EAN: 9783337323790

Printed in Europe, USA, Canada, Australia, Japan

Cover: Foto ©Andreas Hilbeck / pixelio.de

More available books at **www.hansebooks.com**

THE VOYAGE OF THE 'FOX'

IN THE

ARCTIC SEAS

IN SEARCH OF

FRANKLIN AND HIS COMPANIONS.

BY CAPT. SIR F. LEOPOLD M'CLINTOCK, R.N.,

A.D.C.; D.C.L. OXON.; LL.D. DUB. ET CANTAB.; F.R.S.; F.R.G.S.;
HON. MEMBER OF THE GEOGRAPHICAL AND STATISTICAL SOCIETY OF NEW YORK;
OF THE GEOGRAPHICAL SOCIETY OF BERLIN; AND OF THE ROYAL
DUBLIN SOCIETY; ETC. ETC. ETC.

THIRD EDITION, REVISED AND ENLARGED.

WITH MAPS AND ILLUSTRATIONS.

LONDON:
JOHN MURRAY, ALBEMARLE STREET,
PUBLISHER TO THE ADMIRALTY.

1869.

The right of Translation is reserved.

PRINTED BY WILLIAM CLOWES AND SONS, DUKE STREET, STAMFORD STREET,
AND CHARING CROSS.

DEDICATION.

My dear Lady Franklin,

There is no one to whom I could with so much propriety or willingness dedicate my Journal as to you. For you it was originally written, and to please you it now appears in print.

To our mutual friend, Sherard Osborn, I am greatly obliged for his kindness in seeing it through the press—a labour I could not have settled down to so soon after my return; and also for pointing out some omissions and technicalities which would have rendered parts of it unintelligible to an ordinary reader. These kind hints have been but partially attended to, and, as time presses, it appears with the mass of its original imperfections, as when you read it in manuscript. Such as it is, however, it affords me this valued opportunity of assuring you of the real gratification I feel in having been instrumental in accomplishing an object so dear to you. To your devotion and self-sacrifice the world is indebted for the deeply interesting revelation unfolded by the voyage of the 'Fox.'

Believe me to be,
With sincere respect, most faithfully yours,
F. L. M'CLINTOCK.

London, 24th Nov. 1859.

LIST OF OFFICERS AND SHIP'S COMPANY OF THE 'FOX.'

F. L. M'CLINTOCK ..	Captain R.N.
W. R. HOBSON	Lieutenant R.N.
ALLEN W. YOUNG ..	Captain, Mercantile Marine.
DAVID WALKER, M.D.	Surgeon and Naturalist.
GEORGE BRAND	Engineer .. .. .. { Died 6th Nov., 1858 (Apoplexy).
CARL PETERSEN	Interpreter.
THOMAS BLACKWELL..	Ship's Steward .. .. { Died 14th June, 1859 (Scurvy).
WM. HARVEY	Chief Quartermaster.
HENRY TOMS	Quartermaster.
ALEX. THOMPSON ..	,,
JOHN SIMMONDS . ..	Boatswain's Mate.
GEORGE EDWARDS ..	Carpenter's Mate.
ROBERT SCOTT	Leading Stoker .. .. { Died 4th Dec., 1857 (in consequence of a fall).
THOMAS GRINSTEAD ..	Sailmaker.
GEORGE HOBDAY ..	Captain of Hold.
ROBERT HAMPTON ..	A. B.
JOHN A. HASELTON ..	,,
GEORGE CAREY	,,
BEN. POUND..	,,
WM. WALTERS	Carpenter's Crew.
WM. JONES	Dog-driver.
JAMES PITCHER .. .. THOMAS FLORANCE ..	} Stokers.
RICHARD SHINGLETON	Officers' Steward.
ANTON CHRISTIAN .. SAMUEL EMANUEL ..	} Greenland Esquimaux { Discharged in Greenland.

OFFICIAL ACKNOWLEDGMENT OF THE SERVICES OF THE YACHT 'FOX.'

ADMIRALTY, LONDON,
24th Oct. 1859.

SIR,

I am commanded by my Lords Commissioners of the Admiralty to acquaint you that, in consideration of the important services performed by you in bringing home the only authentic intelligence of the death of the late Sir John Franklin, and of the fate of the crews of the 'Erebus' and 'Terror,' Her Majesty has been pleased, by her order in Council of the 22nd instant, to sanction the time during which you were absent on these discoveries in the Arctic Regions, viz., from the 30th June, 1857, to the 21st September, 1859, to reckon as time served by a captain in command of one of Her Majesty's ships, and my Lords have given the necessary directions accordingly.

I am, Sir,

Your very humble servant,

W. G. ROMAINE,

Secretary to the Admiralty.

Captain Francis L. M'Clintock, R.N.

PREFACE

TO THE FIRST EDITION.

By SIR RODERICK I. MURCHISON, Bart., F.R.S.,

PRESIDENT OF THE ROYAL GEOGRAPHICAL SOCIETY,

&c.   &c.   &c.

THE following narrative of the bold adventure which has successfully revealed the last discoveries and the fate of Franklin is published at the request of the friends of that illustrious navigator. The gallant M'Clintock, when he penned his journal amid the arctic ices, had no idea whatever of publishing it; and yet there can be no doubt that the reader will peruse with the deepest interest the simple tale of how, in a little vessel of 170 tons burthen, he and his well-chosen companions have cleared up this great mystery.

To the honour of the British nation, and also, let it be said, to that of the United States of America, many have been the efforts made to discover the route followed by our missing explorers. The highly deserving men who have so zealously searched the arctic seas and lands in this cause must now rejoice that, after all their anxious toils, the merit of rescuing from the frozen North the record of the last days of Franklin has fallen to the share of his noble-minded widow.

Lady Franklin has, indeed, well shown what a devoted and true-hearted Englishwoman can accomplish. The moment that relics of the expedition commanded by her husband were brought home (in 1854) by Rae, and that she heard of the account given to him by the Esquimaux of a large party of Englishmen having been seen struggling with difficulties on the ice near the mouth of the Back or Great Fish River, she resolved to expend all her available means (already much exhausted in four other independent expeditions) in an exploration of the limited area to which the search must thenceforward be necessarily restricted.

Whilst the supporters of Lady Franklin's efforts were of opinion that the Government ought to have undertaken a search, the extent of which was, for the first time, definitely limited, it is but rendering justice to the then Prime Minister[1] to state that he had every desire to carry out the wishes of the men of science[2] who appealed to him, and that he was precluded from acceding to their petition by nothing but the strongly expressed opinion of official authorities, that after so many failures the Government were no longer justified in sending out more brave men to encounter fresh dangers in a cause which was viewed as hopeless. Hence it devolved on Lady Franklin and her friends to be the sole means of endeavouring to bring to light the true history of her husband's voyage and fate.

Looking to the list of Naval worthies who, during the preceding years, had been exploring the Arctic Regions, Lady Franklin was highly gratified when she obtained the willing services of Captain M'Clintock to command the

---

[1] Viscount Palmerston.

[2] See the Memorial (Appendix) [First Edition] addressed to the First Lord of the Treasury, headed by Admiral Sir F. Beaufort, General Sabine, and many other men of science, and which, as President of the Royal Geographical Society, I presented to the Prime Minister; and also the speech of Lord Wrottesley, the President of the Royal Society, who, in the absence of the lamented Earl of Ellesmere, brought the subject earnestly under the notice of the House of Lords on the 18th of July, 1856.

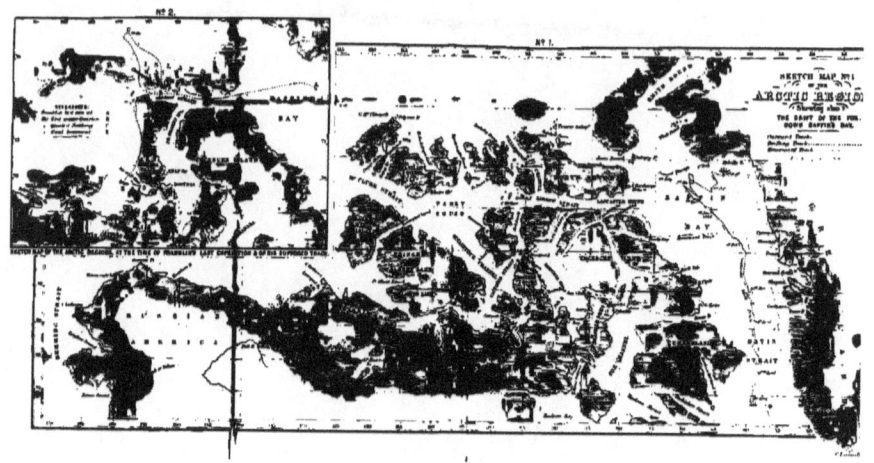

yacht 'Fox,' which she had purchased; for that officer had signally distinguished himself in the voyages of Sir James Ross and Captain (now Admiral) Austin, and especially in his extensive journeys on the ice when associated with Captain Kellett. With such a leader she could not but entertain sanguine hopes of success when the fast and well-adapted little vessel sailed from Aberdeen on the 1st of July, 1857, upon this eventful enterprise.

Deep, indeed, was the mortification experienced by every one who shared the feelings and anticipations of Lady Franklin when the untoward news came, in the summer of 1858, that, the preceding winter having set in earlier than usual, the 'Fox' had been beset in the ice off Melville Bay, on the coast of Greenland, and after a dreary winter, various narrow escapes, and eight months of imprisonment, had been carried back by the floating ice nearly twelve hundred geographical miles—even to $63\frac{1}{2}°$ N. lat. in the Atlantic! See the sketch-map, No. 1.

But although the good little yacht had been most roughly handled among the ice-floes (see Frontispiece), we were cheered up by the information from Disco that, with the exception of the death of the engine-driver, in consequence of a fall into the hold, the crew were in stout health and full of energy, and that, provided with sufficient fuel and provisions, a good supply of sledging dogs, two tried Esquimaux, and the excellent interpreter Petersen the Dane,[1] ample grounds yet remained to lead us to hope for a successful issue. Above all, we were encouraged by the proofs of the self-possession and calm resolve of M'Clintock, who held steadily to the accomplishment of his

[1] Since his return to Copenhagen, Petersen has been worthily honoured by his Sovereign with the silver cross of Dannebrog.

original project; the more so as he had then tested and recognised the value of the services of Lieutenant (now Commander) Hobson, his able second in command; of Captain Allen Young, his generous volunteer associate;[1] and of Dr. Walker, his accomplished Surgeon.

Despite, however, of these reassuring data, many an advocate of this search was anxiously alive to the chance of the failure of the venture of one unassisted yacht, which after sundry mishaps was again starting to cross Baffin Bay, with the foreknowledge that, when she reached the opposite coast, the real difficulties of the enterprise were to commence.

Any such misgivings were happily illusory; and the reader who follows M'Clintock across the "middle ice" of Baffin Bay to Ponds Inlet, thence to Beechey Island, down a portion of Peel Strait, and then through the hitherto unnavigated waters of Bellot Strait in one summer season, may reasonably expect the success which followed.

Whilst the revelation obtained from the long-sought records, which were discovered by Lieutenant Hobson, is most satisfactory to those who speculated on the probability of Franklin having, in the first instance, tried to force his way northwards through Wellington Channel (as we now learn he did), those who held a different hypothesis, namely, that he followed his instructions, which directed him to the S.-W., may be amply satisfied that in the following season the ships did pursue this southerly course till they were finally beset in N. lat. 70° 05'.[2]

---

[1] Captain Allen Young, of the merchant marine, not only threw his services into this cause, and subscribed munificently in furtherance of the expedition, but, abandoning lucrative appointments in command, generously accepted a subordinate post.

[2] For a *résumé* of all the plans of research and the speculations of seamen and geographers, see the interesting and most useful volume

At the same time, the public should fully understand the motive which prompted the supporters of Lady Franklin in advocating this last search. Putting aside the hope which some of us entertained, that a few of the younger men of the missing expedition might still be found to be living among the Esquimaux, we had every reason to expect that, if the ships were discovered, the scientific documents of the voyage, including valuable magnetic observations, would be recovered.

In the absence of such good fortune, we may, however, well be gladdened by the discovery of that one precious document which gives us a true outline of the voyage of the 'Erebus' and 'Terror.'

That the reader may comprehend the vast extent of sea traversed by Franklin in the two summers before his ships were beset, a small map (No. 2) is introduced, representing all the lands and seas of the arctic regions to the west of Lancaster Sound which were known and laid down when he sailed. The dotted lines and arrows, which extend from the then known seas and lands into the unknown waters or blank spaces on this old map indicate Franklin's route, the novelty, range, rapidity, and boldness of which, as thus delineated, may well surprise the geographer, and even the most enterprising arctic sailor.[1] For, those who have

of Mr. John Brown, entitled 'The North-West Passage and Search after Sir John Franklin,' 1858. In an Appendix to this work we learn that from the earliest polar researches by John Cabot, at the end of the 15th century, to the voyage of M'Clintock, there have been about 130 expeditions, illustrated by 250 books and printed documents, of which 150 have been issued in England. Amidst the various recent publications, it is but rendering justice to Dr. King, the former companion of Sir George Back, to state that he suggested and always maintained the necessity of a search for the missing navigators at or near the mouth of the Back River.

[1] The letter A in Baffin Bay (Map No. 2) indicates the spot where

not closely attended to the results of other arctic voyages may be informed that rarely has an expedition in the first year accomplished more by its ships than the establishing of good winter quarters, from whence the real researches began by sledge-work in the ensuing spring. Franklin, however, not only reached Beechey Island, but ascended Wellington Channel, then an unknown sea, to 77° N. lat., a more northern latitude in this meridian than that attained long afterwards in ships by Sir Edward Belcher, and much to the north of the points reached by Penny and De Haven. Next, though most scantily provided with steam-power, Franklin navigated round Cornwallis Land, which he thus proved to be an island. This last discovery of a navigable channel throughout, between Cornwallis and Bathurst Islands, though made in the very summer he left England, has remained even to this day unknown to other navigators!

Franklin then, in obedience to his orders, steered to the south-west. Passing, as M'Clintock believes, down Peel Strait in 1846, and reaching as far as lat. 70° 05' N., and long. 98° 23' W., where the ships were beset, it is clear that he, who, with others, had previously ascertained the existence of a channel along the north coast of America, with which the sea wherein he was interred had a direct communication, was the *first real discoverer of the North-West Passage.* This great fact must therefore be inscribed upon the monument of Franklin.

The adventurous M'Clure, who has been worthily honoured for working out another North-Western passage, which we

---

Franklin was last seen. In Map No. 2, B is the winter rendezvous at Beechey Island; C, the greatest northing of the expedition, viz., 77° N. lat. ; Z, the final beset of the 'Erebus' and 'Terror;' the extreme north and south points of their voyage being represented by two small ships.

now know to have been of subsequent date,[1] as well as Collinson, who, taking the 'Enterprise' along the north coast of America, and afterwards bringing her home, reached with sledges the western edge of the area recently laid open by M'Clintock, will, I have no doubt, unite with their arctic associates, Richardson, Sherard Osborn, and M'Clintock, in affirming that "Franklin and his followers secured the honour for which they died—that of being the first discoverers of the North-West Passage."[2]

Again, when we turn from the discoveries of Franklin to those of M'Clintock, as mapped in red colours on the general map, on which is represented the amount of outline laid down by all other arctic explorers from the days when these modern researches originated with Sir John Barrow, we perceive that, in addition to the discovery of the course followed by the 'Erebus' and 'Terror,' some most important geographical data have been accumulated by the last expedition of Lady Franklin.

Thus, M'Clintock has proved that the strait named by Kennedy in an earlier private expedition of Lady Franklin

---

[1] In 1850.

[2] See a most heart-stirring sketch of the last voyage of Sir John Franklin by Captain Sherard Osborn, in the periodical 'Once a Week,' of the 22nd and 29th October and 5th November last. Possessing a thorough acquaintance with the arctic regions, this distinguished seaman has shown more than his ordinary power of description, in placing before the public his conception of what may have been the chief occurrences in the voyage of the 'Erebus' and 'Terror,' and the last days of Franklin, as founded upon an acquaintance with the character of the chief and his associates, and the record and relics obtained by M'Clintock. This sketch is prefaced by a spirited and graceful outline of all previous geographical discoveries, from the day when they were originated by the father of all modern arctic enterprise, Sir John Barrow, to whom, and to many other eminent persons, from Sir Edward Parry downwards, I have in various Geographical Addressess offered the tribute of my admiration.

after his companion, the brave Lieutenant Bellot, and which has hitherto been regarded only as an impassable frozen channel, or ignored as a channel at all, is a navigable strait, the south shore of which is thus seen to be the northernmost land of the continent of America.

M'Clintock has also laid down the hitherto unknown coast-line of Boothia, southwards from Bellot Strait to the Magnetic Pole, has delineated the whole of King William's Island, and opened a new and capacious, though ice-choked, channel, suspected before, but not proved, to exist, extending from Victoria Strait in a north-west direction to Melville or Parry Sound. The latter discovery rewarded the individual exertions of Captain Allen Young, but will very properly, at Lady Franklin's request, bear the name of the leader of the 'Fox' expedition, who had himself assigned to it the name of the widow of Franklin.[1]

Neither has the expedition been unproductive of scientific results. For, whilst many persons will be interested in the popular descriptions of the native Esquimaux, as well as of the lower animals, the man of science will hereafter be further gratified by having presented to him, in the form of an additional Appendix,[2] most valuable details relating to the zoology, botany, meteorology, and especially to the terrestrial magnetism, of the region examined.

Lastly, M'Clintock has convinced himself that the best

[1] In his volume before cited, p. xii., Mr. John Brown gave strong reasons (which he had held for some time) for believing in the existence of the very channel which now bears the name of M'Clintock. It is, however, the opinion both of that officer and his associates, as also of Captain Sherard Osborn, that Franklin could not have reached the spot where his ships were beset by proceeding down that ice-choked channel, but that he must have sailed down Peel Sound.

[2] Much of this Appendix [First Edition] will be prepared by Dr. David Walker.

way of securing the passage of a ship from the Atlantic to the Pacific is by following, as near as possible, the coast-line of North America: indeed, it is his opinion, founded upon a large experience, that no passage by a ship can ever be accomplished in a more northern direction. This, it is well known, was the favourite theory of Franklin, who had himself, along with Richardson, Back, Beechey, and Dease and Simpson, surveyed the whole of that same North American coast from the Back or Great Fish River to Behring Strait. Thus, when Franklin sailed in 1845, the discovery of a North-West Passage was reduced to the finding a link between the latter survey and the discoveries of Parry, who had already, to his great renown, opened the first half of a more northern course from east to west, when he was arrested by the impenetrable ice-barrier at Melville Island.

And here it is to be remembered that the tract in which the record and the relics have been found is just that to which Lady Franklin herself specially directed Kennedy, the commander of the 'Prince Albert,' in her second private expedition in 1852; and had that intrepid explorer not been induced to search northwards of Bellot Strait, but had felt himself able to follow the course indicated by his sagacious employer, there can be no doubt that much more satisfactory results would have been obtained than those which, after a lapse of seven years, have now been realized by the undaunted perseverance of Lady Franklin, and the skill and courage of M'Clintock.

The natural modesty of this commander has, I am bound to say, prevented his doing common justice, in the following journal, to his own conduct—conduct which can be estimated by those only who have listened to the testimony of the officers serving with and under the man whose great qualities in moments of extreme peril elicited their heartiest admiration and ensured their perfect confidence.

In writing this Preface (which I do at the request of the promoters of the last search), I may state that, having occupied the Chair of the Royal Geographical Society in 1845, when my cherished friend, Sir John Franklin, went forth for the third time to seek a North-West Passage, it became my bounden duty in subsequent years, when his absence created much anxiety, and when I re-occupied the same position, ardently to promote the employment of searching expeditions, and warmly to sustain Lady Franklin's endeavours in this holy cause.

Imbued with such feelings, I must be permitted to say that no event in my life gave me purer delight than when Captain Collinson, whose labours to support and carry out this last search have been signally serviceable, forwarded to me a telegram to be communicated to the British Association at Aberdeen announcing the success of M'Clintock. That document reached Balmoral on the 22nd of September last, when the men of science were invited thither by their Sovereign. Great was the satisfaction caused by the diffusion of these good tidings among my associates (the distinguished arctic explorers Admiral Sir James Ross and General Sabine being present); and it was most cheering to us to know that the Queen and our Royal President[1] took the deepest

---

[1] At the Aberdeen meeting the Prince Consort thus spoke:—" The Aberdeen whaler braves the icy regions of the polar sea to seek and to battle with the great monster of the deep; he has materially assisted in opening these ice-bound regions to the researches of science; he fearlessly aided in the search after Sir John Franklin and his gallant companions whom their country sent forth on this mission; but to whom Providence, alas! has denied the reward of their labours, the

interest in this intelligence — such as, indeed, they have always evinced whenever the search for the missing navigators has been brought under their consideration. The immediate bestowal of the Arctic Medal upon all the officers and men of the 'Fox' is a pleasing proof that this interest is well sustained.

But these few introductory sentences must not be extended; and I invite the reader at once to peruse the Journal of M'Clintock, which will gratify every lover of truthful and ardent research, though it will leave him impressed with the sad belief that the end of the companions of Franklin has been truly recorded by the native Esquimaux, who saw these noble fellows "fall down and die as they walked along the ice."

Looking to the fact that little or no fresh food could have been obtained by the crews of the 'Erebus' and 'Terror' during their long imprisonment of twenty months, in so frightfully sterile a region as that in which the ships were abandoned—so sterile that it is even deserted by the Esquimaux—and also to the want of sustenance in spring at the mouth of the Back River, all the arctic naval authorities with whom I have conversed coincide with M'Clintock and his associates in the belief that none of the missing navigators can be now living.

Painful as is the realisation of this tragic event, let us now dwell only on the reflection that, while the North-West Passage has been solved by the heroic self-sacrifice of Franklin, Crozier, Fitzjames, and their associates, the searches after them, which are now terminated, have, at a very small loss of life, not only added prodigiously to

return to their homes, to the affectionate embrace of their families and friends, and the acknowledgments of a grateful nation."

b

geographical knowledge, but have, in times of peace, been the best school for testing, by the severest trials, the skill and endurance of many a brave seaman. In her hour of need—should need arise—England knows that such men will nobly do their duty.

RODERICK I. MURCHISON.

November, 1859.

CONTENTS.

INTRODUCTION .. .. Page xxv

CHAPTER I.

Cause of delay in equipment — Fittings of the 'Fox' — Volunteers for arctic service — Assistance from public departments — Reflections upon the undertaking — Instructions and departure — Orkneys and Greenland — Fine arctic scenery — Danish establishments in Greenland — Frederickshaab, in Davis' Strait 1

CHAPTER II.

Fiskernaes and Esquimaux — The 'Fox' reaches Disco — Disco Fiord — Summer scenery — Waigat Strait — Coaling from the mine — Purchasing Esquimaux dogs — Heavy gale off Upernivik — Melville Bay — The middle ice — The great glacier of Greenland — Do Reindeer cross the glacier? 16

CHAPTER III.

Melville Bay — Crow's-nest — Beset in Melville Bay — Signs of winter — The coming storm — Drifting in the pack — Canine appetite — Resigned to a winter in the pack — Dinner stolen by sharks — The arctic shark — White whales and Killers 29

CHAPTER IV.

Snow crystals — Dogs will not eat raven — An arctic school — The dogs invade us — Bear-hunting by night — Ice-artillery — Arctic palates — Sudden rise of temperature — Freezing of salt-water — Harvey's idea of a sortie 43

CHAPTER V.

Burial in the pack — Musk oxen in lat. 80° north — Habits of the arctic fox — The aurora affects the electrometer — An arctic Christmas — Sufferings of Dr. Hayes' boat party — Ice acted on by wind only — How the sun ought to be welcomed — Constant action of the ice — Return of the seals — Revolving storm 59

CHAPTER VI.

A bear-fight — An ice-nip — Strong gales, rapid drift — Breaking up of the ice — Hanging on to floe-edge — The arctic bear — An ice tournament — Escape out of the pack — A storm in the pack — Description of the escape .. .. Page 74

CHAPTER VII.

A holiday in Greenland — A lady blue with cold — The loves of Greenlanders — Close shaving — Meet the whalers — Information of whalers — Disco — Danish hospitality — Sail from Disco — Coaling — Kindness of the whalers — Danish establishments in Greenland 90

CHAPTER VIII.

'Fox' nearly wrecked — Afloat, and push ahead — Arctic hair-breadth escapes — Nearly caught in the pack — Shooting little auks — The arctic highlanders — Cape York — Crimson snow — Struggling to the westward — Reach the West-land — Off the entrance of Lancaster Sound 105

CHAPTER IX.

Off Cape Warrender — Sight the whalers again — Enter Pond's Bay — Communicate with Esquimaux — Ascend Pond's Inlet — Esquimaux information — Arctic summer abode — An arctic village — No intelligence of Franklin's ships — Arctic trading — Geographical information of natives — Information of Rae's visit — Improvidence of Esquimaux — Travels of Esquimaux 124

CHAPTER X.

Leave Pond's Bay — A gale in Lancaster Sound — The Beechey Island depot — An arctic monument — Reflections at Beechey Island — Proceed up Barrow's Strait — Peel Sound — Port Leopold — Prince Regent's Inlet — Bellot Strait — Flood-tide from the west — Unsuccessful efforts — Fox's Hole — No water to the west — Precautionary measures — Fourth attempt to pass through 142

CHAPTER XI.

Proceed westward in a boat — Unpromising state of the western sea — Struggles in Bellot Strait — Falcons, good arctic fare — The resources of Boothia Felix — Future sledge travelling — Heavy gales — Hobson's party start — Winter quarters — Bellot Strait — Advanced depot established — Observatories — Intense cold — Autumn travellers — Ravens — Narrow escape — Wolves .. Page 165

CHAPTER XII.

Death of our engineer — Scarcity of game — The cold unusually trying — Jolly, under adverse circumstances — Petersen's information — Return of the sun of 1859 — Early spring sledge parties — Unusual severity of the winter — Severe hardships of early sledging — The western shores of Boothia — Meet the Esquimaux — Intelligence of Franklin's ships — Return to the 'Fox' — Allen Young returns 185

CHAPTER XIII.

Dr. Walker's sledge journey — Snow-blindness attacks Young's party — Departure of all sledge-parties — Equipment of sledge-parties — Meet the same party of natives — Intelligence of the second ship — My depot robbed — Part company from Hobson — Matty Island — Deserted snow-huts — Native sledges — Land on King William's Land 210

CHAPTER XIV.

Meet Esquimaux — News of Franklin's people — Frighten a solitary party — Reach the Great Fish River — On Montreal Island — Total absence of all relics — Dog-driving — Examine Ogle Peninsula — Discover a skeleton — Vagueness of Esquimaux information — Cape Herschel — Cairn 226

CHAPTER XV.

The cairn found empty — Discover Hobson's letter — Discovery of Crozier's record — The deserted boat — Articles discovered about the boat — The skeletons and relics — The boat belonged to the 'Erebus' — Conjectures 242

CHAPTER XVI.

Errors in Franklin's records — Relics found at the cairn — Reflections on the retreat — Returning homeward — Geological remarks — Difficulties of summer sledging — Arrive on board the 'Fox' — Navigable N.W. Passage — Death from scurvy — Anxiety for Captain Young — Young returns safely .. .. .. Page 256

CHAPTER XVII.

Signs of release — Seal-stalking — Dearth of animal life — Birthdays — Break out of winter quarters — Game lists — Steam out of port — Escape from Regent's Inlet — In Baffin's Bay — Bears — Captain Allen Young's journey — Hobson's journey — Disco; sad disappointment — Part from our Esquimaux friends — Adieu to Greenland — Arrive home 273

CONCLUSION 309

APPENDIX.

No. I.—List of Relics of the Franklin Expedition brought to England in the 'Fox,' and deposited in the Museum of the United Service Institution 315

No. II.—Reports of Scientific Observations obtained during the voyage of the 'Fox;' or References to such of these Reports as are published elsewhere 321

INDEX 328

LIST OF ILLUSTRATIONS.

The Escape out of the Pack, page 86. *Drawn by Captain W. W. May, R.N.* .. .. *Frontispiece.*

Sketch Map of the Arctic Regions, showing the Track of the 'Fox,' and her Drift down Baffin's Bay; also, Sketch Map of the Arctic Regions at the time of Franklin's Departure, and showing his supposed Track .. .. *To face p.* ix

	PAGE
The Governor in his Oomiak. *By Captain W. W. May, R.N.*	15
Our Summer Costume	27
The crow's-nest. *By Captain W. W. May, R.N.*	42
Funeral on the Ice—Paraselenæ and Lunar halos, 4th December, 1857. *By Captain W. W. May, R.N.*	58
Section of Seal's Cave in the Ice	75
The Greenlander's Supper appropriated by a Bear	83
Perilous Position of the 'Fox' near Buchan Island, 7th June, 1858. *By Captain W. W. May, R.N.*	104
Esquimaux near Cape York watching the Approach of the 'Fox;' also Christian in his kayak. *From a Sketch by Captain Allen Young*	112
Final Liberation from the Melville Bay ice, 2nd July, 1858. *From a Sketch by Captain Allen Young*	118
Village and Glacier of Kaparōktolik, 4th August, 1858. *By Captain W. W. May, R.N.*	133
The Three Graves, and Depot House, Beechey Island. *By Captain W. W. May, R.N.*	147
Departure from Beechey Island, 16th August, 1858. *By Captain W. W. May, R.N.*	149
Stranded mass of heavy floe ice. *By P. Skelton, from a Sketch by Captain Allen Young*	155
Bellot Strait, 1st September, 1858. *By Captain W. W. May, R.N.*	164
Greenland dog-sledge	172
Interior of the Magnetic Observatory. *By Captain W. W. May, R.N.*	179

	PAGE
Top of Funnel of our stove-pipe	191
Travelling Costume	195
Boothian Mother and Infant	209
Starting of the Exploring Parties, 2nd April, 1859. *Drawn from a Photograph, by Captain W. W. May, R.N.*	215
Plan of the Snow Huts	219
Sledge under Sail. *By Captain W. W. May, R.N.*	225
Cape Herschel, and Remains of Simpson's Cairn. *By Captain W. W. May, R.N.*	239
Facsimile of the Record of Franklin's Expedition, found at Point Victory. *Copied by F. G. Netherclift* .. *To face*	244
Diagram of the stem of the Boat	249
Pattern of worked slippers found in the Boat	251
Christian Seal-stalking. *By Captain W. W. May, R.N.*	275
Moonlight, 25th August, 1859	293
Belles of Disco. *From a Photograph by Dr. J. J. Hayes, kindly lent by the late C. Grinnell, Esq.*	305
Map to illustrate the Voyage, and the Geographical Discoveries of the 'Fox.' *By J. Arrowsmith, Esq.* .. *At the end.*	

INTRODUCTION.

A NEW EDITION of this narrative having been called for, I gladly avail myself of the opportunity to make some few alterations and additions which I trust will render it more acceptable to the public. Much of the Appendix has been omitted, in order to bring the volume to its present reduced size. The illustrations are more numerous, the text has been corrected, and some new matter dispersed through its pages chiefly descriptive of the habits of arctic animals, of our tent life on the floe, and of our sledging journeys.

The latter, being the special means by which arctic exploration is now-a-days mainly carried on, deserve more than a passing notice.

In these details, which I have introduced at the suggestion of some valued friends, I have had recourse to my rough journal kept on board the 'Fox,' and to my diaries in three preceding polar expeditions of search.[1]

In submitting this new edition to the notice of the public, I feel it incumbent on me, not only to acknowledge the indulgence with which the narrative was originally received, but to fulfil the higher duty of expressing the deep sense entertained by my officers and men, as well as myself, of our country's sympathy and approbation, and of the generous reception we met with on returning to our native shores. We had not done all that we desired, but we had done our

[1] Under Sir James Ross, Sir Horatio Austin, and Sir Edward Belcher.

best; and the lapse of time and other adverse circumstances considered, we had, perhaps, met with as much success as could have reasonably been expected.

It is with hesitation that I allude to the honours personally conferred upon me, by our gracious Sovereign, and by the Universities of Oxford, Cambridge, and Dublin. I mention with less reserve other tokens of the national feeling, for these prove how well it was understood that the success of the 'Fox' expedition—or rather the measure of success which it achieved—was mainly owing to the high spirit of loyalty to the cause which animated all my companions, and to their untiring exertions.

It will be remembered that in March, 1860, Parliament voted 5000*l.* for the public services the 'Fox' had rendered. And, when the Royal Geographical Society conferred their Patron's Gold Medal on the commander, it was, to use the words of Earl de Grey, the President, "for having in the 'Fox' yacht, with your gallant companions, not only enlarged our acquaintance with arctic geography, but having also brought to light the *precious record* which has revealed to us the voyage and final abandonment of the 'Erebus' and 'Terror.'"[1]

The City of London also, when it conferred upon me the rare honour (for a naval officer) of the Freedom of the City,

---

[1] On this occasion the Founder's Gold Medal was, by exceptional favour (but with admirable justice), awarded to Lady Franklin in the following terms :—" Desirous of commemorating in an especial manner the arctic researches of our associate, the late Sir John Franklin, and of testifying to the fact that his expedition was the first to discover a North-West Passage, the Council of the Royal Geographical Society have awarded the Founder's Gold Medal to his widow, Lady Franklin, in token of their admiration of her noble and self-sacrificing perseverance in sending out at her own cost several searching expeditions, until at length the fate of her husband has been ascertained."

was not unmindful of those brave men by whose zeal and devotion I was enabled, under Providence, to bring our expedition to a successful issue. The document expressly records "their thanks to the officers and crew composing it, for the bravery and self-sacrifice which distinguished their conduct on this patriotic occasion."

Many other most honourable and gratifying recognitions of our common services might be mentioned; but I forbear from doing so. To say less, however, than I have done, would be a failure of respect to the public, as well as an inadequate expression of my own feelings and those of my companions.

Ten years have elapsed since the discoveries made during the voyage of the 'Fox' were made public. Gallant efforts have not been wanting during that period to glean further information of the lost crews of the 'Erebus' and 'Terror;' yet no additional light has been obtained, and beyond vague rumours current among Esquimaux remote from the scene of the final catastrophe, nothing whatever has come to our knowledge. We must, therefore, I greatly fear, relinquish all hope of recovering any of the official documents or private journals of the officers; the long interval of twenty-one years since the abandonment of the 'Erebus' and 'Terror' almost precludes the possibility of their existence.

As a fitting sequel to the subjoined list of the officers of the Franklin expedition, I have endeavoured to give an outline of their services. This outline in some instances is necessarily of the briefest description.

The ships selected were the 'EREBUS' and 'TERROR.' Originally constructed for bomb vessels, they were enormously strong, their timbers being as massive as those of a seventy-four-gun ship. Moreover, they had been especially fortified for the antarctic voyage, from which they had but recently returned. Before sailing for the discovery of the North-West Passage, screw propellers and very small engines were adapted to them, being just sufficient to propel them at the rate of three miles an hour in calm weather. They were commissioned and fitted out at Woolwich Dockyard, and sailed from the Thames, 19th May, 1845; and they were last seen 26th July, of that year, in Melville Bay.

H.M.S. EREBUS. 370 Tons. 20 H.-P. Screw.

Captain .. SIR JOHN FRANKLIN, K.C.H. &c.
Commander JAMES FITZJAMES .. .. Captain, Dec. 1845.
Lieutenant . GRAHAM GORE .. .. Commr., Nov. 1846.
  ,,   H. T. D. LE VESCONTE.
  ,,   JAMES W. FAIRHOLME.
Ice Master . JAMES READ.
Surgeon .. STEPHEN SAMUEL STANLEY.
Purser .. CHARLES HAMILTON OSMER.
Mate.. .. ROBERT ORME SARGENT .. .. Lieut., May, 1846.
  ,, ... CHARLES FREDERICK DES VŒUX   ,, Nov. 1846.
  ,, ... EDWARD COUCH .. .. ,, May, 1847.
Asst.-Surg. (Acting, for Arctic Expedition only), HENRY D. S. GOODSIR.
2nd Master, HENRY FOSTER COLLINS.

H.M.S. TERROR. 340 Tons. 20 H.-P. Screw.

Captain .. FRANCIS RAWDON MOIRA CROZIER.
Lieutenant . EDWARD LITTLE .. .. Commr., Nov. 1846.
  ,,   G. H. HODGSON.
  ,,   JOHN IRVING.
Ice Master . THOMAS BLANKY.
Surgeon (Acting), JOHN SMART PEDDIE .. .. Surgeon, Dec. 1845.
Mate.. .. FREDERICK J. HORNBY .. .. .. Lieut., May, 1846.
  ,, ... ROBERT THOMAS .. .. ,, April, 1847.
Assistant-Surgeon, ALEXANDER M'DONALD.
2nd Master, GILLIES ALEXANDER MACBEAN.
Clerk in Charge, E. J. H. HELPMAN.

Of the illustrious leader of the expedition, SIR JOHN FRANKLIN, it is almost superfluous to speak, his career being interwoven with the history of his country. In his earliest years he had an opportunity of distinguishing himself in war; but it was during a period of profound peace that he entered on that arctic career with which his name is especially connected, and in which he won the imperishable fame of solving the vexed problem of centuries. The martyr's palm is his, and theirs who followed him, for "they forged the last link of the North-West Passage with their lives."

Born at Spilsby, in Lincolnshire, in 1786, young FRANKLIN entered the Navy as a midshipman on board H.M.S. 'Polyphemus' in 1800, and was serving in that ship when it led the line at the battle of Copenhagen in 1801. He afterwards was appointed to H.M.S. 'Investigator,' under his distinguished relative, Captain Matthew Flinders, R.N., who was at that time engaged in the discovery and survey of the coasts of Australia; and after two years was wrecked with his commander in H.M.S. 'Porpoise' on one of the innumerable coral reefs on its northern coast.

Franklin, now separated from his chief, was returning home in the fleet of Indiamen under Commodore Dance, when it was attacked by the French squadron under Admiral Linois. In the action, which put the French to flight, Franklin took a conspicuous part.

On his return home he was appointed to H.M.S. 'Bellerophon,' Captain Cook, and served as signal midshipman at the battle of Trafalgar, where he was remarked for his imperturbable coolness and intrepidity in a position of great danger. Without enumerating his intermediate services, we find him in 1814 lieutenant in H.M.S. 'Bedford,' commanding the boats from that ship in the attack upon New Orleans, when he was the first to board and capture one of the enemy's gun-boats.

It was in 1818 that he commenced his arctic career in command of H.M.S. 'Trent,' consort to the 'Dorothea,' Captain Buchan, R.N., in an attempt to reach the North Pole. Disappointed in his desire to continue this voyage alone, when the 'Dorothea' became disabled, Franklin had not long to wait on his return home before he was appointed to command an overland and boat expedition (coincident with the ship expedition of Parry, for the discovery of the North-West Passage), the object of which was to determine the limits and direction of the arctic shores of America, where only two or three isolated points had hitherto been ascertained.

In this expedition he was accompanied by his faithful friend and able coadjutor, Dr. (afterwards Sir John) Richardson. Together they surveyed 555 geographical miles of arctic coast, and traversed, to reach it, a still greater extent of inland country, carrying their boats with them, and depending for food on the casual supplies of the chase, which sometimes failed them altogether. The narrative of their return from the Arctic Sea over the "Barren Grounds" of the interior, in order to reach the nearest Hudson Bay Company's settlement, is a tale of suffering and endeavour which flushes the cheek and dims the eye of the most phlegmatic of readers. The lichens on the rock, and occasional bits of soaked shoe-leather, alone saved the party from absolute starvation. What a foreshadowing of that still deeper tragedy which was to close the career of the gallant leader and his followers in later years! But the future was veiled from his eyes.

Our adventurous explorers returned after four years of absence to meet, when they landed in Europe, with the sympathy and admiration of their countrymen. Franklin, who had been made a commander during his absence, was now raised to the rank of captain, and elected a Fellow of the Royal Society.

Undaunted by his late bitter experience, Franklin started again in 1825 at the head of another canoe expedition (of which he had submitted the plan to Government), and in which he was again accompanied by his friend Richardson, who acted in this, as in the former search, as surgeon and naturalist and second in command.

By their united exertions, though in separate parties, thirty-seven degrees of longitude were surveyed along the arctic shore of the American continent; and the conviction must have been more and more impressed upon their minds that this was the real pathway for ships striving to get from sea to sea, if only a gap to the eastward, which would connect it with the older discoveries on the Atlantic side, could be found.

On their return, Franklin enjoyed an interval of two or three years of repose, and during this time received with his friend Parry (who had secured a world-wide fame by his arctic discoveries in a higher latitude) the honour of knighthood, and that of the honorary degree of D.C.L. conferred upon them both by the University of Oxford. The Geographical Society of Paris also adjudged its annual gold medal to Franklin. He met with less liberality at home from the Board of Longitude, which declined to admit his and Richardson's claims to the pecuniary reward which had been offered for attaining certain degrees of longitude (or portions of the North-West Passage), on the ground, mainly, that their work had been performed in boats instead of ships![1]

[1] Twenty thousand pounds had by the same Act of Parliament been

Arctic expeditions being now suspended, Franklin sought employment in the ordinary line of his profession, and was immediately appointed to commission H.M.S. 'Rainbow' for the Mediterranean station, when the Greek war of independence was closing, but whilst Greece was still disorganised, and a prey to foreign intrigues and internal disturbance. Whilst on duty in Greece, where his ship was chiefly stationed, he received the warm acknowledgments of that distinguished officer, the late Admiral Sir Henry Hotham, for the diplomatic skill and judgment with which he conducted the services entrusted to him. Otho, the young King of Greece, conferred on him the Order of the Cross of the Redeemer, and on his return to England he was created by William IV. a Knight Commander of the Guelphic Order of Hanover.

Shortly after the expiration of his commission, having no immediate prospect of another ship, he accepted the important government of the colony of Tasmania (then called Van Diemen's Land), which was offered to him by the late Lord Glenelg in terms which he greatly appreciated. True to his old profession, however, he stipulated with the Secretary of State for the Colonies that he might be allowed to resign the government if, on a war breaking out, he were offered the command of a ship. Franklin arrived in Tasmania in January, 1837, and administered the government during seven years. That his memory is held in great respect and affection by the colonists there is evinced by the unanimous vote of the Legislature for the erection of a

held out as a reward for the discovery of the North-West Passage, but immediately following the decision against Franklin, a Bill was brought into Parliament abrogating the former Act altogether; not, however, before Parry had established his own indisputable claim to a portion of the reward.

statue to his honour, which now occupies the site of the old Government House.

Within a year of his return from Tasmania, Franklin left England for the last time (May 19, 1845), in command of the expedition which Government had, after much deliberation, resolved upon for the completion of the discovery of the North-West Passage.

This was, perhaps, the proudest moment of Franklin's life. He would not solicit the appointment, deeming it due to his own long career of arctic experience that it should be tendered to him if younger men had not the preference; but when sent for by the First Lord of the Admiralty, and offered the command, in terms which showed that his former laurels were still fresh in remembrance, he felt a proud satisfaction which compensated him for many previous trials.

For his guidance in this momentous undertaking, Franklin had Parry's and Ross's charts and narratives, and his own Admiralty Instructions: but the charts, compared with those which subsequent explorations have filled with well-defined coast-lines, were little more than sheets of blank paper particularly in that direction to which his efforts were to be mainly directed.[1] He had to launch into the wide unknown space, and find his way as best he might. His Admiralty Instructions could aid him but little; suggested mainly by himself, they were the result of the united deliberations of the most eminent men who had already distinguished themselves in earlier explorations, or who had made the subject a field of earnest and careful study: amongst the latter the late Sir John Barrow, Secretary to the Admiralty, was the most conspicuous.

[1] See the sketch-map in Preface, at page ix.

The Instructions were rather warnings what to avoid than orders what to do; but even under the latter head the language is sufficiently explicit. "Therefore" (after assuming from the experience of Parry that all attempts to penetrate westward of longitude 98° in the direction of Melville Island would be useless), "you will not stop to examine any openings either to the northward or southward in that (Barrow) Strait, but continue to push to the westward without loss of time, in the latitude of 74°¼ N., till you have reached that portion of land on which Cape Walker is situated, or about 98° W. From that point we desire that every effort be used to penetrate to the southward and westward in a course as direct towards Behring Strait as the position and extent of the ice or the existence of land, at present unknown, may admit."

Franklin was last seen by a whaling ship which communicated with him in Baffin's Bay on 26th of July, little more than two months after his departure from England. At that time all was well with the expedition; and letters from Disco, of a few days' earlier date, from himself and his officers, attest their confidence under Providence of final success, and their mutual satisfaction with each other.[1]

CAPTAIN FRANCIS R. M. CROZIER, F.R.S., F.S.A., was born at Banbridge, Ireland, in September, 1796.

---

[1] For further details of Franklin's life, the reader is referred to the 'Encyclopedia Britannica,' 8th edition, in which there is an admirable article—under the head of Franklin—written by his friend and relative, Sir John Richardson, the companion of his earlier explorations, and who knew and loved him as a brother; also, to the very interesting memoir in French, by M. de la Roquette, late Vice-President of the Geographical Society of Paris, published by desire of that society, before the final expedition of the 'Fox' had enabled the biographer to bring his record to an authentic close.

He entered the Navy as a midshipman in 1810, and served in it almost without cessation for the remainder of his singularly adventurous life. He accompanied Sir Edward Parry in his second, third, and fourth polar voyages, and attained his lieutenancy in 1826.

When Sir James Ross was suddenly despatched to the arctic regions, in the depth of winter, for the relief of several missing whale ships, Crozier accompanied him, as senior lieutenant, and was promoted to commander on their return home in 1836. He commanded the 'Terror, consort to the 'Erebus,' Captain Sir James C. Ross, throughout the antarctic voyage—the most remarkable and important expedition of discovery since the days of Cook. Commander Crozier was made captain shortly after their departure; but services like his were too valuable to be dispensed with, therefore he was retained in his command until the return of the expedition in 1843.

Captain Crozier had now achieved the highest professional reputation; he had also contributed largely, more especially in the department of terrestrial magnetism, to the various scientific observations of the exploring voyages —both arctic and antarctic—in which he had been for so many years engaged. Therefore, when an expedition for the discovery of the North-West Passage, and for general scientific research in the arctic regions, was determined upon, Sir John Franklin naturally sought for, and obtained, the nomination of Crozier as his second in command, Franklin being in the 'Erebus,' and Crozier in his former ship, the 'Terror.'

They sailed from the Thames, 19th May, 1845.

For all that we know of him, or any of his companions,

subsequently to the following July, we are alone indebted to the Crozier record, found on Point Victory in 1859.[1]

[1] Whilst these pages were going through the press, the public journals announced the return of the American explorer, Captain C. F. Hall, after an absence of five years; I am therefore enabled to notice that portion of his report (published in the New York 'Tribune,' 30th September) which relates to his search for our long lost countrymen.

During the spring of this year, Captain Hall reached King William's Island, and explored a portion of their line of retreat, along its southern shore. His experience, and also the native information he has collected, agrees in all important points with that previously obtained, but without adding thereto.

According to these latest accounts, the place called Oot-loo-lik, where one of the ships was stranded (*Narrative*, p. 220), is on the shore of the continent some thirty or forty miles south-westward of Cape Herschel.

And it appears that, subsequently to the examination of King William's Island by sledge parties from the ' Fox,' the Esquimaux visited its north-western shores, thus leaving no part of it unsearched, and of course removing or destroying every relic and trace of the lost crews—those seen by us as well as others which the snow concealed from our view.

Captain Hall's report fully confirms the opinion expressed in this Narrative (p. 312), that their sufferings could not have been materially prolonged beyond the short period for which the provisions, brought from their ships, would support them.

Deriving his information from the Esquimaux, he states that one of the parties seen to pass Cape Herschel, reached the continent near Point Richardson, about 12 or 15 miles westward of the Great Fish River. Captain Hall also states that none of the lost crews reached Montreal Island, in the mouth of that river, notwithstanding that Mr. Anderson's evidence, repeatedly corroborated by Esquimaux testimony, seems conclusive that a boat-party did reach it, and that their boat was eventually cut up there by the natives.

He further tells us, that in the overwhelming thirst for plunder, even their graves (so called, but merely superficial constructions of loose stones as a protection against wild animals—*See Narrative*, p. 254) were not respected.

His journey has resulted in additional relics and reports obtained from the natives, but no *documents* or *writings* whatever. And it shows us conclusively that, had the ' Fox ' expedition been delayed even for a couple of years, we should have been deprived of the only reliable information respecting the voyage and abandonment of the ' Erebus ' and ' Terror,' which has ever come to light; for the ruthless Esquimaux would have plundered the only remaining cairns, and have destroyed those precious records, which for eleven years lay sheltered beneath them.

Upon the death of Franklin (11th June, 1847), Crozier succeeded to the chief command. On him devolved the terrible necessity of abandoning the ships, and endeavouring to save their crews by a desperate attempt to reach the Hudson Bay territories.

Crozier's record—written upon the march—is dated 25th April, 1848.

The reader may perhaps picture to himself that last fearful march, and the heroic bearing of its undaunted leader, whose nobleness of character and warmth of heart had ever won for him universal esteem and affection.

CAPTAIN JAMES FITZJAMES entered the Navy as a midshipman in 1825. After serving in various ships, he was attached to Colonel Chesney's celebrated expedition to the River Euphrates, and took an active part as mate of the 'Euphrates' steamer upon that river. On the return of the expedition in 1838, and after two years and a half of distinguished service, Mr. Fitzjames was promoted to the rank of lieutenant.

He served on board H.M.S. 'Ganges' throughout the Syrian campaign (1840), again particularly distinguishing himself.

His next appointment was to the 'Cornwallis,' the flagship of Vice-Admiral Sir Wm. Parker, the naval commander-in-chief on the East Indian station. During the Chinese hostilities in 1842, Lieutenant Fitzjames's brilliant conduct was such that he was five times gazetted! He participated in all the operations on the River Yang-tse-kiang both afloat and on shore, his conspicuous exertions and gallantry repeatedly calling forth the warm approbation of the General Sir Hugh (afterward Viscount) Gough, as well as of the Admiral. At the storming and capture of Ching-kiang-Foo, Fitzjames received four bullet wounds; one of these balls passed through his body, and was subsequently extracted from beneath his shoulder blade.

In December, 1842, he was promoted to the rank of commander, and appointed to H.M.S. 'Clio,' a command which he retained until the termination of her period of commission in October, 1844.

In the following March, he was appointed to the 'Erebus' with Franklin, and was gazetted a captain a few months after the departure of the expedition.

Captain Fitzjames was a man of rare talent as well as gallantry; his sketches, and his writings, exhibit remarkable vigour and accuracy; frank, warm-hearted, and ever cheerful, he was deservedly one of the most popular officers in the Navy; most enterprising, active, and endowed with rare powers of endurance, he was eminently constituted for that peculiar service in which unhappily has terminated a career of the highest promise.

COMMANDER GRAHAM GORE entered the Navy in 1820. As midshipman, on board H.M.S. 'Albion,' he was present in the battle of Navarin (1827); became lieutenant in 1837, upon his return from an arctic voyage in the 'Terror' with Captain (now Admiral Sir George) Back. Lieutenant Gore was present at the capture of Aden in 1839; also present at the capture of the Bogue Forts, and Chusan, in 1840. He continued to serve in various ships up to March, 1845, the date of his appointment as senior lieutenant to the 'Erebus.'

His promotion to the rank of commander took place in November, 1846.

Commander Gore's name appears in both the Franklin records. In the more recent one he is alluded to as "the late Commander Gore;" his death therefore occurred between their dates, viz. 28th May, 1847, and 25th April, 1848.

He had seen much active service; he was an accomplished as well as an excellent officer, and one in whom remarkable evenness of temper was combined with great stability of character.

COMMANDER EDWARD LITTLE joined the Navy in 1825; was made lieutenant in 1837, and served in various ships up to March, 1845, when he was appointed to the 'Terror' as senior lieutenant. In November, 1846, he was promoted to the rank of commander. In his last letters from Greenland, Captain Crozier writes in terms of warm praise of his senior lieutenant, Mr. Little.

LIEUTENANT H. T. D. LE VESCONTE entered the Navy in 1829; served throughout the Chinese war, distinguishing himself on several occasions, and by repeated acts of conspicuous gallantry winning his lieutenancy in 1841.

As lieutenant, he continued in active service, and was appointed to the 'Erebus' in 1845.

LIEUTENANT JAMES W. FAIRHOLME joined the Navy in 1834. When despatched in a captured slaver, he was wrecked on the coast of Africa, and taken prisoner by the Moors; most fortunately he was rescued within a few days.

Mr. Fairholme served in the Syrian war in 1840. In 1841 he accompanied Captain Trotter in a most perilous expedition up the River Niger. He attained his lieutenancy in 1842, and served without cessation up to his appointment to the 'Erebus' in 1845.

LIEUTENANT G. H. HODGSON commenced his naval career in 1832. Mr. Hodgson served under Admiral Sir William Parker in China, where he distinguished himself during the war by his personal gallantry, and was also wounded. In 1842 he was made lieutenant, and again distinguished himself in an attack on pirates.

LIEUTENANT JOHN IRVING entered the Navy in 1828, obtained his lieutenant's commission in 1843, and joined the 'Terror' in 1845. His name is mentioned in the Point Victory record. In the interval between passing his examinations for lieutenant and obtaining that rank, Mr. Irving spent a few years in Australia, where he acquired experience of bush life and its attendant hardships. He possessed an iron constitution, was a talented draftsman, and in every respect well adapted for arctic service.

ICE-MASTERS. — JAMES READ and THOMAS BLANKY. Previously commanders of Greenland whaleships, distinguished for their intimate knowledge of the arctic seas, and their experience in ice-navigation. Owing to these valuable acquirements, they were selected and appointed to the 'Erebus' and 'Terror' respectively. Mr. Blanky had, moreover, served in the 'Griper,' Captain G. F. Lyon, R.N., in 1824, when an attempt was made to reach Repulse Bay. He also served in the 'Hecla' in 1827 under Sir E. Parry, when that officer tried to reach the North Pole. And we find Mr. Blanky for the third time engaged in an arctic expedition, as first mate of the 'Victory' with Sir John Ross, in 1829-34; the three years he then passed amongst the Boothian Esquimaux enabled him to acquire a valuable knowledge of their language and habits.

SURGEONS.—STEPHEN SAMUEL STANLEY and JOHN SMART PEDDIE.

Dr. Stanley entered the Navy as an assistant-surgeon in 1838. He served in China during the war of 1840-42, and was favourably noticed by his Captain—the late Sir Thomas Bouchier—for having, on several occasions, taken medical charge of the men engaged in active operations both in the boats and on shore. Dr. Stanley was specially gazetted for his services, and promoted to the rank of surgeon in June, 1842. He had also attained to some distinction by his knowledge of natural history.

Dr. Peddie had served as an assistant-surgeon from 1836, the date of his entry, until appointed to the 'Terror' in March 1845 as acting surgeon; he was confirmed in this rank the following December. It is pleasant to be able to record, that Captain Crozier's last letters make very favourable mention of Dr. Peddie.

PURSER.—CHARLES HAMILTON OSMER. This gentleman commenced his naval career as a clerk, in 1819. In 1836 he was promoted to the rank of purser. He served in the 'Blossom' throughout her memorable voyage to Behring Strait in 1825-8, under Captain F. W. Beechey, R.N.

In 1839, when it became expedient to re-establish our naval power upon the lakes of North America, Mr. Osmer was appointed as purser to the senior officer's ship, the 'Niagara,' which appointment he retained for nearly four years. Having acquired most extensive and varied experience, Mr. Osmer was selected to accompany Sir J. Franklin's expedition.

ASSISTANT-SURGEONS.—ALEX. M'DONALD and HENRY D. S. GOODSIR.

Dr. M'Donald, I believe, had previously visited the arctic seas, as surgeon of a whaler. He entered the Navy as assistant-surgeon in 1841, and served for nearly four years in H.M.S. 'Belvidera,' previously to joining the 'Terror.'

Dr. Goodsir was an anatomist, and a naturalist of the highest promise. In 1843 he succeeded his brother John (the late eminent Professor of Anatomy to the Edinburgh University) in the curatorship of the Royal College of

Surgeons, Edinburgh, which position he gave up on joining the Franklin expedition, in 1845. Ostensibly, he embarked as an assistant-surgeon, "acting, for Arctic Expedition only," but really as a naturalist, the wide field for scientific research which the voyage offered, proving as irresistible to his enthusiastic mind as the antarctic voyage had previously been to the present distinguished botanist, R. D. Hooker, F.R.S.

Very early in life Dr. Goodsir made himself known to science by contributing, in conjunction with his brother John, some papers to the Wernerian Society of Edinburgh.

His younger brother Robert twice visited the arctic regions in search of the Franklin expedition, the second time as surgeon of a Government expedition, under the command of Captain William Penny.

The junior officers were all young men; consequently, of their previous services there is but little to record; but the fact of their having been selected to form part of so difficult and hazardous an expedition is proof of their general merits and rising qualifications.

MR. HORNBY passed his examinations for lieutenant's rank in 1841; SARGENT, in 1843; DES VŒUX, in 1844; THOMAS, and COUCH, in 1845.

They were all promoted within two years of their departure from England.

Mr. Des Vœux served under Sir Charles Napier in the Syrian war of 1840.

He proceeded to China in the flag-ship of Admiral Sir William Parker, and served in the 'Endymion,' under the present Admiral Sir Frederick Grey, during the Chinese war. At one period of this war he was employed as a naval aide-de-camp to General Sir Hugh Gough, the commander-in-chief of the forces. Thus early had he distinguished himself by his intelligence, gallantry, and zeal. His name occurs in both the Franklin records.

The seamen composing the crews of the two ships had been carefully selected; they were, for the most part, hardy north-countrymen, the remainder being men-of-war's men.

I cannot better conclude this imperfect notice of the gallant men whose sad fate has moved with sympathy the whole civilized world, than by giving a few extracts from some of their last letters (from the oldest to the youngest officer on board) written to friends at home, whilst upon their outward voyage and during their short detention in Greenland, at the Whalefish Islands; the last letter received from them is dated 12th July. These extracts will convey to the reader, far better than any description could do, an idea of the delightful tone of feeling which existed amongst them, and of their devoted loyalty, I may with truth say, affection, for their renowned leader.

Gallant spirits eminently worthy of their heroic chief! Higher praise than this it is alike impossible to win or to bestow.

EXTRACTS.

(1). "Sir John is delightful, active, energetic, and evidently even now persevering; what he *has been*, we all know. I think it will turn out that he is in no way altered."

(2). "I would not lose him for the command of the expedition, for I have a real regard—I might say *affection*—for him, and believe this is felt by all of us."

(3). "Of all men he is the most fitted for the command of an enterprise requiring sound sense and great perseverance; and he is full of benevolence and kindness withal. You have no conception how happy we are."

(4). "Yesterday we had the highest sea I ever saw; it was very fine. I know nothing finer than a gale of wind, particularly when you are running before it. We had a few seas over our decks, one of which found its way down on our table just as we had done dinner. We are packed so closely we can't move very far; but the good humour of every one is perfect, and we do dance before it (the gale) finely."[1]

(5). "I wish I could, however, convey to you a just idea of the immense stock of good feeling, good humour, and real kindliness of heart in our small mess. We are very happy, and very fond of Sir John Franklin, who improves very much as we come to know more of him. He is anything but nervous or fidgety; in fact, I should say remarkable for energetic decision in sudden emergencies. Our men are all fine hearty fellows."

(6). "'Tis a rare thing to find met together twelve men of different ranks and ages who combine the scholar with the gentleman, such as these which it has been my fortunate lot to mix with; and I do most fervently pray that nothing may occur to loosen the ties which at present so happily bind us to each other. With such a man to command us, 'tis next to impossible that we shall be aught else than most happy and comfortable."

(7). "I had omitted to mention that we have had Divine Service every Sunday since we left Greenhithe; and you would be perfectly delighted at the beautiful and impressive manner in which Sir John reads both the Service and the Sermon. I assure you it was with unalloyed feelings of delight that I witnessed their fervent and audible responses (the entire crew); every individual on board has a Bible and Prayer-Book."

(8). "11 P.M., Lat. 63° N. The air is delightfully cool and bracing, and everybody is in good humour, either with himself or his neighbours. Goodsir is catching the most extraordinary animals in a net, and is in ecstacies. Gore and Des Vœux are over the side with nets and long poles. We take it in turns to fish with a net at the end of a long pole, and bring up most strange animals."

(9). "The more I see of our worthy chief the more I like and admire him; in fact, he is deservedly *beloved* by us *all*, seamen as well as officers. As this day (Sunday) will serve as a sample of what has already taken place on the Lord's Day, and which will no doubt be strictly adhered to for the future, I will describe our observance of it :—We assemble at Prayers at ten o'clock, the beautiful Service of the Church of England is read by Sir John in the most impressive manner, after which a Sermon adapted to our pursuits is also most impressively delivered. At seven in the evening all those who are desirous assemble in Sir John's cabin, when the Evening Service is read, and another

---

[1] This extract is dated 23rd June, off Cape Desolation, Davis Strait.

Sermon delivered. We look forward to the coming of the Sabbath with much gratification, and 'tis rarely you will miss the attendance of even *one*, except when duty occurs, and then these absentees are sure to be of the evening congregation."

(10). "To-day we have had a sea smooth as glass; very cloudy, and a cold air, thermometer 35°; passed several icebergs, within a mile of a large one. The effect was very fine, for the horizon happened to be a dark distinct line; and these bergs, catching an occasional gleam of sunshine, shone like a twelfth-cake. I had fancied icebergs were large transparent lumps, or rocks of ice. They look like huge masses of pure snow, furrowed with caverns and dark ravines. I went on board the 'Terror' in the evening, for it was quite calm, and found Hodgson better. When we came on board, we pulled up for Goodsir—beasts, starfish, mud, and shells, from a depth of 250 fathoms, and caught more cod."

(11). "We are now (eight o'clock, evening, 3rd July) slowly approaching our anchorage; comparatively mild weather, with 192 icebergs, large and small, in sight. We have chess, backgammon, draughts, and 1700 books on board to amuse us."

(12). "I cannot tell you—more than I have done—how truly and deservedly beloved Sir John is by us *all*."

(13). "We are all very happy and comfortable on board, Sir John is such a good old fellow. We all have perfect confidence in him."

(14). "Sunday. Whalefish Islands. A fine sunshiny night, and we have had a delightful sunshiny day, quite warm, the air clear, ice glistening in all directions. The fine bold land of Disco, black, and topped with snow; the sea covered with bits of ice which are rushing through the channel as they break off from the icebergs, falling with a noise like thunder. Every man nearly on shore, running about for a sort of holiday, getting eider duck's eggs, &c.; curious mosses and plants being collected, also shells."

(15). "All is getting on as well as I could wish. Officers full of youth and zeal, and, indeed, everything going on most smoothly. The Admiralty were exceedingly kind to us, all our demands were readily granted; if we can only do something worthy of the country which has so munificently fitted us out, I will only be too happy; it will be an ample reward for all my anxieties, and believe me, Henry, there will be no lack of them."

The last of these extracts is from a letter of Captain Crozier's, written from the Whalefish Islands, and was one of the last letters ever received from the expedition.

It was not until the close of 1847, when no further news had arrived of the absent ships, that anxiety began to be felt as to their safety, or rather, that apprehensions were awakened of their being in some predicament which required assistance and relief.

In November of that year, Lord Auckland, then at the head of the Admiralty, kindly communicated to Lady Franklin his intention of sending out an expedition in their behalf in the following spring, and invited her to express any views she might entertain in connection with it.

It is not my purpose to enter here into a history of the several expeditions which under successive administrations, and commanded by various distinguished officers, were despatched in quest of the missing navigators; neither will I touch upon the supplementary efforts made by Lady Franklin herself with the assistance of sympathising friends. This auxiliary search was rendered necessary in the opinion of Lady Franklin, by the failure of the Government expeditions to penetrate into those particular parts of the field of search where she believed the 'Erebus' and 'Terror' would be found: an opinion which gained increased force, when in 1854 Dr. Rae arrived in England with news derived from the Esquimaux, and confirmed by relics obtained from them, of some fatal catastrophe that had taken place within the area on which her anxious attention had always been fixed.

On the arrival of this sad rumour, confirmed by such painful symbols, the Admiralty deemed it time to recall, if it were possible, their searching vessels.

To Lady Franklin, however, it was only an incentive to renewed exertions, directed to the place (ever circumscribed, and now plainly ascertained) where alone there was a chance of success.

The reduced dimensions of this work have prevented me from inserting, as in former editions, the letter of Lady Franklin to Lord Palmerston, and the memorial also addressed to the Prime Minister by all the leading men of science then in London, strenuously advocating this final effort. I will give one passage only from Lady Franklin's letter above alluded to, and will conclude with a few touching words from her appeal to the Admiralty :—

"I submit to your Lordship that this is a case of no ordinary exigency. These 135 men of the 'Erebus' and 'Terror' (or perhaps I should rather say the greater part of them, for we do not yet know that there are no survivors) have laid down their lives after sufferings doubtless of unexampled severity, in the service of their country, as truly as if they had perished by the rifle, the cannon-ball, or the bayonet.

"Nay, more, by attaining the northern and already surveyed coast of America, it is clear that they solved the problem which was the object of their labours, or, in the beautiful words of Sir John Richardson, that they 'forged the last link of the North-West Passage with their lives.' Surely, then, I may plead for such men that a careful search be made for any possible survivor, that the bones of the dead be sought for and gathered together, that their buried records be unearthed or recovered from the hands of the Esquimaux, and above all, that the last written words, so precious to their bereaved families and friends, be saved from destruction.

"A mission so sacred is worthy of a Government which has grudged and spared nothing for its heroic soldiers and sailors in other fields of warfare, and will surely be approved by our gracious Queen, who overlooks none of her loyal subjects suffering and dying for their country's honour.[1]

"This final and exhausting search is all I seek in behalf of the first and only martyrs to arctic discovery in modern times, and it is all I ever intend to ask. . . . ."

"It is my humble hope and fervent prayer, that the Government of my country will themselves complete the work of search which they have begun, and not leave it to a weak and helpless woman to attempt the doing that imperfectly which they themselves can do so easily and well; yet, if need be, such is my painful resolve, God helping me."

Had the prayer of this petition been granted, it is needless to say that the expedition of the 'Fox' would not have taken place.

The national monument commemorative of this—perhaps the noblest episode in England's naval history—has been erected in Waterloo Place. Upon the pedestal beneath his statue is the following inscription :—

FRANKLIN.

TO THE GREAT NAVIGATOR
AND HIS BRAVE COMPANIONS
WHO SACRIFICED THEIR LIVES IN
COMPLETING THE DISCOVERY OF
THE NORTH-WEST PASSAGE.

A.D. 1847–8.

ERECTED BY THE UNANIMOUS VOTE
OF PARLIAMENT.

---

[1] Written at the close of the Crimean War.

H. M. S. ships Erebus and Terror
{ Wintered in the Ice in
28 of May 1847 { Lat. 70° 5' N Long. 98° 23' W

Having wintered in 1846–7 at Beechey Island
in Lat 74° 43' 28" N. Long 91° 39' 15" W after having
ascended Wellington Channel to Lat 77° and returned
by the West side of Cornwallis Island.

Sir John Franklin commanding the Expedition.
All well.

Party consisting of 2 Officers and 6 Men
left the Ships on Monday 24th May 1847.

Gm. Gore, Lieut.
Chas. F. Des Voeux, Mate.

WHOEVER finds this paper is requested to forward it to the Secretary of the Admiralty, London, with a note of the time and place at which it was found: or, if more convenient, to deliver it for that purpose to the British Consul at the nearest Port.

QUINCONQUE trouvera ce papier est prié d'y marquer le tems et lieu où il l'aura trouvé, et de le faire parvenir au plutot au Secretaire de l'Amirauté Britannique à Londres.

CUALQUIERA que hallare este Papel, se le suplica de enviarlo al Secretario del Almirantazgo, en Londrés, con una nota del tiempo y del lugar en donde se halló.

EEN ieder die dit Papier mogt vinden, wordt hiermede verzogt, om het zelve, ten spoedigste, te willen zenden aan den Heer Minister van de Marine der Nederlanden in 's Gravenhage, of wel aan den Secretaris der Britsche Admiraliteit, te London, en daar by te voegen eene Nota, inhoudende de tyd en de plaats alwaar dit Papier is gevonden geworden.

FINDEREN af dette Papiir ombedes, naar Leilighed gives, at sende samme til Admiralitets Secretairen i London, eller nærmeste Embedsmand i Danmark, Norge, eller Sverrig. Tiden og Stædit hvor dette er funden önskes venskabeligt paategnet.

WER diesen Zettel findet, wird hier-durch ersucht denselben an den Secretair des Admiralitets in London einzusenden, mit gefälliger angabe an welchen ort und zu welcher zeit er gefunden worden ist.

London John Murray, Albemarle Street. 1859.

JOURNAL OF THE SEARCH

FOR

SIR JOHN FRANKLIN.

CHAPTER I.

Cause of delay in equipment — Fittings of the 'Fox' — Volunteers for arctic service — Assistance from public departments — Reflections upon the undertaking — Instructions and departure — Orkneys and Greenland — Fine arctic scenery — Danish establishments in Greenland — Frederickshaab, in Davis' Strait.

It is now a matter of history how Government and private expeditions prosecuted with unprecedented zeal and perseverance the search for Sir John Franklin's ships, between the years 1847-55; and that the only ray of information gleaned was that afforded by the inscriptions upon three tombstones at Beechey Island, briefly recording the names and dates of the deaths of those individuals of the lost expedition, who thus early fell in the cause of science and in the service of their country.

In this manner were we made aware of the locality where the Franklin expedition passed its first Arctic winter. The traces assuring us of that fact were discovered in August, 1850, by Captain Ommanney, R.N., of H.M.S. 'Assistance,' and by Captain Penny of the 'Lady Franklin.'

In October, 1854, Dr. Rae brought home the only additional information respecting them, which had ever reached us. From the Esquimaux of Boothia Felix he learned that a party of about forty white men were met on the west coast of King William's Island, who from thence travelled on to the mouth of the Great Fish River, where they all perished of starvation, and that this tragic event occurred apparently in the spring of 1850.

Some relics obtained from these natives, and brought home by Dr. Rae, were proved to have belonged to Sir John Franklin and several of his associates.

The Government caused an exploring party to descend the Fish River in 1855; but, although sufficient traces were found to prove that some portion of the crews of the 'Erebus' and 'Terror' had actually landed on the banks of that river, and traces existed of them up to Franklin Rapids, no additional information was obtained either by the discovery of Records, or through the Esquimaux. Mr. Anderson, the Hudson Bay Company's officer in charge, and his small party, deserve credit for their perseverance and skill; but they were not furnished with the necessary means of accomplishing their mission. Mr. Anderson could not obtain an interpreter, and the two frail bark canoes in which his whole party embarked were almost worn out before they reached the locality to be searched. It is not surprising that such an expedition caused very considerable disappointment at home.

Lady Franklin, and the advocates for further search, now pressed upon Government the necessity of following up, in a more effectual manner, the traces accidentally found by Dr. Rae, and, in fact, of rendering the search complete by one more effort, involving but little of hazard or expense. It was not until April, 1857, that any decisive answer was given to Lady Franklin's appeal.[1]

[1] Lady Franklin's letter to Viscount Palmerston, here alluded to, was published in the Appendix of the former editions of this work.

Sir Charles Wood then stated "that the members of Her Majesty's Government, having come, with great regret, to the conclusion that there was no prospect of saving life, would not be justified, for any objects which in their opinion could be obtained by an expedition to the arctic seas, in exposing the lives of officers and men to the risk inseparable from such an enterprise."

Lady Franklin, upon this final disappointment of her hopes, had no hesitation in immediately preparing to send out a searching expedition, equipped and stored at her own cost. But she was not without ardent supporters. Many friends of the cause—including some of the most distinguished scientific men in England, and especially Sir Roderick Murchison, whose zeal was as practical as it was enlightened—hastened to tender their aid, and soon a very considerable sum was raised in furtherance of so truly noble an effort.

On the 18th April, 1857, Lady Franklin offered me the command of the proposed expedition,—it was of course most cheerfully accepted. As a post of honour and of some difficulty it possessed quite sufficient charms for a naval officer who had already served in three consecutive expeditions from 1848 to 1854. I was thoroughly conversant with all the details of this peculiar service; and I confess, moreover, that my whole heart was in the cause. How could I do otherwise than devote myself to save at least the record of faithful service, even unto death, of my brother officers and seamen? and being one of those by whose united efforts not only the Franklin search, but the geography of arctic America, had been brought so nearly to completion, I could not willingly resign to posterity, the honour of filling up even the small remaining blanks upon our maps.

To leave these discoveries incomplete, more especially in a quarter through which the tidal stream actually demonstrates the existence of a channel—the only remaining hope of a practicable north-west passage—would indeed be leaving strong inducement for future explorers to reap the rich reward of our long-continued exertions.

I immediately applied to the Admiralty for leave of absence to complete the Franklin search; and on the 23rd received at Dublin the telegraphic message from Lady Franklin: "Your leave is granted; the 'Fox' is mine; the refit will commence immediately." She had already purchased the screw-yacht 'Fox,' of 177 tons burthen, and now placed her, together with the necessary funds, at my disposal.

Let me explain what is here implied by the simple word "refit." The velvet hangings and splendid furniture of the yacht, and also everything not constituting a part of the vessel's strengthening, were to be removed; the large skylights and capacious ladderways had to be reduced to limits more adapted to a polar clime; the whole vessel to be externally sheathed with stout planking, and internally fortified by strong cross beams, longitudinal beams, iron stanchions, and diagonal fastenings; the false keel taken off, the slender brass propeller replaced by a massive iron one, the boiler taken out, altered, and enlarged; the sharp stem to be cased in iron until it resembled a ponderous chisel set up edgeways; even the yacht's rig had to be altered.

She was placed in the hands of her builders, Messrs. Hall and Co., of Aberdeen, who displayed even more than their usual activity in effecting these necessary alterations, for it was determined that the 'Fox' should sail by the 1st July.

Internally she was fitted up with the strictest economy in every sense, and the officers were crammed into pigeon-holes, styled cabins, in order to make room for provisions and stores; our mess-room, for five persons, measured 8 feet square. The ordinary heating apparatus for winter use was dispensed with, and its place supplied by a few very small stoves. The 'Fox' had been the property of the late Sir Richard Sutton, Bart., who made but one trip to Norway in her, and she was purchased by Lady Franklin from his executors for 2000*l*.

Having thus far commenced the refit of the vessel, I turned my attention to the selection of a crew and to the requisite clothing and provisions for our voyage.

Many worthy old shipmates, my companions in previous arctic voyages, most readily volunteered their services: and they were as cheerfully accepted, for it was my anxious wish to gather around me well-tried men, who were aware of the duties expected of them, and accustomed to naval discipline. Hence, out of the twenty-five souls composing our small company, seventeen had previously served in the arctic search.

Expeditions of this nature are always popular with seamen, and innumerable were the applications made to me; but still more abundant were the offers to "serve in any capacity" which poured in from all parts of the country, from people of all classes, many of whom had never seen the sea. It was, of course, impossible to accede to any of these latter proposals, yet, for my own part, I could not but feel gratified at such convincing proofs that the spirit of the country was favourable to us, and that the ardent love of hardy enterprise still lives amongst Englishmen, to be cherished, I trust, as the most valuable of our national characteristics—that which has so largely contributed to make England what she is.

My second in command was Lieutenant W. R. Hobson, R.N., an officer already distinguished in arctic service. Captain Allen Young joined me as sailing-master, contributing not only his valuable services but largely of his private funds to the expedition. This gentleman had previously commanded some of our very finest merchant ships, the latest being the steam-transport 'Adelaide,' of 2500 tons: he had but recently returned, in ill-health, from the Black Sea, where he was most actively employed during the greater part of the Crimean campaign. Nothing that I could say would add to the merit of such singularly generous and disinterested conduct. David Walker, M.D., volunteered for the post of surgeon and naturalist; he also undertook the photographic department; and just before sailing, Carl Petersen, now so well known to arctic readers as the Esquimaux interpreter in the expeditions of Captain Penny and Dr. Kane, came to join me from Copenhagen, although landed there from Greenland only six days previously, after an absence of a year from his family: we were indebted to Sir Roderick Murchison and the electric telegraph for securing his valuable services.

Like the Paris omnibuses we were at length *au complet*, and quite as anxious to make a start.

Ample provisions for twenty-eight months were embarked, including preserved vegetables, lemon-juice, and pickles, for daily consumption, and preserved meats for every third day: also as much of Messrs. Allsopp's stoutest ale as we could find room for. The Government, although declining to send out an expedition, yet now contributed liberally to our supplies. All our arms, powder, shot, powder for ice-blasting, rockets, maroons, and signal-mortar, were furnished by the Board of Ordnance. The Admiralty caused 6682 lbs. of pemmican to be prepared for our use. Not less than 85,000 lbs. of this invaluable food have been prepared since 1845 at the Royal Clarence Victualling Yard, Gosport, for the use of the arctic Expeditions. It is composed of prime beef cut into thin slices and dried over a wood fire; then pounded up and mixed with about an equal weight of melted beef fat. The warm pemmican is then run into strong tin cases and becomes hard on cooling; our cases contained 42 lbs. each, they were oblong in shape, but with convex ends, this form giving them greater strength to resist the claws of the Bears.

The Admiralty supplied us also with all the requisite ice-gear, such as saws from ten to eighteen feet in length, ice-anchors, and ice-claws: also with our winter housing, medicines, pure lemon-juice, seamen's library, hydrographical instruments, charts, chronometers, and an ample supply of arctic clothing which had remained in store from former expeditions. The Board of Trade contributed a variety of meteorological and nautical instruments and journals; and I found that I had but to ask of these departments for what was required, and if in store it was at once granted. I asked, however, for such things only as were indispensably necessary.

The President and Council of the Royal Society voted the sum of 50*l*. from their donation fund for the purchase of magnetic and other scientific instruments, in order that our anticipated approach to so interesting a locality as the Magnetic Pole might not be altogether barren of results.

I was desirous to retain for my vessel the privileges she formerly enjoyed as a yacht, and my wishes were very promptly gratified: in the first instance by the Royal Harwich Yacht Club, of which my officers and myself were enrolled as members—the Commodore, A. Arcedeckne, Esq., presenting my vessel with the handsome ensign and burgee of the Club; and shortly afterwards by my being elected a member of the Royal Victoria Yacht Club for the period of my voyage. Lastly, upon the very day of sailing, I was proposed for the Royal Yacht Squadron, to which the yacht had previously belonged when the property of Sir Richard Sutton.

Throughout the whole period required for our equipment I constantly experienced the heartiest co-operation and earnest goodwill from all with whom my varied duties brought me in contact. Deep sympathy with Lady Franklin in her distress, her self-devotion and sacrifice of fortune, and an earnest desire to extend succour to any chance survivors of the missing expedition who might still exist, or at least, to ascertain their fate, and rescue from oblivion their heroic deeds, seemed the natural promptings of every honest English heart.

It is needless to add that this experience of public opinion confirmed my own impression that the glorious mission intrusted to me was in reality a *great national duty*. I could not but feel that, if the gigantic and admirably equipped national expeditions sent out upon precisely the same duty, and reflecting so much credit upon the Board of Admiralty, were ranked amongst the noblest efforts in the cause of humanity any nation ever engaged in, and that, if high honour was awarded to all composing these splendid expeditions, surely the effort became still more remarkable and worthy of approbation when its means were limited to one little vessel, containing but twenty-five souls, equipped and provisioned (although efficiently, yet) in a manner more according with the limited resources of a private individual than with those of the public purse. The less the means, the more arduous I felt was the achievement. The greater the risk—for the 'Fox' was to be launched alone into those dangerous seas from which every other vessel had long since been withdrawn—the more glorious would be the success, the more honourable even the defeat, if again defeat awaited us.

Upon the last day of June Lady Franklin, accompanied by her niece Miss Sophia Cracroft, and my esteemed friend and brother officer Rochfort Maguire,[1] came on board at

[1] The late Commodore Maguire. This brave, generous, and humane

Aberdeen to bid us farewell, for we purposed sailing in the evening. Seeing how deeply agitated Lady Franklin was on leaving the ship, I endeavoured to repress the enthusiasm of my crew, but without avail; it found vent in three prolonged hearty cheers. The strong feeling which prompted them was truly sincere; and this unbidden exhibition of it can hardly have gratified her for whom it was intended more than it did myself.

I must here insert the only written instructions I could prevail upon Lady Franklin to give me; they were not read until the 'Fox' was fairly in the Atlantic.

My dear Captain M'Clintock, *Aberdeen, June* 29, 1857.

You have kindly invited me to give you "Instructions," but I cannot bring myself to feel that it would be right in me in any way to influence your judgment in the conduct of your noble undertaking; and indeed I have no temptation to do so, since it appears to me that your views are almost identical with those which I had independently formed before I had the advantage of being thoroughly possessed of yours. But had this been otherwise, I trust you would have found me ready to prove the implicit confidence I place in you by yielding my own views to your more enlightened judgment; knowing too as I do that your whole heart also is in the cause, even as my own is.

As to the objects of the expedition and their relative importance, I am sure you know that the rescue of any possible survivor of the 'Erebus' and 'Terror' would be to me, as it would be to you, the noblest result of our efforts.

To this object I wish every other to be subordinate; and next to it in importance is the recovery of the unspeakably precious documents of the expedition, public and private, and the personal relics of my dear husband and his companions.

And lastly, I trust it may be in your power to confirm, directly or in-

---

officer was universally respected and beloved. Scarcely had he reached the meridian of life when a protracted and most painful malady terminated his career in 1867, a few days only after his return from Australia, where he held the chief naval command. In 1840 he was most severely wounded at the taking of Sidon. When engaged in arctic service, 1852-3-4, he particularly distinguished himself by his noble forbearance towards the natives at Point Barrow who attacked H.M.S. 'Plover' under his command: his admirable narrative is published in the Appendix to McClure's 'North-West Passage.'

ferentially, the claims of my husband's expedition to the earliest discovery of the N.W. passage, which, if Dr. Rae's report be true (and the Government of our country has accepted and rewarded it as such), these martyrs in a noble cause achieved at their last extremity, after five long years of labour and suffering, if not at an earlier period.

I am sure you will do all that man can do for the attainment of all these objects; my only fear is that you may spend yourselves too much in the effort; and you must therefore let me tell you how much dearer to me even than any of them is the preservation of the valuable lives of the little band of heroes who are your companions and followers.

May God in his great mercy preserve you all from harm amidst the labours and perils which await you, and restore you to us in health and safety as well as honour! As to the honour I can have *no* misgiving. It will be yours as much if you fail (since you *may* fail in spite of every effort) as if you succeed; and be assured that, under *any and all circumstances whatever*, such is my unbounded confidence in you, you will possess and be entitled to the enduring gratitude of your sincere and attached friend,

JANE FRANKLIN.

We were not destined to get to sea that evening. The 'Fox,' hitherto during her brief career, accustomed only to the restraint imposed upon a gilded pet in summer seas, seemed to have got an inkling that her duty henceforth was to combat with difficulties, and, entering fully into the spirit of the cruize, answered her helm so much more readily than the pilot expected, that she ran aground upon the bar. She was promptly shored up, and remained in that position until next morning, when she floated off unhurt at high water, and commenced her long and lonely voyage.

Scarcely had we left the busy world behind us when we were actively engaged in making arrangements for present comfort and future exertion. How busy, how happy, and how full of hope we all were then!

On the night of the 2nd of July we passed through the Pentland Firth, where the tide rushing impetuously against a strong wind raised up a tremendous sea, amid which the little vessel struggled bravely under steam and canvas. The bleak wild shores of Orkney, the uncouth aspect, hoarse screams and unintelligible dialect of the Pilots' crew, the shrill cry of innumerable sea-birds, the howling breeze and angry sea, made us feel as if we had suddenly awakened in Greenland itself.

The southern extremity of that ice-locked continent became visible on the 12th. It is quaintly named Cape Farewell; but whether by some sanguine outward-bound adventurer who fancied that in leaving Greenland behind him he had already secured his passage to Cathay; or whether by the wearied homesick mariner, barely escaping in his shattered bark from the grasp of winter, and firmly purposing to bid a long *farewell* to this cheerless land, history altogether fails to enlighten us.

From January until July this coast is usually rendered unapproachable by a broad margin of heavy ice, which drifts there from the vicinity of Spitzbergen, and, lapping round the Cape, extends alongshore to the northward about as far as Baal's River, a distance of 250 miles. Although it effectually blockades the ports of South Greenland for the greater part of the summer, and is justly dreaded by the captains of the Greenland traders, it confers important benefits upon the Greenlander by bearing to his shores immense numbers of seals and many bears. The same current which conveys hither all this ice is also freighted with a scarcely less valuable supply of driftwood from the Siberian rivers.

About this time, one of my crew showing symptoms of diseased lungs, I determined to embrace the earliest opportunity of sending him home out of a climate so fatal to those who are thus affected; and having learnt from Mr. Petersen, who had quitted Greenland only in April last, that a vessel would very soon leave Frederickshaab for Copenhagen, I resolved to go to that place in order to catch this homeward-bound ship.

It was necessary to push through the Spitzbergen ice, and we fortunately succeeded in doing so after eighteen hours of buffeting with this formidable enemy; at first we found it tolerably loose, and the wind being strong and favourable, we thumped along pleasantly enough; but as we advanced, the ice became much more closely packed, a thick fog came on, and many hard knocks were exchanged; at length our steam carried us through into the broad belt of clear water between the ice and land, which Petersen assured me always exists here at this season.

The dense fog now prevented further progress, and as evening closed in I gave up all hope of improvement for the night: when suddenly, the fog rolled back upon the land disclosing some islets close to us, then the rugged points of mainland, and at length, the distant snowy mountain-peaks against a deep blue sky. We found ourselves to be upon the Tallard Bank, 30 miles north of our port, having been rapidly carried northward by the Spitzbergen current.

The evening became bright and delightful; the whole extent of coast was fringed with innumerable islets, backed by lofty mountains, and, being richly tinted by a glorious western sun, formed an unusually splendid sight. Greenland unveiled to our anxious gaze, that memorable evening, all the magnificence of her wondrous natural beauty. It almost seemed as if to welcome us, she thus suddenly cast off her dingy mantle and shone forth with an impressive grandeur which alpine scenery alone can equal.

A faint streak apparently of mist, which we could not account for, still extended across a low wide interval in the mountain range; the telescope revealed its true character,—it was a portion of the distant mighty glacier.

July 20*th*.—This morning the chief trader of the settlement, or, as he is more usually styled by the English, the Governor, came off to us, and his pilot soon conducted us into the safe little harbour of Frederickshaab. I was much gratified to learn that we were just in time to secure a passage home for our ailing shipmate.

For trading purposes Greenland is monopolized by the Danish Government; its Esquimaux and mixed population amount to about 7000 souls. Some 400 or 500 Danes reside constantly there for the purpose of conducting the trade, which consists almost exclusively in the exchange of European goods for oil and the skins of seals, reindeer, and a few other animals.

The Esquimaux are not subject to Danish laws, and they pride themselves upon this mere show of independence; they are, however, sincerely attached to the Danes, and with abundant reason; a Lutheran clergyman, a doctor, and a schoolmaster, whose several duties it is to give them gratuitous instruction and relief, are attached to each district, and supported by the Danish Government; and when these improvident people are in distress, which not unfrequently happens during the long winters, provisions are issued to them free of cost: spirits are strictly prohibited. All of them have become Christians, and many can read and write.

Have we English done as much for the aborigines in any of our numerous colonies, even in far more favoured climes? We have thousands of Esquimaux within our own territories of Labrador and of the Hudson's Bay Company, have we ever attempted to do anything for their welfare?—and thousands more of them inhabit the north shore of Hudson's Strait and the west shore of Davis' Strait, within three weeks' sail of us, and in annual communication with our whaling ships.

Greenland is divided into two inspectorates, the northern and southern; the inspector of the latter division, Dr. Rink, had arrived at Frederickshaab upon his summer round of visits only the day previous to ourselves. He came on board to call upon me, and after Divine Service I landed, and enjoyed a ramble with him over the moss-clad hills. Our first meeting was in North Greenland in 1848; we had not seen one another since, so we had much to talk about. Dr. Rink is a gentleman of acknowledged talent, a distinguished traveller, and is thoroughly conversant with the sciences of geology and botany. Unfortunately for me his excellent work on Greenland has not been translated into English.

Huge granitic boulders are not uncommon; we met some during our walk; the largest measured fifty feet in circumference by eight feet in height.

We were kindly permitted to purchase eight tons of coals, and such small things as were required; the only fresh supplies to be obtained besides codfish, which was abundant, consisted of a very few ptarmigan and hares, and a couple of kids; these last are scarce. Some goats exist, but for eight months out of the year they are shut up in a house, and even now—in midsummer—are only let out in the daytime. We also purchased of the Esquimaux some specimens of Esquimaux workmanship, such as models of the native dresses, kayaks, &c., also birds' skins and eggs. I saw fine specimens of the white swan, and of a bird said to be extremely rare in Greenland,—it was a species of grebe, *Podiceps cristatus*, I imagine. Frederickshaab is just now well supplied with wood: besides an unseaworthy brig, the wreck of a large timber-ship lay on the beach, and an abandoned timber-vessel, which was met with between Iceland and Greenland in July by Prince Napoleon, drifted upon the coast 30 miles to the northward in the following September.

21st.—Dr. Rink paid me a visit when starting upon a boat-voyage to visit some settlements at several days' journey to the southward. His boat was constructed of a wooden frame covered with stout seal-skin; it was about thirty feet long, very narrow, and flat at the bottom. The crew consisted of six smartly dressed young women,—hence, I suppose, the Esquimaux name of *Oomiak*, or woman's boat;—and the coxswain, or pilot, was a sedate old man, whose patience must often have been sorely tried by these frisky damsels.

Esquimaux matrons remain at home attending to household affairs. The men and lads employ themselves in hunting and fishing—they are too dignified and lazy to labour in rowing;—so it is amongst the disposable young women one must look for a boat's crew, and it seemed to us that the worthy inspector had selected the belles of the place. The difficulty of *discipline* amongst them once got over, boating in South Greenland may be pleasant enough; we naturally regarded such a boat and boat's crew as an interesting novelty, and were immensely amused by observing the amount of coquettishness, combined with very graceful skill, which these emulous rowers contrived to display upon this rare and fitting occasion,—the Governor's State visit to the 'Fox'!

The Governor in his Oomiak

CHAPTER II.

Fiskernaes and Esquimaux — The 'Fox' reaches Disco — Disco Fiord — Summer scenery — Waigat Strait — Coaling from the mine — Purchasing Esquimaux dogs — Heavy gale off Upernivik — Melville Bay — The middle ice — The great glacier of Greenland — Do Reindeer cross the glacier?

23rd July.—SAILED the day before yesterday for Godhaab. The fog was thick, and wind strong and contrary, but the current being favourable we found ourselves off the small out-station of Fiskernaes, when early this morning our fore topmast was carried away; this accident induced me to run in and anchor for the purpose of repairing the damage.

After passing within the outer islets, the Moravian settlement of Lichtenfels came in view upon the right hand; it consists of a large sombre-looking wooden house over which is a belfry, a smaller wooden house, and about a dozen native huts roofed with sods, and scarcely distinguishable from the ground they stand on, even at a very short distance. The land immediately behind is a barren rocky steep, now just sufficiently denuded of snow to look desolate in the extreme. A strong tide was setting out of the fiord, as we approached and anchored in the rocky little cove of Fiskernaes; here we were not only sheltered from the wind, but the steep dark rocks within a ship's length on each side of us reflected a strong heat, whilst large mosquitoes lost no time in paying us their annoying visits. This remote spot has been visited by the arctic voyagers Captain Inglefield, R.N., and Dr. Kane, U.S.N., and still more recently by Prince Napoleon. Dr. Kane's account of his visit is full and very interesting.

Cod-fishing was now in full activity, and the few men not so employed had gone up the fiord to hunt reindeer.

The solitary dwelling-house belongs of course to the chief trader, and is a model of cleanliness and order; built of wood, it exhibits all the resources of the painter's art; the exterior is a dull red, the window-frames are white, floors yellow, wooden partitions and low ceilings pale blue. The lady of the house had resided here for about eight years, and appeared to us to be, and acknowledged she was, heartily tired of the solitude. She gave me coffee, and some seeds for cultivation at our winter quarters: these were lettuce, spinach, turnips, carraway, and peas, the latter being the common kind used on board ship; usually they have only produced leaves on this spot, but once the young peas grew large enough for the table. I expressed a wish to see the interior of an Esquimaux tent. Petersen pulled aside the thin membrane of some animal, which hung across a doorway, and served to exclude the wind, but admitted light; for, although past midnight, there was good daylight. Some seven or eight individuals lay within closely packed upon the ground; the heads of old and young, males and females, being just visible above the common covering. Going to bed here only means lying down with your clothes on, upon a reindeer skin, wherever you can find room, and pulling another fur-robe over you.

Fiskernaes appeared to be a sunny little nook, yet all the people we saw there were suffering from colds and coughs, and many deaths had occurred during the spring. The boys brought us handfuls of rough garnets, some of them as large as walnuts, receiving with evident satisfaction biscuits in exchange.

By next morning we were able to put to sea, and early on the day following arrived off the large settlement of Godhaab; it is in the "Gilbert Sound" of Davis, and appears in many old charts as Baal's River. Almost adjoining Godhaab is the Moravian settlement of New Herrnhut. Here it was that Hans Egede, the missionary father of Greenland, established himself in 1721, and thus re-opened the communication between Europe and Greenland, which had ceased upon the extinction of its early Scandinavian settlers in the 14th century.

A few years after Egede's successful beginning, the Moravian mission still existing under the name of New Herrnhut was established. At present the Moravians support four missions in Greenland; they are not subject to the Danish authorities, nor are they permitted in any way to trade.

As we were about to enter the harbour, the Danish vessel —the sole object of our visit—came out, so not a moment was lost in sending on board our invalid[1] and our letter-bag, and in landing our coasting pilot. This man had brought us up from Frederickshaab for the very moderate sum of three pounds; he was an Esquimaux, and, as the brother of poor Hans, Dr. Kane's unhappy dog-driver, was received with favour amongst us, and soon won our esteem by his quiet obliging disposition, as also by his ability in the discharge of his duty; he was so keensighted and so vigilant, it was quite a comfort to have him on board during the foggy weather, for he could recognise on the instant every rock or point, even when dimly looming through the mist. We were not long in discovering that his absence was a loss to us.

When passing out to the north of the Kookornen islands, the wind suddenly failed, and at the same time a swell from to seaward reached us; we therefore had considerable diffi-

---

[1] This man was in a rapid decline; his shipmates kindly prepared for him a few bottles of cod liver oil from the fish obtained at Frederickshaab; to this oil, he subsequently told me, he attributed his speedy and complete recovery.

culty in towing the ship clear of the rocks; for nearly half an hour our position was most critical.

July 31*st.*—Anchored at Godhavn (or Lively), in Disco, for a few hours. I presented a letter from the Directors of the Royal Greenland Company to the Inspector of North Greenland, Mr. C. S. M. Olrik, authorising him to furnish us with any needful supplies. Our only wants were sledge-dogs and a native to manage them. We soon obtained ten of the former, but were advised to go into Disco Fiord, where many of the Esquimaux were busy in taking and drying salmon-trout, and where one of the latter would most probably be obtained.

I was much pleased with Mr. Olrik's kind reception of me, and soon found him to be not only agreeable but well informed. Born in Greenland of Danish parents, he is thoroughly conversant with the language and habits of the Esquimaux, and has devoted much of his leisure time in collecting rare specimens of the animal, vegetable, and mineral productions of the country. I came away enriched by some fossils from the fossilized forest of Atanekerdluk, also with specimens of native coal.

It was here I met with the commanders of the late whalers 'Gipsy' and 'Undaunted,' of Peterhead, which had been crushed by the ice in Melville Bay five or six weeks previously: all the other whalers had returned from the north along the pack edge, and passed south of Disco. They said that the ice in Melville Bay was all broken up, and that they thought we should find but little difficulty at this late period in passing through it into the North Water.

Although the crews of the lost whalers were here, awaiting a passage home in the Danish ship, yet I could not induce any of them to volunteer for the 'Fox.'

Leaving Godhavn in the afternoon with a native pilot, we found ourselves some 10 or 12 miles up Disco Fiord at an early hour next morning. After despatching the pilot to announce our arrival to his countrymen at their fishing station, 7 or 8 miles further up, the Doctor and I landed upon the north side to explore.

The scenery is charming, lofty hills of trap rock, with slopes unusually rich in grass and moss for the 70th parallel, descending to the fiord, and strewed with boulders of gneiss and granite. We found the blue campanula holding a conspicuous place amongst the wild flowers. I do not know a more enticing spot in Greenland for a week's shooting, fishing, and yachting than Disco Fiord; hares and ptarmigan may be found along the bases of the hills: ducks are most abundant about the fiord, and delicious salmon-trout very plentiful in the rivers. Formerly Disco was famed for the large size and abundance of its reindeer; but for some unexplained reason they now confine themselves to the mainland.

At this season the natives of Godhavn resort here and enjoy the trout fishery,—it is truly their season of harvest: the weather is pleasant, food delicious and abundant, and labour an agreeable pastime.

Some kayaks soon came off to the ship, bringing salmon-trout, both fresh and smoked.

A young Esquimaux, named Christian, volunteered his services as our dog-driver, and was accepted; he is about 23 years of age, unmarried, and an orphan. The men soon thoroughly cleansed and cropped him: soap and scissars being novelties to an Esquimaux; they then rigged him in sailor's clothes; he was evidently not at home in them, but was not the less proud of his improved appearance, as reflected in the admiring glances of his countrymen.

We now hastened away to the Waigat Strait to complete our coals. When passing Godhavn, the pilot was launched off our deck in his little kayak without stopping the ship!

As a kayak is usually about 18 feet long, 8 inches deep, and only 15 or 16 inches wide, it requires great expertness to perform such a feat without the addition of a capsize.

4th August. — Entered the Waigat yesterday morning, slowly steaming through a sea of glass. Its surface was only rippled by the myriads of eider-ducks which extended over it for several miles : most of them were immature in plumage, and were probably the birds of last year.

After running about 24 miles, towards evening we approached a low range of sandstone cliffs on the Disco shore, in which horizontal seams of coal were seen. Here we anchored, and immediately commenced coaling. It was fortunate we did so, for soon it began to blow hard ; and ere noon to-day we were obliged, for the safety of the ship, to leave our exposed anchorage, having, however, secured eight or nine tons of tolerable coal. Formerly these coal-seams were worked for the supply of the neighbouring settlements, but for several years past it has been found more profitable and convenient to send out coals from Denmark, and thus permit the natives to devote their whole time to the seal-fishery.

The Waigat scenery is unusually grand ; the strait varies from 3 to 5 leagues in width ; on each side are mountains of 3000 feet in height. The Disco side, upon which we landed, is composed of trap, sandstone appearing only at the beach, and occasionally rising in cliffs to about 100 feet. Upon the moss-clad slopes many fragments of quartz and zoolite were met with. The north end of Disco is almost a precipice, the snow-capped summit of which is 4000 feet high.

5th.—A pleasant fair wind carries us rapidly northward, passing many icebergs. Our rigging is richly garnished with split codfish, which we hoped would dry and keep ; but a warm day in Disco Fiord, and much rain with a southerly gale in the Waigat, have destroyed it for our own use. It is, however, still valuable as food for our dogs. I am very anxious to complete my stock of these our native auxiliaries, as without them we cannot hope to explore all the lands which it is the object of our voyage to search. We could only obtain ten at Godhavn, and we require twenty more.

6th.—By Petersen's intimate knowledge of the coast we were enabled to run close in to the little settlement of Proven during the night,[1] and obtain a few dogs and some dogs' food. This morning we reached the extreme station of Upernivik, the last trace of civilization we shall meet with for some time. It is in lat. $72\frac{3}{4}$ N. Here Petersen resided for twelve of the eighteen years he has spent in Greenland, and his unlooked-for reappearance astonished and delighted the small community, more especially Governor Fliescher and his household, who received us with a most hearty welcome. On a previous visit to this place I was tempted to measure an Esquimaux's mouth as he stood on the deck, grinning frightfully and offering a couple of speared looms for sale; it measured four inches and a half across! Flattered by this attention, he begged for rum, and a small wineglassful was given him,—he literally chucked it into this yawning crater, as a dog catches the crumb thrown to him, and, quick as thought, held the glass out for more, which of course he did not get.

7th.—Yesterday, when we hove to off Upernivik, the weather was very bad and rapidly growing worse, therefore our stay was limited to a couple of hours. The last letters for home were landed, fourteen dogs and a quantity of seal's flesh for them embarked, and the ship's head was turned seaward.

It was then blowing a southerly gale, with overcast murky sky, and a heavy sea running. When four miles outside the

---

[1] It is hardly necessary to remind the reader that at this season, and in this high latitude, the daylight is constant.

outer island, breakers were *suddenly* discovered ahead, only just in time to avoid the ledge of sunken rocks upon which the sea was beating most violently. Many such rocks lie at considerable distances beyond the islands which border this coast, and greatly add to the dangers of its navigation. Being now fairly at sea, and the ship under easy sail for the night, I went early to bed in the hope of sleeping. I had been up all the previous night, naturally anxious about the ship threading her way through so many dangers, uncertain about being able to complete the number of our sledge-dogs, and much occupied in closing my correspondence, to which there would be an end for at least a year. All this over, the uncertain future loomed ominously before me. The great responsibilities I had undertaken seemed now and at once to fall with all their weight upon me. A mental whirlpool was the consequence, which, backed by the material storm, and the howling of the wretched dogs in concert on deck, together with the tumbling about of everything below, long kept sleep in abeyance. One thought and feeling predominated: it was gratitude, deep and humble, for the success which had hitherto attended us, and for some narrow escapes which I must ever regard as providential.

Yesterday's gale has given place to calm foggy weather. An occasional iceberg is seen. The officers amuse themselves in trying new guns, and shooting sea-birds for our dogs.

Governor Fliescher told me yesterday that for the last four weeks southerly winds had prevailed, and that only a fortnight ago his boat was unable to reach the Loom Cliffs at Cape Shackleton, 50 miles north of Upernivik, in consequence of the ice being pressed in against the land. I fear these same winds have closed together the ice which occupies the middle of Davis' Strait (hence called the middle ice), so that we shall not be able to penetrate it. However, we are standing out to make the attempt.

To the uninitiated it may be as well to observe that each winter the sea called Baffin's Bay freezes over; in spring this vast body of ice breaks up, and drifting southward in a mass—called the main-pack, or the middle ice—obstructs the passage across from east to west.

The "North Passage" is made by sailing round the north end of this pack; the "Middle Passage," by pushing through it; and the "Southern Passage," by passing round its southern extreme; but seasons do occur when none of these routes is practicable.

It is very remarkable that southward of Disco northerly winds have prevailed. They greatly impeded our progress up Davis' Strait, but we cheered ourselves with the hope that they would effectually clear a path for us across the northern part of Baffin's Bay.

8th.—Last night we reached the edge of the middle ice, about 70 miles to the west of Upernivik, and ran southward along its edge all night. This morning, in thick fog, the ship was caught in its margin of loose ice. The fog soon after cleared off, and we saw the clear sea about two miles to the eastward, whilst all to the west was impenetrable closely-packed floe-pieces. After steaming out of our predicament (a matter which we could not accomplish under sail) we ran on to the southward until evening, but found the pack edge still composed of light ice very closely pressed together.

Having now closely examined it for an extent of 40 miles, I was satisfied that we could not force a passage through it across Baffin's Bay, as is frequently done in ordinary seasons: therefore, taking advantage of a fair wind, we steered to the northward, in order to seek an opening in that direction.

12th.—*Position* 75° 6' *N.*, 59° 20' *W.* We are in Melville Bay; made fast this afternoon to an iceberg, which lies aground in 58 fathoms water, about two miles from Browne's Islands, and between them and the great glacier which here takes the place of the coast-line.

We have got thus far without any difficulty, sailing along the edge of the middle ice; but here we find it pressing in against Browne's Islands, and covering the whole bay to the northward, quite in to the steep face of the glacier. This is evidently the result of long-continued southerly winds; but as the ice is very much broken up, we may expect it to move off rapidly before the autumnal northerly winds now due, and these winds invariably remove the previous season's ice. All that we know of Melville Bay navigation in August is derived from the experience of exploring voyages, and is limited to eight or nine seasons. My own three previous transits across it were made in this month. The whalers either get through in June or July, or give up the attempt as being too late for their fishing. It frequently happens that they get round the south end of the middle ice, between latitudes 66° and 69° N., and up the west coast of Baffin's Bay late in the season; but we have no accounts of these voyages, nor should I be justified, at this late period of the season, in abandoning the prospect before me, in order to attempt a route which, even if successful, would lengthen our voyage to Barrow's Strait by 700 or 800 miles. We have already passed what is usually the most difficult and dangerous part of the Melville Bay transit.

There is much to excite intense admiration and wonder around us; one cannot at once appreciate the grandeur of this mighty glacier, extending, coastwise, unbroken for 40 or 50 miles. Its sea-cliffs, about 5 or 6 miles from us, appear comparatively low, yet the icebergs detached from it are of the loftiest description. Here, on the spot, it does not seem incorrect to compare the icebergs to mere chippings off its edge, and the floe-ice to the thinnest shavings.

The far-off outline of glacier, seen against the eastern sky, has a faint tinge of yellow: it is almost horizontal, and of unknown distance and elevation; roughly, we may estimate it to be thirty or forty miles off, and 1500 or 2000 feet high.

There is an unusual dearth of birds and seals; everything around us is painfully still, excepting when an occasional iceberg splits off from the parent glacier; then we hear a rumbling crash like distant thunder, and the wave occasioned by the launch reaches us in six or seven minutes, and makes the ship roll lazily for a similar period. I cannot imagine that within the whole compass of nature's varied aspects there is presented to the human eye a scene so well adapted for promoting deep and serious reflection, for lifting one's thoughts from trivial things of everyday life to others of the highest moment.

The glacier reminds us at once of Time and Eternity—of time, for we see portions of it break off to drift and melt away; and of eternity, since its downward march is so extremely slow, and its augmentations behind so regular, that no change in its appearance is perceptible from age to age. If even the untaught savages of luxuriant tropical regions regard the earth merely as a temporary abode, surely all who gaze upon this ice-overwhelmed region, this wide expanse of "terrestrial wreck," must be similarly assured that here we have no abiding place, "no continuing city."

During daytime the strong glare is very distressing, hence the subdued light of midnight, when the sun just skims along the northern horizon, is much the most agreeable part of the twenty-four hours; the temperature varies between 30° and 40° of Fahrenheit.

The drift-ice of various descriptions about us is constantly in motion under the influence of mysterious surface and under currents (according to their relative depths of floatation), which whirl them about in every possible direction.

To the S.E. are two small islands, almost enveloped in the glacier, and far within it an occasional mountain-peak protrudes from beneath.

Our Summer Costume.

From observing closely the variations in the glacier surface, I think we may safely infer that where it lies unbroken and smooth, the supporting land is level; and where much crevassed the land beneath is uneven. The crevassed parts are of course impassable, but, by following the windings of the smooth surface, I think the interior could be reached. Some attempts to cross the glacier in

South Greenland have failed, yet, by studying its character and attending to this remark, I think places might be found where an attempt would succeed. Mr. Petersen tells me that the Esquimaux of Upernivik are unable to account for occasional disappearances and reappearances of immense herds of reindeer, except by assuming that they migrate at intervals to feeding-grounds beyond the glacier, the surface of which he also says is smooth enough in many places even for dog-sledges to travel upon. As there is much uninhabited land both to the northward and southward of Upernivik, I do not see the necessity for this supposition. The habits of the Esquimaux confine them almost exclusively to the islands and sea-coasts.

CHAPTER III.

Melville Bay — Crow's-nest — Beset in Melville Bay — Signs of winter — The coming storm — Drifting in the pack — Canine appetite — Resigned to a winter in the pack — Dinner stolen by sharks — The arctic shark — White whales and Killers.

15th Aug.—THREE days of the most perfect calm have sadly taxed our patience. Lovely bright weather, but scarcely a living creature seen. This afternoon the anxiously-looked-for north wind sprang up, and immediately the light ice began to drift away before it, but it is not strong enough to influence the icebergs, and they greatly retard the clearing-out of the bay. We have noticed a constant wind off the glacier, probably the result of its cooling effect upon the atmosphere; this wind does not extend more than 3 or 4 miles out from it. We are lying alongside an iceberg; from the pools upon its surface we obtain the most delicious water: the Doctor has clambered all over it in search for extraneous matter, boulders, mud, &c., but without success. The dogs have been put upon it, and they enjoy the comparative freedom of space which it affords; occasionally they survey the prospect from its loftiest peak, frequently they fight, and, then unwarily approaching too near to its glassy slopes, tumble into the sea; when this happens the whole pack give us notice by setting up a prolonged melancholy howl, peculiar to wolves and Esquimaux dogs;— What's the row now? Oh, it's only another dog overboard! The dog swims to the ship, allows himself to be pulled up in the bight of a rope, and for the time tranquillity is restored.

So great is the discharge of fresh water from the glacier and the innumerable icebergs, and so calm has been the weather, that we find the surface of the sea covered to a depth of three inches by water which is perfectly fresh!

16th.—One of the loveliest mornings imaginable; the icebergs sparkled in the sun, and the breeze was just sufficiently strong to ripple the patches of dark blue sea; beyond this, there was nothing to cheer one in the prospect from the crow's-nest at four o'clock; but little change had taken place in the ice; I therefore determined to run back along the pack-edge to the south-westward, in the hope that some favourable change might have taken place further off shore. The barometer was unusually low, yet no indication of any change of weather. A seaman's chest was picked up; it contained only a spoon, a fork, and some tin canisters, and probably drifted here from the southward, where the two whale-ships were crushed in June, affording another proof of the prevalence of southerly winds. As we steamed on, the ice was found to have opened considerably; it fell calm, and mist was observed rolling along the glacier from the southward. By noon a S.E. wind reached us; all sail was set, the leads or lanes of water became wider, and our hopes of speedily crossing Melville Bay rose in proportion as our speed increased. We are pursuing our course without let or hindrance.

The "crow's-nest" is a peculiarity of arctic ships; it is merely a secure and sheltered look-out post, as high up the mast as possible. Here on this lofty perch the commander spends anxious hours watching the ice-movements, and tracing out in the ever-changing labyrinth the most secure and continuous "leads" or "lanes" of water in the direction of his course. It resembles a cask about $4\frac{1}{2}$ feet high, and wide enough for a man to turn round in freely; it has a trap-door in the bottom through which he enters it, a small moveable screen on the top to keep off the biting winds, and contains a narrow flat seat; a light iron rod extends round from its upper rim on which to rest a telescope. The extent of vision over the sea-level, of course, varies with the observer's elevation, and is in actual sea-miles but slightly more than the square-root of that elevation in feet.

17th.—The fog overtook us yesterday evening, and at length, unable to see our way, we made fast at eleven o'clock to the ice. The wind had freshened, it was evidently blowing a gale outside the ice. During the night we drifted rapidly together with the ice, and this morning, on the clearing off of the fog, we steamed and sailed on again, threading our way between the floes, which are larger and much covered with *dry* snow. This evening we again made fast, the floes having closed together, cutting off advance and retreat. A wintry night, much wind and snow.

19th. — Continued strong S.E. winds, pressing the ice closely together, dark sky and snow; everything wears a wintry and threatening aspect; we are closely hemmed in, and have our rudder and screw unshipped. This recommencement of S.E. winds and rapid ebbing of the small remaining portion of summer, makes me more anxious about the future than the present. Yesterday the weather improved, and by working for thirteen hours we got the ship out of her small ice-creek into a larger space of water, and in so doing advanced a mile and a half. It is now calm, but the ice still drifts, as we would wish it, to the N.W. Yesterday we were within 12 miles of the position of the 'Enterprise' upon the same day in 1848, and under very similar conditions of weather and ice also.

20th.—*Position*, 75° 17' N., 62° 16' W. No favourable ice-drift: this detention has become most painful. The 'Enterprise' reached the open water upon this day in 1848, within 50 miles of our present position; unfortunately, our prospects are not so cheering. There is no relative motion in the floes of ice, except a gradual closing together, the small spaces and creaks of water being still further diminished. The temperature has fallen, and is usually below the freezing-point. I feel most keenly the difficulty of my position; we cannot afford to lose many more days. Of all the voyages to Barrow Strait, there are but two which were delayed beyond this date, viz., Parry's in 1824, and the 'Prince Albert's' in 1851. Should we not be released, and therefore be compelled to winter in this pack, notwithstanding all our efforts, I shall repeat the trial next year, and in the end, with God's aid, perform my sacred duty.

The men enjoy a game of rounders on the ice each evening; Petersen and Christian are constantly on the look-out for seals, as well as Hobson and Young occasionally; if in good condition and killed instantaneously, the seals float; several have already been shot; the liver fried with bacon is excellent.

Birds have become scarce,—the few we see are returning southward. How anxiously I watch the ice, weather, barometer, and thermometer! Wind from any other quarter than S.E. would oblige the floe-pieces to rearrange themselves, in doing which they would become loose, and then would be our opportunity to proceed.

24*th*.—Fine weather with very light northerly winds. We have drifted 7 miles to the west in the last two days. The ice is now a close pack, so close that one may walk for many miles over it in any direction, by merely turning a little to the right or left to avoid the small water spaces. My frequent visits to the crow's-nest are not inspiring: how absolutely distressing this imprisonment is to me, no one without similar experience can form any idea. As yet the crew have but little suspicion how blighted our prospects are.

27th.—We daily make attempts to push on, and sometimes get a ship's length, but yesterday evening we made a mile and a half! the ice then closed against the ship's sides and lifted her about a foot. We have had a fresh east wind for two days, but no corresponding ice-drift to the west; this is most discouraging, and can only be accounted for by supposing the existence of much ice or grounded icebergs in that direction.

The dreaded reality of wintering in the pack is gradually forcing itself upon my mind,—but I must not write on this subject, it is bad enough to brood over it unceasingly. We can see the land all round Melville Bay, from Cape Walker nearly to Cape York. Petersen is indefatigable at seal-shooting, he is so anxious to secure them for our dogs; he says they must be hit in the head; "if you hit him in the beef that is not good," meaning that a flesh-wound does not prevent their escaping under the ice. Petersen and Christian practise an Esquimaux mode of attracting the seals; they scrape the ice, thus making a noise like that produced by a seal in making a hole with its flippers, and then place one end of a pole in the water and put their mouths close to the other end, making noises in imitation of the snorts and grunts of their intended victims; whether the device is successful or not I do not know, but it looks laughable enough.

Christian came back a few days ago, like a true seal-hunter, carrying his kayak on his head, and dragging a seal behind him. Only two years ago Petersen returned across this bay with Dr. Kane's retreating party; he shot a seal which they devoured raw, and which, under providence, saved their lives. Petersen is a good ice-pilot, knows all these coasts as well as, or better than any man living, and, from long experience and habits of observation, is almost unerring in his prognostications of the weather. Besides his great value to us as interpreter, few men are better adapted for arctic work,—an ardent sportsman, an agreeable companion, never at a loss for occupation or amusement, and always contented and sanguine. Happily we have many such dispositions in the 'Fox.'

30th.—Position, 75° 30' N., 64° 4' W. The whole distance across Melville Bay is 170 miles: of this we have performed about 120, 40 of which we have drifted in the last fourteen days. The 'Isabel' sailed freely over this spot on 20th August, 1852; but the 'North Star' was beset on 30th July, 1849, to the southward of Melville Bay, and carried in the ice across it and some 70 or 80 miles beyond, when she was set free on 26th September, and went into winter quarters in Wolstenholme Sound. What a precedent for us!

Yesterday we set to work as usual to warp the ship along, and moved her ten feet: an insignificant hummock then blocked up the narrow passage; as we could not push it before us, a two-pound blasting charge was exploded, and the surface ice was shattered, but such an immense quantity of broken ice came up from beneath, that the difficulty was greatly increased instead of being removed. This is one of the many instances in which our small vessel labours under very great disadvantages in ice-navigation—we have neither sufficient manual power, steam power, nor impetus to force the floes asunder. I am convinced that a steamer of moderate size and power, with a crew of forty or fifty men, would have got through a hundred miles of such ice in less time than we have been beset.

The temperature fell to 25° last night, and the pools are strongly frozen over. I now look matters steadily and calmly in the face; whilst reasonable ground for hope remained I was anxious in the extreme. The dismal prospect of a "winter in the pack" has scarcely begun to dawn upon the crew; however, I do not think they will be much upset by it. They had some exciting foot-races on the ice yesterday evening.

1st Sept.—The indications of an approaching S.E. gale are at all times sufficiently apparent here, and fortunately so, as it is the dangerous wind in Melville Bay. It was on the morning of the 30th, before church-time, that they attracted our attention: the wind was very light, but barometer low and falling; very threatening appearances in the S.E. quarter, dark-blue sky, and grey detached clouds slowly rising; when the wind commenced the barometer began to rise. This gale lasted forty-eight hours, and closed up every little space of water; at first all the ice drifted before the wind, but latterly remained stationary. Twenty seals have been shot up to this time.

On comparing Petersen's experience with my own, and that of the 'North Star' in 1849, it seems probable that the ice along the shores of Melville Bay, at this season, will drift northward close along the land as far as Cape Parry, where it probably meets with a southerly current out of Smith's Sound; it will be carried away into the middle of Baffin's Bay, and thence during the winter down Davis' Strait into the Atlantic. From Cape Dudley Digges to Cape Parry, including Wolstenholme Sound, open water remains until October. It is strange that we have ceased to drift lately to the westward.

6th.—Position, 75° 24′ N., 64° 31′ W. During the last week we have only drifted 9 miles to the west. Obtained soundings in 88 fathoms; this is a discovery, and not an agreeable one. Of the six or seven icebergs in sight, the nearest are to the west of us; they are very large, and appear to be aground; we approach them slowly. Pleasant weather, but the winds are much too gentle to be of service to us; although the nights are cold, yet during the day our men occasionally do their sewing on deck. Our companions, the seals, are larger and fatter than formerly, therefore they float when shot; we are disposed to attribute their improved condition to better feeding upon this bank. The dredge brought up some few shellfish, starfish, stones, and much soft mud.

9th.—On this day in 1824 Sir Edward Parry got out of the middle ice, and succeeded in reaching Port Bowen. To continue hoping for release in time to reach Bellot Strait would be absurd; yet, to employ the men, we continue our preparation of tents, sledges, and gear for travelling. Two days ago the ice became more slack than usual, and a long lane opened; its western termination could not be seen from aloft. Every effort was made to get into this water, and by the aid of steam and blasting-powder we advanced 100 yards out of the intervening 170 yards of ice, when the floes began to close together, a S.E. wind having sprung up. Had we succeeded in reaching the water, I think we should have extricated ourselves completely, and perhaps ere this have reached Barrow Strait, but S.E. and S.W. gales succeeded, and it now blows a S.S.E. gale, with sleet.

10th.—Young went to the large icebergs to-day; the nearest of them is 250 feet high, and in 83 fathoms water; it is therefore probably aground, except at spring-tide; the floe ice was drifting past it to the westward, and was crushing up against its sides to a height of 50 feet. Since we first became beset, and consequently the sudden destruction of the ship a contingency which we should be prepared for, provisions have been kept at hand on deck, boats and sledges in readiness for instant use. In such a dire extremity we should of course endeavour to reach the nearest inhabited land.

13th.—Thermometer has fallen to 17° at noon. We have drifted 18 miles to the W. in the last week; therefore our neighbours, the icebergs, are not always aground, but even when afloat drift more slowly than the light ice. There is a water-sky to the W. and N.W.; it is nearest to us in the direction of Cape York: *could we only advance 12 or 15 miles in that direction, I am convinced we should be free to steer for Barrow Strait.*

Forty-three seals have been secured for the dogs; one dog is missing, the remaining twenty-nine devoured their two days' allowance of seal's flesh (60 or 65 lbs.) in forty-two seconds! it contained no bone, and had been cut up into small pieces, and spread out upon the snow, before they were permitted to rush to dinner; in this way the weak enjoy a fair chance, as there is no time for fighting. We do not allow them on board.

16*th.*—*Position*, 75° 33' N., 64° 52' W. At length we have drifted past the large icebergs, obtaining soundings in 69 fathoms within a mile of them; they must now be aground, and have frequently been so during the last three weeks; and being directly upon our line of drift, are probably the immediate cause of our still remaining in Melville Bay. The ice is slack everywhere, but the temperature having fallen to 3°, new ice rapidly forms, so that the change comes too late. The western limit of the bay— Cape York—is very distinct, and not more than 25 miles from us.

18*th.*—Lanes of water in all directions; but the nearest is half-a-mile from us. They come too late, as do also the N.W. winds which have now succeeded the fatal southeasters. The temperature fell to 2° below zero last night. We are now at length in the "North Water"; the old ice has spread out in all directions, so that it is only the young ice—formed within the last fortnight—which detains us prisoners here.

The icebergs, the chief cause of our unfortunate detention, and which for more than three weeks were in advance of us to the westward, are now, in the short space of two days, nearly out of sight to the eastward.

The preparations for wintering and sledge-travelling go on with unabated alacrity; the latter will be useful should it become necessary to abandon the ship.

Notwithstanding such a withering blight to my dearest hopes, yet I cannot overlook the many sources of gratification which do exist; we have not only the necessaries, but also a fair portion of the luxuries of ordinary sea-life; our provisions and clothing are abundant and well suited to the climate. Our whole equipment, though upon so small a scale, is perfect in its way. We all enjoy excellent health, and the men are most cheerful and willing.

Our "native auxiliaries," consisting of Christian and his twenty-nine dogs, are capable of performing immense service; whilst Mr. Petersen from his great arctic experience is of much use to me, besides being all that I could wish as an interpreter. Humanly speaking, we were not unreasonable in confidently looking forward to a successful issue of this season's operations, and I greatly fear that poor Lady Franklin's disappointment will consequently be the more severely felt.

We are doomed to pass a long winter of absolute inutility, if not of idleness, in comparative peril and privation; nevertheless the men seem very happy,—thoughtless of course, as true sailors always are.

We have drifted off the bank into much deeper water, and suppose this is the reason that seals have become more scarce.

22nd.—Constant N.W. winds continue to drift us slowly southward. Strong indications of water in the N.W., W., and S.E.; its vicinity may account for a rise in the temperature, without apparent cause, to 27° at noon to-day.

The newly-formed ice affords us delightful walking; the

old ice on the contrary is covered with a foot of soft snow. We have no shooting; scarcely a living creature has been seen for a week.

24th.—Position, 75° 8' N., 65° 20' W. Yesterday I thought I saw two of our men walking at a distance, and beyond some unsafe ice, but on inquiry found that all were on board: Petersen and I set off to reconnoitre the strangers; they proved to be bears, but much too wary to let us come within shot. It was dark when we returned on board after a brisk walk over the new ice. The calm air felt agreeably mild, we were without mittens and but that the breath froze upon mustachios and beard, one could have readily imagined the night was comfortably warm; yet the thermometer stood at 27° below the freezing point. I feel more inclined to pardon the man who remarked, "the thermometer had no influence whatever on the cold," than to bear with people who take for granted that it indicates the sensation of heat or cold appreciable by our feelings.

To-day when walking in a fresh breeze the wind felt very cold, and kept one on the look-out for frost-bites, although the thermometer was up to 10°. Games upon the ice and skating are our afternoon amusements; but we also have some few lovers of music, who embrace the opportunity for vigorous execution, without fear of being reminded that others may have ears more sensitive and discriminating than their own. But I must not omit to mention the cat, for she affords us quite as much amusement as the concertina. The Doctor has been very zealous in arranging the specimens of dried plants, and tells me that now he has got them all packed up and ready for *delivery!*

26th.—The mountain to the north of Melville Bay, known as the "Snowy Peak," was visible yesterday, although 90 miles distant; I have calculated its height to be 6000 feet. A raven was shot to-day.

27th.—Our salt meat is usually soaked for some days before being used; for this purpose it is put into a net, and lowered through a hole in the ice; this morning the net had been torn, and only a fragment of it remained! We suppose our twenty-two pounds of salt meat have been devoured by a shark; it would be curious to know how such fare agrees with him, as a full meal of salted provision will kill an Esquimaux dog, which thrives on almost anything. I used to remonstrate upon the skins of sea-birds being given to our dogs, but was told the feathers were good for them! Here all sea-birds are skinned before being cooked, otherwise our ducks, divers, and looms would be intolerably fishy. A well-baited shark-hook has been substituted for the net of salt-meat; I much wish to capture one of the monsters, as wonderful stories are told us of their doings in Greenland: whether they are the white shark, or the basking shark of natural history, I cannot find out. It is only of late years that the shark fishery has been carried on to any extent in Greenland; they are captured for the sake of their livers, which yield a considerable quantity of oil. It has very recently been ascertained that a valuable substance resembling spermaceti may be expressed from the carcase, and for this purpose powerful screw presses are now employed. In early winter the sharks are caught with hook and line through holes in the ice.

The Esquimaux assert that they are insensible to pain; and Petersen assures me he has plunged a long knife several times into the head of one whilst it continued to feed upon a white whale entangled in his net!! It is not sufficient to drive them away with sundry thrusts of spears or knives, but they must be towed away to some distance from the nets, otherwise they will return to feed. It must be remembered that the brain of a shark is extremely small in proportion to the size of its huge head. I have seen bullets fired through them with very little apparent effect; but if these creatures *can* feel, the devices practised upon them by the Esquimaux must be cruel indeed.

It is only in certain localities that sharks are found, and in these places they are often attracted to the nets by the animals entangled in them. The dogs are not suffered to eat either the skin or the head, the former in consequence of its extreme roughness, and the latter because it causes giddiness and makes them sick.

The nets alluded to are set for the white whale or the seal; if for the former, they are attached to the shore and extend off at right angles, so as to intercept them in their autumnal southern migration, when they swim close along the rocks to avoid their direst foe, the grampus, or "killer," the *Delphinus orca* of naturalists. When the white whale is stopped by the net it often appears at first to be unconscious of the fact, and continues to swim against it, affording time for the approach of the boat and deadly harpoon from behind. If entangled in the net a very short time suffices to drown them, as, like all the whale tribe, they are obliged to come to the surface to breathe.

The killer is also a cetacean of considerable size, 15 to 20 feet in length, but of very different habits; it is very swift, is armed with powerful teeth, and is gregarious. When in sufficient numbers they even attack the whale, impeding his progress by fastening on his fins and tail. In summer they appear in the Greenland seas, and the seals instantly seek refuge from them in the various creeks and inner harbours; and the Esquimaux hunter in his frail kayak, when he sees the huge pointed dorsal fin swiftly cleaving the surface of the sea, is scarcely less anxious to shun such dangerous company. With such stories as these Petersen beguiles the time; I never tire of listening to them, and now amuse myself in jotting scraps of them down.

Once only have I seen these dreaded monsters; when in the crow's-nest contemplating the chequered surface of ice and sea, some eight or ten of them swam rapidly past us, close to the surface, and occasionally displaying out of water the whole of their very remarkable dorsal fin, which appeared to be at least four or five feet in length.

The crow's-nest.

CHAPTER IV.

Snow crystals — Dogs will not eat raven — An arctic school — The dogs invade us — Bear-hunting by night — Ice-artillery — Arctic palates — Sudden rise of temperature — Freezing of salt-water — Harvey's idea of a sortie.

3rd Oct.—Position, 74° 58' N., 65° 52' W. SEPTEMBER has passed away and left us as a legacy to the pack; what a month have we had of anxious hopes and fears!

Up to the 17th S.E. winds prevailed, forcing the ice into a compact body, and urging it north-westward; subsequently N.W. winds set in, drifting it southward, and separating the floe-pieces; but the change of wind being accompanied by a considerable fall of temperature, they were either quickly cemented together again, or young ice formed over the newly-opened lanes of water, almost as rapidly as the surface of the sea became exposed. During the month the thermometer ranged between + 36° and − 2°. Two more bears and a raven have been seen. A wearied ptarmigan alighted near the ship, but before it could take wing again the dogs caught it, and scarcely a feather remained by the time I could rush on deck.

Our beautiful little organ was taken out of its case to-day, and put up on the lower deck; the men enjoy its pleasing tones, whilst Christian unceasingly turns the handle in a state of intense delight; he regards it with such awe and admiration, and is so entranced, that one cannot help envying him; of course he never saw one before. The instrument was presented by the Prince Consort to the searching vessel bearing his name which was sent out by

Lady Franklin in 1851; it is now about to pass its third winter in the frozen regions.

Two dogs ran off yesterday, in the vain hope, I suppose, of bettering their condition,—we only feed them three times a week at present; they returned this morning.

Seals are daily seen upon the new ice, but in this doubtful sort of light they are extremely timid, therefore our sportsmen cannot get within shot. The bears scent or hear our dogs, and so keep aloof; even the shark has deserted us, the bait remains intact. The snow crystals of last night are extremely beautiful; the largest kind is an inch in length; its form exactly resembles the end of a pointed feather. Stellar crystals two-tenths of an inch in diameter have also fallen; these have six points, and are the most exquisite things when seen under a microscope. I remember noticing them at Melville Island in March, 1853, when the temperature rose to $+8°$; as these were formed last night between the temperatures of $+6°$ and $+12°$, it would appear that the form is due to a certain fixed temperature. In the sun, or even in moonlight, all these crystals glisten most brilliantly; and as our masts and rigging are abundantly covered with them, the 'Fox' never was so gorgeously arrayed as she now appears.

13*th*.—One day is very like another; we have to battle stoutly with monotony; and but that each twenty-four hours brings with it necessary, though trivial duties, it would be difficult to remember the date. We take our guns and walk long distances, but see nothing. Two of the dogs go hunting on their own account, sometimes remaining absent all night. What they find or do is a mystery. The weather is generally calm and cold,—very favourable for freezing purposes at all events,—for the ice of only three weeks' growth is two feet thick.

Our well is exhausted; for nearly a month we have drawn

our whole supply of fresh water from one of those pools of thawed snow so common upon old ice in the summer; it had become frozen over and was covered with a foot of snow.

A week ago this *well* was 33 inches deep, and contained 16 inches of water. Of course this fresh water did not in the most remote degree owe its origin to the sea.

I hardly expect any considerable disruption of the ice before the general break-up in the spring, yet we do not trust any of our provisions upon it, nor is it sufficiently still to set up a magnetic observatory, for which purpose the instruments have been supplied to us.

Petersen still hopes we may escape and get into Upernivik, as the sea is not permanently frozen over there before December. I am surprised to hear that eagles have been seen so far north as Upernivik, although it is but twice in twenty-four years that specimens have been noticed there. In Richardson's 'Fauna Boreali-Americana' the extreme northern limit of these birds is given as 66°; but Upernivik is in $72\frac{3}{4}°$.

A few bear and fox tracks have been seen, but no living creatures for several days, except a flock of ducks hastening southward, and a solitary raven.

It is said that Esquimaux dogs will eat everything except fox and raven. There are exceptions, however; one of ours, old "Harness Jack," devoured a raven with much gusto some days ago. All the other dogs allowed their harness to be taken off when they were brought on board; but old Jack will not permit himself to be unrobed; when attempted he very plainly threatens to use his teeth. This canine oddity suddenly became immensely popular, by constituting himself protecting head of the establishment when one of his tribe littered; he took up a most uncomfortable position on top of the family cask (our *impromptu* kennel), and prevented the approach of all the other dogs : but for his timely interference on behalf of the poor little puppies, I verily believe they would all have been stolen and devoured! Dogs may do even worse than eat raven.

I have attempted some experiments for the purpose of determining the mean hourly change of oscillation of a pendulum due to the earth's diurnal motion; but as mine was only 11½ feet in length, I failed of any approach to accuracy. The mean of several observations gave 17° 47', whereas the change due to our latitude is about 14° 30'. A single experiment gave 14° 10', and this was the longest in point of time of any of them, the pendulum having swung for thirty-six minutes.

24th.—Position, 75° 27' N., 68° 41' W. Furious N.W. and S.E. gales have alternated of late; the ship is housed over, to keep out the driving snow; so high is the snow carried in the air that a little box perforated with small holes and triced up 50 feet high is soon filled up; this box is supplied morning and evening with a piece of prepared paper to detect the presence and comparative amount of ozone in the atmosphere; it is a peculiar pet of the Doctor's.

At eight o'clock this evening I noticed the falling of a very brilliant meteor; it passed through the constellation of Cassiopeia in a N.N.E. direction before terminating its visible existence, which it did very much like a huge rocket; the flash was so brilliant that a man whose back was turned to it mistook the illumination for lightning.

26th.—Our school opened this evening, under the auspices of Dr. Walker. He reports eight or nine pupils, and is much gratified by their zeal. At present their studies are limited to the three R's—reading, 'riting, and 'rithmetic. They have asked him to read and explain something instructive, so he intends to make them acquainted with the trade-winds and atmosphere. This subject affords an opportunity of explaining the uses of our thermometer, barometer, ozonometer, and electrometer, which they see us take much interest in. It is delightful to find a spirit of inquiry amongst them. Apart from scholastic occupation, I give them healthful exercise in spreading a thick layer of snow over the deck, and encasing the ship all round with a bank of the same non-conducting material.

28*th*.—Midnight. This evening, to our great astonishment, there occurred a disruption and movement of the ice within 200 yards of the ship. The night was calm; the reflection of a bright moon, aided by the more than ordinary brilliancy of the stars upon the snowy expanse, made it appear to us almost daylight. As I sit now in my cabin I can distinctly hear the ice crushing; it resembles the continued roar of distant surf, and there are many other occasional sounds; some of them remind one of the low moaning of the wind, others are loud and harsh, as if trains of heavy waggons with ungreased axles were slowly labouring along. Upon a less-favoured night these sounds might be appalling; even as it is they are sufficiently ominous to invite reflection. Cape York has been in sight for some days past.

29*th*.—Another heavenly night, and still greater ice disturbance; some of the crushed-up pieces are nearly four feet thick. The currents, icebergs, and changes of temperature, may contribute to this ice action; but I think the tides are the chief cause, and for these reasons; that it wants but two days to the full moon, and that the ice-movements are almost confined to the night, and change their direction morning and evening. Now we know that the night-tides in Greenland greatly exceed the day-tides. One thing is evident—the weather continues calm, therefore the winds are not concerned in the matter.

2*nd Nov*.—*Position*, 75° 13' N., 68° 50' W. Having observed some days ago that a few of the dogs were falling away—from some cause or other not having acquired their natural winter clothing before the recent cold weather set in —they were all allowed on board, and given a good extra meal. Since then we can scarcely keep them out. One calm night they made a charge, and boarded the ship so suddenly that several of the men rushed up, very scantily clothed, to see what was the matter. Vigorous measures were adopted to expel the intruders, and there was desperate chasing round the deck with broomsticks, &c. Many of them retreated into holes and corners, and two hours elapsed before they were all driven out; but though the chase was hot, it was cold enough work for the half-clad men.

Sailors use quaint expressions. They describe the nightly foraging expeditions as "sorties:" they point out to me the various corners between decks where the "ice corrodes," *i.e.* the moisture condenses and forms frost; a ramble over the ice is called "a bit of a peruse." I presume this indignity is offered to the word perambulation.

There was a very sudden call "to arms" this evening. Whether sleeping, prosing, or schooling, every one flew out upon the ice on the instant, as if the magazine or the boiler was on the point of explosion. The alarm of "A bear close-to, fighting with the dogs," was the cause. The luckless beast had approached within 25 yards of the ship ere the quartermaster's eye detected his indistinct outline against the snow; so silently had he crept up that he was within 10 yards of some of the dogs. A shout started them up, and they at once flew round the bear and embarrassed his retreat. In crossing some very thin ice he broke through, and there I found him surrounded by yelping dogs. Poor fellow! Hobson, Young, and Petersen had each lodged a bullet in him; but these only seemed to increase his rage. He succeeded in getting out of the water, when, fearing harm to the numerous bystanders and dogs, or that he might escape, I fired, and luckily the bullet passed through his brain. He proved to be a full-grown male, 7 feet 3 inches in length As we all aided in the capture, it was decided that the skin should be offered to Lady Franklin.

The carcase will feed our dogs for nearly a month; they were rewarded on the spot with the offal. All of them, however, had not shown equal pluck; some ran off in evident fright, but others betrayed no symptom of fear, plunging or falling into the water with Bruin. Poor old Sophy was amongst the latter, and received a deep cut in the shoulder from one of his claws. The established authorities on all canine matters — *i.e.*, Petersen, Christian, and Alexander Thompson—have prescribed double allowance of food for her, and say she will soon recover.

For the few moments of its duration the chase and death was exciting. And how strange and novel the scene! A misty moon affording but scanty light—dark figures gliding singly about, not daring to approach each other, for the ice trembled under their feet—the enraged bear, the wolfish howling dogs, and the bright flashes of the deadly rifles.

3rd.—I remained up the greater part of last night taking observations, for the evening mists had passed away, and a lovely moon reigned over a calm enchanting night; through a powerful telescope[1] she resembled a huge frosted-silver melon, the large crater-like depression answering to that part from which the footstalk had been detached. Not a sound to break the stillness around, excepting when some hungry dog would return to the late battlefield to gnaw into the bloodstained ice.

On the 1st the sun paid us his last visit for the year, and now we take all our meals by lamplight.

5th.—In order to vary our monotonous routine, we determined to celebrate the day; extra grog was issued to the

---

[1] Most kindly lent to the Expedition by the late Lord Wrottesley, then President of the Royal Society.

crew, and also for the first time a proportion of preserved plum-pudding. Lady Franklin most thoughtfully and kindly sent it on board for occasional use. It is excellent.

This evening a well-got-up procession sallied forth, marched round the ship with drum, gong, and discord, and then proceeded to burn the effigy of Guy Fawkes. Their blackened faces, extravagant costumes, flaring torches, and savage yells, frightened away all the dogs; nor was it until after the fireworks were let off and the traitor consumed that they crept back again. It was school-night, but the men were up for fun, so gave the Doctor a holiday.

12th.—Position 74° 42' N., 68° 6' W. Yesterday I had the good fortune to shoot two seals; they were very fat, and their stomachs were filled with shrimps.[1] To-day Young and Petersen shot three more, and many others have been seen. This is cheering, and entices people out for hours daily. There is just enough movement in the ice to keep a few narrow lanes and small pools of water open; the floes or fields of ice are more inclined to spread out from each other than to close. We have latterly been drifting before northerly winds. William Jones, our dog-driver, spent some years on the Labrador coast, in the Hudson's Bay Company's service; he there developed a taste for seal's flesh, and doubtless obtained some distinction for cooking it; at all events he has placed on our table a novel roast joint, viz., a stuffed shoulder of seal—very good and tender, although its colour was very dark. Somebody once said that the man who invents a new dish is a benefactor to the whole human race; such our dog-driver has been to us, his zeal and skill have received the commendations they deserve; if seal and all else were to fail, I can hardly doubt he would exercise his genius upon some of his own team!

---

[1] This is worthy of remark, for with our longest sounding-line, measuring 220 fathoms, we could not reach the bottom.

16th.—A renewal of ice-crushing within a few hundred yards of us. I can hear it in my bed. The ordinary sound resembles the roar of distant surf breaking heavily and continuously; but when heavy masses come in collision with much impetus, it fully realizes the justness of Dr. Kane's descriptive epithet, "ice-artillery." Fortunately for us, our poor little 'Fox' is well within the margin of a stout old floe : we are therefore undisturbed spectators of ice-conflicts, which would be irresistible to anything of human construction. Immediately about the ship all is still, and, as far as appearances go, she is precisely as she would be in a secure harbour—housed all over, banked up with snow to her gunwales. In fact, her winter plumage is so complete that the masts alone are visible. The deck and the now useless skylights are covered with hard snow. Below hatches we are warm and dry; all are in excellent health and spirits, looking forward to an active campaign next winter. God grant it may be realized!

Yesterday Young shot the fiftieth seal, an event duly celebrated by our drinking *the* bottle of champagne which had been set apart in more hopeful times to be drunk on reaching the "North Water"—our unhappy failure, the more keenly felt from being so very unexpected!

Petersen saw and fired a shot into a narwhal, which brought the blubber out. When most arctic creatures are wounded in the water, blubber more frequently than blood appears, particularly if the wound is superficial—it spreads over the surface of the water like oil. Bills of fare vary much, even in Greenland. I have enquired of Petersen, and he tells me that the Greenland Esquimaux (there are many Greenlanders of Danish origin) are not agreed as to which of their animals affords the most delicious food; some of them prefer reindeer venison, others think more favourably of young dog, the flesh of which, he asserts, is "just like the beef of sheep." He says a Danish captain, who had acquired the taste, provided some for his guests, and they praised his *mutton!* after dinner he sent for the skin of the animal, which was no other than a large red dog! This occurred in Greenland, where his Danish guests had resided for many years, far removed from European *mutton*. Baked puppy is a real delicacy all over Polynesia: at the Sandwich Islands I was once invited to a feast, and had to feign great disappointment when told that puppy was so extremely scarce it could not be procured in time, and therefore sucking-pig was substituted!

19*th*.—A heavy southerly gale has increased the ice movements; happily we are undisturbed. As Young was seated under the lee of a hummock, watching for seals to pop up for breath, the ice under him suddenly cracked and separated! He escaped with a ducking, and was just able to reach his gun from the bank ere it sank through the sludgy mixture of snow and water.

Yesterday we were all out; I saw only one seal, but was refreshed by the sight of a dozen narwhals. It is a positive treat to see a living creature of any kind. The only birds which remain are dovekies, but they are scarce, and being white are very rarely observed.

The dogs are fed every second day, when 2 lbs. of seal's flesh—previously thawed when possible—is given to each; the weaker ones get additional food, and they all pick up whatever scraps are thrown out; this is enough to sustain, but not to satisfy them, so they are continually on the lookout for anything eatable. Hobson made one very happy without intending it; he meant only to give him a kick, but his slipper being down at heel, flew off, and was instantly snapped up and carried off in triumph by this lucky dog, who demolished it at his leisure, away amongst the hummocks.

Two large icebergs drift in company with us; our relative positions have remained pretty nearly the same for the last month.

23rd.—A heavy gale commenced at N.E. on the 21st, and continued for thirty-six hours unabated in force, but changed in direction to S.S.W. It appears to have been a revolving storm, moving to the N.W. Yesterday, as the wind approached S.E., the temperature rose to $+ 32°$; the upper deck sloppy; the lower deck temperature during Divine Service was $75°$!! As the wind veered round to the S.S.W. it moderated, and temperature fell; this evening it is $- 7°$. How is it that the S.E. wind has brought us such a very high temperature? Even if it traversed an unfrozen sea it could not have derived from thence a higher temperature than $29°$. Has it swept across Greenland—that vast superficies partly enveloped in glacier, partly in snow? No, it must have been borne in the higher regions of the atmosphere from the far south, in order to mitigate the severity of this northern climate.

Petersen tells me the same warm S.E. wind suddenly sweeps over Upernivik in midwinter, bringing with it abundance of rain; and that it always shifts to the S.W., and then the temperature rapidly falls: this is precisely the change we have experienced in lat. $75°$. I believe a somewhat similar, but less remarkable, change of temperature was noticed in Smith's Sound, lat. $78\frac{3}{4}°$ N.

25th.—Position, $75°$ 2' N., $70°$ 22' W. Mild, " Madeira weather," as Hobson calls it, temperature up to $+ 7°$. It is commonly asserted that sea ice produces fresh water; and even Dr. Kane, who had the opportunity of testing the fact, states (at page 377 of his narrative of 'The Grinnell Expedition, 1850–51') that "it will produce from salt water a fresh, pure, and drinkable element."

By my desire, Dr. Walker is occupied upon making a

series of experiments upon the freezing of salt water; I will here briefly state the process he found necessary, in order to procure fresh water from sea ice.

Finding that sea ice contained less salt than the sea water, he collected and thawed a considerable quantity of it; he then exposed it in tubs until coated over with half-inch ice; he gathered this second crop of ice, thawed it, and found that it also was less salt than the water which produced it. Again repeating the process of exposure in tubs, he obtained a third crop of ice, which was found to yield drinkable water; and repeating this process a fourth time, a small quantity of nearly pure fresh water was obtained.

He found that the ice would contain less salt when frozen slowly than when exposed to a very low temperature, and therefore rapidly frozen.

A very beautiful frosty efflorescence appears upon sea ice when formed at low temperatures in calm weather, it is in fact a portion of the brine expressed by the action of freezing.

No wonder, then, that sledge dogs, when driven hard over this ice, which soon cuts their feet, suffer intense pain, often falling down in fits; nor that snow thinly covering such ice wholly or partially thaws so frequently, even when the temperature is far below the freezing point. Should it then rise to near the freezing point, the young ice, thus coated with sludge so saline as to resist the ordinary freezing temperature, not unfrequently becomes so weakened, as to be unsafe.[1]

29th.—Keen, biting, N.W. winds. No cracks in the ice,

---

[1] In a paper read before the Royal Geographical Society on 12th April, 1869, from Captain Montgomery of the Indian Survey, it is stated, that at the gold diggings in Thibet, first visited by our explorers in 1867, it is the custom of the miners to use melted ice for drinking, as the water is too salt! These mines are at an elevation of 16,300 feet, and the cold is very considerable.

therefore no seals. Grey dawn at ten o'clock, and dark at two; the moon, everywhere the sailor's friend, is a source of great comfort to us here. Nothing to excite conversation, except an occasional inroad of the dogs in search of food; this generally occurs at night. Whenever the deck-light which burns under the housing happens to go out, they scale the steep snow banking, and rush round the deck like wolves. "Why, bless you, Sir, the wery moment that there light goes out, and the quartermaster turns his back, they makes a regular sortæ, and in they all comes." "But *where* do they come in, Harvey?" "Where, Sir? why everywheres; they makes no more to do, but in they comes, clean over all." Not long ago old Harvey was chief quartermaster in a line-of-battle ship, where, during the long nightwatches, the younger midshipmen would gather round him and eagerly listen while he spun them long tough yarns by the hour about the arctic regions,—its bears, its icebergs, and still more terrific "auroras, roaring and flashing about the ship enough to frighten a fellow!"

30*th.*—*Position*, 74° 41' N., 69° 10' W. Severe cold has arrived with the full moon; eight days ago the thermometer stood at the freezing-point, it is now 64° below it! So dark is it now that I was able to observe an eclipse of Jupiter's first satellite before three o'clock to-day. For the last two months we have drifted freely backwards and forwards before N.W. and S.E. winds; each time we have gained a more off-shore position, being gradually separated further and further from the land by fresh growths of ice, which invariably follow up every ice-movement. In this manner we have been thrust out to the S.W. 80 miles from the nearest land, and into that free space which in autumn was open water, and which we then vainly struggled to reach.

That the ice has been most free to move in this direction

is additional evidence of the recent proximity of an open sea, and shows that in all probability—I had almost said certainty—we should have sailed, or at least drifted into it, had it not been for those enemies to our progress, the grounded bergs.

CHAPTER V.

Burial in the pack — Musk oxen in lat. 80° north — Habits of the arctic fox — The aurora affects the electrometer — An arctic Christmas — Sufferings of Dr. Hayes' boat party — Ice acted on by wind only — How the sun ought to be welcomed — Constant action of the ice — Return of the seals — Revolving storm.

4th Dec.—I HAVE just returned on board from the performance of the most solemn duty a commander can be called upon to fulfil. A funeral at sea is always peculiarly impressive; but this evening at seven o'clock, as we gathered around the sad remains of poor Scott, reposing under an Union Jack, and read the Burial Service by the light of lanterns, the effect could not fail to awaken very serious emotions.

The greater part of the Church Service was read on board, under shelter of the housing; the body was then placed upon a sledge, and drawn by the messmates of the deceased to a distance from the ship, where a hole through the ice had been cut: it was then "committed to the deep," and the Service completed. What a scene it was! I shall never forget it. The lonely 'Fox,' almost buried in snow, completely isolated from the habitable world, her colours half-mast high, and bell mournfully tolling: our little procession slowly marching over the rough surface of the frozen deep, guided by lanterns and direction-posts, amid the dreary darkness of an arctic winter; the death-like stillness around, the intense cold, and the threatening aspect of a murky, overcast sky; and all this heightened by one of those strange lunar phenomena which are but seldom seen even here, a complete halo encircling the moon, through which passed a horizontal band of pale light that encompassed the heavens; above the moon appeared the segments of two other halos, and there were also mock moons or paraselenæ to the number of six. The misty atmosphere lent a very ghastly hue to this singular display, which lasted for rather more than an hour.

Scarcely had the Burial Service been completed, when our poor dogs, discovering that the ship was deserted, set up a most dismal unearthly moaning, continuing it until we returned on board. Coming to us from a distance across the ice, at such a solemn moment, this most strange and mournful sound was both startling and impressive.

Poor Scott fell down a hatchway two days only before his death, which was occasioned by the internal injuries then received; he was a steady serious man; a widow and family will mourn his loss. He was our engine-driver; we cannot replace him, therefore the whole duty of working the engines will devolve upon the engineer, Mr. Brand.

11th.—Position, 74° 31′ N., 68° 21′ W. Calm, clear weather, pleasant for exercise, but steadily cold; thermometer varies between − 20° and − 30°. At noon the blush of dawn tints the southern horizon, to the north the sky remains inky blue, whilst overhead it is bright and clear, the stars shining, and the pole-star near the zenith very distinct. Although there is a light north wind, thin mackerel-clouds are passing from south to north, and the temperature has risen 10°.

I have been questioning Petersen about the bones of the musk oxen found in Smith's Sound by Dr. Kane's expedition; he says the decayed skulls of about twenty were found, all of them to the north of the 79th parallel. As they were all without lower jaws, he says they were killed by Esquimaux, who leave upon the spot the skulls of large animals, but the weight of the lower jaw being so trifling it is allowed to remain attached to the flesh and tongue. The skull of a musk ox with its massive horns cannot weigh less than 30 lbs.

Although it has been abundantly proved by the existence of raised beaches and fossils, that the shores of Smith's Sound have been elevated within a comparatively recent geological period, yet Petersen tells me that there exist numerous ruins of Esquimaux buildings, probably one or two centuries old, all of which are situated upon very low points, only just sufficiently raised above the reach of the sea; such sites, in fact, as would at present be selected by the natives. These ruins show that no perceptible change has taken place in the relative level of sea and land since they were originally constructed. At Petersen's Greenland home, Upernivik, the land has sunk, as is plainly shown by similar ruins over which the tides now flow.

Anything which illustrates the habits of animals in such extremely high latitudes I think is most interesting; their instincts must be quickened in proportion as the difficulty of subsisting increases. Foxes, white, and sooty or dingy-blue, are very numerous; all the birds are merely summer visitors, therefore the hare is the only creature remaining upon which foxes can prey; but the hares are comparatively scarce, how then do the foxes live for eight months of each year? Petersen thinks they store up provisions during the summer in various holes and crevices, and thus manage to eke out an existence during the dark winter's season; he once saw a fox carry off eggs in his mouth from an eider-duck's nest, one at a time, until the whole were removed; and in winter he has observed a fox scratch a hole down through very deep snow, to a cache of eggs beneath.

Both these kinds of foxes have been found in all arctic lands; they are very small, and in their winter fur are beautiful animals, full of tricks and impudence.

We once captured a litter of three cubs (early in September, 1853); they were exactly the colour of the dark greyish-brown stones amongst which they were found; such fierce little fellows, with most restless eyes, and pliant weasel-shaped bodies.

Not unfrequently foxes would venture on board our ships during the winter nights, and even be caught in traps set for them on deck. I find in my journal for December, 1852, at Melville Island, that, "a wretched-looking, but most lucky fox has been caught three times, and each time hunted by the dogs; the last time Lion opened his huge mouth to seize it, but the spirited little creature turned, bit him in the foot, and escaped. Had this miserable little fox been worth the skinning, its life would have paid the forfeit of its first capture. We consider a fox which weighs eight pounds to be a large one." When irritated they give a short half-suppressed bark, and sometimes when hunting they utter a strange cry, which always puzzled our men, who would take it for that of a hawk, a goose, or a gull.

I fancy that birds and lemmings form their ordinary prey. Captain Collinson attributed the success of his hunting-parties at Walker Bay, in shooting hares, to their having killed off all the foxes.

Besides hunting on their own account, they appear to follow the bears to pick up their scraps. Yet how this brave little fellow lives is a marvel; he is so small that the geese and larger gulls often successfully resist his attempts upon their broods.

The men are exercised at building snow huts; for winter or early spring travelling, this knowledge is almost indispensable. Upon a calm day the temperature of the external air being $-33°$, *within* a snow hut the thermometer stood $17°$ higher, this important difference being due to the transmission of heat through the ice from the sea beneath.

Evaporation goes on through ice from the water underneath it. The interior of each snow-hut is coated with crystals, although the ice upon which the huts are built is four feet thick : but when no longer in contact with, that is, floating upon, the water, I cannot discover any evaporation from ice. For instance, a canvas screen on deck which became wet by the sudden thaw last month still remains frozen stiff.

14th.—Of late there has been much damp upon the lower deck. This has now been remedied by enclosing the hatchway within a commodious snow-porch; and, instead of the steam and vapour of the inhabited deck being condensed into moisture about the hatchway as heretofore, it now meets the downward rush of cold air in the porch, and is there converted into minute particles of snow; this porch also diminishes the escape of heat.

19th.—*Position*, 74° 5′ N., 66° 27′ W. Light N.W. winds, with occasional mists; the temperature is comparatively mild :—12° to −25°.

It is now the time of spring-tides; they cause numerous cracks in the ice, but why so, at such a great distance from the land, I cannot explain. The three nearest points of land are respectively 110, 140, and 180 miles distant from us.

Frequent auroras during the last two days. Yesterday morning it was visible until eclipsed by the day-dawn at 10 o'clock. Although we could no longer see it, I do not think it ceased; very thin clouds occupied its place, through which, as through the aurora, stars appeared scarcely dimmed in lustre. I do not imagine that the aurora is ever visible in a *perfectly* clear atmosphere. I often observe it just silvering or rendering luminous the upper edge of low fog or cloud banks, and with a few vertical rays feebly vibrating.

Last evening Dr. Walker called me to witness his success with the electrometer. The electric current was so very weak that the gold-leaves only diverged at intervals of four or five seconds. Some hours afterwards it was strong enough to *keep* them diverged.

21*st.*—Mid-winter day. Out of the arctic regions it is better known as the *shortest* day. At noon we could just read type similar to the leading article of the 'Times.' Few of us could read more than two or three lines without making our eyes ache.

27*th.*—Our Christmas was a very cheerful, merry one. The men were supplied with several additional articles, such as hams, plum-puddings, preserved gooseberries and apples, nuts, sweetmeats, and Burton ale. After Divine Service they decorated the lower deck with flags, and made an immense display of food. The officers came down with me to see their preparations. We were really astonished! Their mess-tables were laid out like the counters in a confectioner's shop, with apple and gooseberry tarts, plum and sponge-cakes in pyramids, besides various other unknown puffs, cakes, and loaves of all sizes and shapes. We bake all our own bread, and excellent it is. In the background were nicely-browned hams, meat-pies, cheeses, and other substantial articles. Rum and water in wine-glasses, and plum-cake were handed to us: we wished them a happy Christmas, and complimented them on their taste and spirit in getting up such a display. Our silken sledge-banners had been borrowed for the occasion, and were regarded with deference and peculiar pride.

In the evening the officers were enticed down amongst the men again, and at a late hour I was requested, as a great favour, to come down and see how much they were enjoying themselves. I found them in the highest good humour with themselves and all the world. They were perfectly sober, and singing songs, each in his turn. I expressed great satisfaction at having seen them enjoying themselves so much and so rationally, I could therefore the better describe it to Lady Franklin, who was so deeply interested in everything relating to them. I drank their healths, and hoped our position next year would be more suitable for our purpose. We all joined in drinking the healths of Lady Franklin and Miss Cracroft, and amid the acclamations which followed I returned to my cabin, immensely gratified by such an exhibition of genuine good feeling, such veneration for Lady Franklin, and such loyalty to the cause of the expedition. It was very pleasant also that they had taken the most cheering view of our future prospects. I verily believe I was the happiest individual on board that happy evening.

Our Christmas-box has come in the shape of northerly winds, which bid fair to drift us southward towards those latitudes wherein we hope for liberation next spring from this icy bondage.

28th.—We have been in expectation of a gale all day. This evening there is still a doubtful sort of truce amongst the elements. Barometer down to 28·83; thermometer up to $+5°$, although the wind has been strong and steady from the N. for twenty-four hours, low scud flying from the E., snow constantly falling. An hour ago the wind suddenly changed to S.S.E.; the snowing has ceased; the sky become clear; the thermometer falls and barometer rises. Here, as on the 23rd November, we have a well-marked instance of a revolving storm passing to north-westward, and occasioning the otherwise unaccountable phenomenon of a *warm* north wind.

2nd Jan., 1858.—New Year's day was a second edition of Christmas, and quite as pleasantly spent. We dwelt much upon the anticipations of the future, being a more agreeable theme than the failure of the past. I confess to a hearty welcome for the new year—anxious, of course, that we may escape uninjured, and sufficiently early to pursue the object of our voyage.

Exactly at midnight on the 31st December the arrival of the new year was announced to me by our *band*—two flutes and an accordion—striking up at my door. There was also a procession, or perhaps I should say a continuation of the band; these performers were grotesquely attired, and armed with frying-pans, gridirons, kettles, pots, and pans, with which to join in and add to the effect of the *other* music!

We have a very level hard walk alongside the ship; it is narrowed to two or three yards in width by a snow-bank four feet high. In the face of this bank some twenty-five holes have been excavated for the dogs, and in them they spend most of their time. It looks very formidable in the moonlight, being a good imitation of a casemated battery.

After our rubber of whist on New Year's night Petersen related to us some of his dreadful sufferings when with the boat party from Dr. Kane's Expedition. They left Rensselaer Harbour in August, 1854, intending to proceed to Upernivik; they spent the months of October and November in Booth Sound, lat. 77°, all that time upon the verge of starvation, unable to advance or retreat. For these two months they had no other fuel than their small cedar boat, the smoke of which was not endurable in their wretched hut, and without light (for the sun left them in October), unless we except one inch and a half of taper daily, which they made out of a lump of bees'-wax that accidentally found its way into their boat before leaving the ship. In December they regained their vessel. I am surprised that no account of the extreme hardships of this party—so far exceeding that of their shipmates on board—has ever appeared; and I regret it, as I believe they owed their lives to the experience and fidelity of their interpreter Petersen.[1] At first the Esquimaux assisted them; latterly they were quite unable to do so, and became anxious to get rid of their visitors. Observing how weakened they had become, the Esquimaux endeavoured to separate them from their guns and from each other, and even used threatening language. It is a pity that these facts are not more fully and generally known, as they bear directly upon two questions very important to arctic explorers :—Can white men find subsistence wherever Esquimaux do? And, Can white men adopt the habits of wild Esquimaux in so far as to become domesticated amongst them? Even when seeking to escape from starvation, this small party could not accomplish either the one or the other; nor has any instance of their ever having been accomplished come to my knowledge.

During December we drifted 67 miles, directly down Baffin's Bay towards the Atlantic, and are now in lat. $74°$. Although it is quite impossible to discriminate between the several influences which probably govern our movements, or to ascertain how much is due to each of them—such as the relative positions of ice, land, and open water, the influence of the winds, currents, and earth's rotation—yet it appears in the present instance that the wind is almost the sole agent in hastening this vast *continent* of ice towards the latitudes of its dissolution. We move before the wind in proportion to its strength; we remain stationary in calm weather. Neither surface nor submarine current has been detected; the large icebergs obey the same influences as the surface ice. We have noticed a slight set to the westward—it is not likely to be produced by current, unless it is the northerly current along the Greenland shore which thus *wedges* us off to the westward, and may be the result of the earth's motion from west to east.

[1] Since the above was written, Dr. I. I. Hayes, one of the party, has published a most interesting account of their journey.

6th.—*Position*, 73° 49′ N., 65° 47′ W. Many lanes of water. A seal has been seen, the only one for six weeks. Of the old ice which so closely hemmed us in, up to the middle of September, there is hardly any within several miles of us except the large floe-piece we are frozen to. Every crack or lane which opens is quickly covered with young ice, so that it cannot close again; and in this manner the old ice has been spread out. I heartily rejoice at its dispersion!

To-day I put a tumblerful of our strong ale (Allsopp's) on deck to freeze: this was soon effected, the temperature being −35°. After bringing it below, and when its temperature had risen to 17°, it was almost all thawed—at 22° it was completely so: it looked muddy, but settled after standing for a couple of hours, when I drank it off, in every way satisfied with my experiment and my beer: it seemed none the worse for its freezing, but rather flat from its long exposure in a tumbler.

17th.—*Position*, 73° 9′ N., 63° 25′ W. Northerly winds blow almost constantly. We have drifted 60 miles since the 1st, and are only 115 miles from Upernivik,—once more upon confines of the habitable world! good light for three hours daily; all this is cheering. We continue our snow-hut practice, and can build one in three-quarters of an hour.

28th.—*Position*, 72° 48′ N., 62° 35′ W. The upper edge of the sun appeared above the horizon to-day, after an absence of eighty-nine days; it was a gladdening sight. I sent for the ship's steward and asked what was the custom on such occasions? "To hoist the colours and serve out an extra half-gill, sir," was the ready reply: accordingly, the Harwich lion soon fluttered in a breeze cool enough to stiffen the limbs of ordinary lions, and in the evening the grog was issued.

30th.—Our messmate Pussy is unwell, and won't eat; in vain has Hobson tempted her with raw seal's flesh, preserved salmon, preserved milk, &c.; at length castor-oil was forcibly administered. Puss is a great favourite. Our finest dog, Sultan, is also sick, and his coat is in bad order; blubber has been prescribed for him;—and poor old Mary has fits, not uncommon after the long winter. Petersen immediately ordered her to be bled by slitting her ear; but Christian, in his fright and haste, for Mary's teeth are sharp, cropped the tip of it off. These are our only medical cases. A dovekie, in its white winter plumage, and two seals have been seen lately.

15th Feb.—Position, 71° 38' N., 61° 31' W. The returning daylight cheers us up wonderfully — not that we were suffering, either mentally or bodily,—but the change is most agreeable, and we can take much longer walks than were possible during the dark period. The men have been supplied with muskets, and go out sporting as ardently as schoolboys. I took a long walk towards one of our iceberg companions, but could not quite reach it as weak ice intervened, each step producing an undulation; finding the point of my knife went through it with but very slight resistance, I gave up the attempt and turned back, the ship's masts being then scarcely visible in the distance; almost the whole of the intervening ice was of this winter's growth, and in many places much crushed up.

Daylight reveals to us evidences of vast ice movements having taken place during the dark months when we fancied all was still and quiet; and we now see how greatly we have been favoured, what innumerable chances of destruction we have unconsciously escaped! A few days ago the ice suddenly cracked within ten yards of the ship, and gave her such a smart shock that every one rushed on deck with astonishing alacrity. One of these sudden disruptions occurred between me and the ship when I was returning from the iceberg; the sun was just setting as I found myself cut off. Had I been upon the other side I would have loitered to enjoy a refreshing gaze upon this dark streak of water; but after a smart run of about a mile along its edge, and finding no place to cross, visions of a patrol on the floe for the long night of fifteen hours began to obtrude themselves! At length I reached a place where the jagged edges of the floes met, so crossed and got safely on board. Nothing was seen during this walk of nearly 25 miles except one seal. Recent gales have drifted us rapidly southward; cracks and lanes are very numerous.

On the 1st a blue (or sooty) fox was shot. Although 130 geographical miles from the nearest land he was very fat, hence we argue dovekies were much more numerous during winter than we supposed. We have often noticed the tracks of foxes following up those of the bears, probably for discarded scraps of the seals upon which they prey. Hobson's favourite dog "Chummie" has returned, after an absence of six days, decidedly hungry, but he can hardly have been without food all that time; some fox may have lured him off. He evinced great delight at getting back, devoted his first attentions to a hearty meal, then rubbed himself up against his own particular associates, after which he sought out and attacked the weakest of his enemies, and, soothed by their howlings, coiled himself up for a long sleep.

1st March.—*Position,* 69° 50′ N., 59° 43′ W. February has been a remarkably mild, cloudy, windy month: the winter temperature may be said to have passed away by the 10th, the average temperature for the first ten days being $-25°$, whilst for the remainder of the month it was $-11°$ Had one fallen asleep for a month at least, he could not reasonably have expected to find a greater change on awaking than that which occurred in the second week in February. Our drift has also been great,—166 miles. We are south of the 70th parallel, and may soon be expelled from our icy home.

On the 24th there was a fearful gale of wind. Had not our housing been very well secured, it must have been blown away. We are preparing for sea, removing the snow from off the deck and round the ship; our skylights have been dug out (for in winter they are always covered with a thick layer of snow), and the flood of light which beams down through them is quite charming. How intolerably sooty and smoke-dried everything looks!

On the 27th the first seal of this year was shot; it came in good time, for the fifty-one seals shot in autumn were finished only two days before: our English supply of dogs' food therefore remains almost untouched. Snow was observed to melt against the ship's side exposed to the sun, the thermometer in the shade standing at $-22°$! A very fine dog has died from eating a quantity of salt fish, which he managed to get at although it was supposed to be quite out of his reach.

One of the two large icebergs which commenced this voyage with us last October, in $75\frac{1}{2}°$ N., has drifted out of sight to the S.E.; the other one is far off in the N.W. I attribute these increased distances solely to the spreading abroad of the intervening ice.

When we were far north, and probably drifting more slowly than the ice in the stream of Lancaster Sound to the westward of us, the ship's head turned very gradually from right to left, in other words, from N.N.W. to W. When about the parallel of $72°$ N., we supposed ourselves to be drifting faster than the western ice (in this, as in the previous case, comparing our drift with that of Lieutenant de Haven), the ship's head slowly shifted back to the right as far as

W.N.W. ; latterly it has not changed at all: we are in a narrower part of Davis' Strait, where the winds probably blow with equal force from shore to shore, and drift the whole pack at an uniform rate.

5th.—On the 2nd, four fat seals and some dovekies were shot; the largest seal weighed 170 lbs.; the smallest 150 lbs.; they were males of the species *Phoca hespida*, or *Phoca fœtida*, the latter epithet being by far the most appropriate at this season; the disagreeable odour resembles garlic, and taints the whole animal so strongly that even Esquimaux are nearly overpowered by it: this is almost the only description of seal we have obtained, but the females are at all seasons free from fetor. Several long lanes of water extend at right angles to the straits.

The Doctor has taken a photograph of the ship by the albumen process on glass; the temperature at the time was below zero. Upon the 3rd and 4th a well-marked revolving storm passed nearly over us to the W.N.W.; its extreme diameter was 30 hours, that of the strength of the gale 18 hours; its centre probably passed about one-tenth of its diameter to the S.W. The barometer was rather high, having risen just before the wind commenced at N.E.; but it now fell half an inch in ten hours, and continued to fall until the wind shifted—almost suddenly—through S.E. to S.S.W., when it immediately commenced a rapid ascent. As the barometer fell, the temperature rose from zero to $+18°$, and fell again after the change of wind. This violent storm brought with it a smart hail-shower.

The depression of the ice about the bows, in consequence of a vast accumulation of snow-drift upon it, brought the ship down by the head considerably; to-day this ice suddenly detached itself, and the fore part of the vessel sprang up; she still remains frozen and held down abaft. The snow-banking looks very woe-begone after this *ice-quake;* it inclines out from the ship, and in many places has been prostrated by the shock.

7th.—*Position*, 69° 55′ N., 59° 11′ W. Early this morning the lofty land of Disco was seen, its distance is upwards of 90 miles.

CHAPTER VI.

A bear-fight — An ice-nip — Strong gales, rapid drift — Breaking up of the ice — Hanging on to floe-edge — The arctic bear — An ice tournament — Escape out of the pack — A storm in the pack — Description of the escape.

9th March.—A BEAR was seen this morning, but as he was going away from us, the dogs were brought out in the hope that they might keep him at bay until the sportsmen came up. It was very pretty to see them take up the scent, and the moment they caught sight of him they set off at full speed. Bruin had seen them first, and increased his pace to a clumsy gallop, yet the dogs were soon around him: he seemed to care but little about them, steadily making off and following the trending of a recently frozen crack in search of clear water, evidently aware that his persecutors would not follow him there.

After five hours all returned on board again; out of the ten dogs four were wounded by his claws,—skin-deep only,—but one of the wounds was seven inches in length, as if made with a sharp knife; this was sewed up, the others were merely trimmed, and nature I am informed will do all the rest. It is really wonderful what cures nature and instinct effect: notwithstanding the extreme cold, no external dressings are applied, because the animal must not be prevented from licking its wound. Petersen says this bear must be very thin, else he could not run so fast. I think it very probable also that he has been hunted before, and that fear lent him wings. A black whale has been seen.

11th.—Two small seals, free from taint, were shot yesterday, so we had fried liver and steaks for breakfast this morning; both were good, but the steaks were preferred; they were very dark and very tender, had been cut thin, deprived of all fat, and washed in two or three waters to get rid of the blubber. I doubt if seals breed in this drifting pack, we have not seen one of their cubs as yet. They contrive to make an excavation or cell in the ice, usually amongst hummocks, and large enough to contain two or three seals; in this "gelid cavern" the young ones are born, it is only a few inches above the water, has a very small breathing hole through the roof, and a large one through which they dive into the sea. When the weather becomes warm enough, they break a hole through the roof and come up on the ice, where they bask in the sun, and—

"Flounce and tremble in unwieldy joy."

I have been into one of these caverns and noticed that the ice admitted quite sufficient light, whilst the icicles hanging

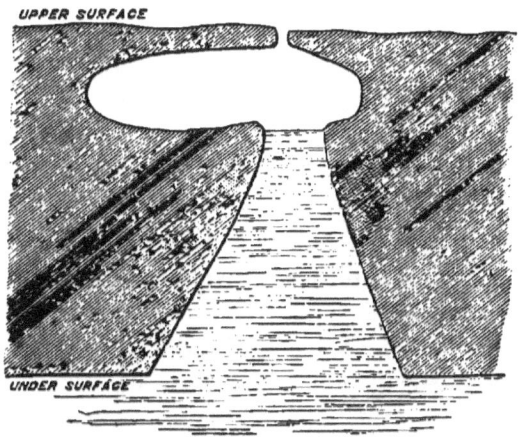

Section of Seal's Cave in the Ice.

from it shewed that it had also enough warmth, imparted from the animals themselves, to occasion a partial thaw.

How often may we not have walked unconsciously over

these sub-glacial dwellings, alarming their timid inmates and causing them to plunge terror-stricken into the sea! The breathing-hole is invariably covered with snow, and therefore invisible.

16th.—*Position*, 69° 38' N., 59° 14' W. Several long lanes of water have again opened, all of them parallel to the direction of the straits; one lane passes within 120 yards of the ship; its extremes are not visible even from aloft; the ice upon its east side has a more rapid southerly motion than that upon its west side.

18th.—Last night the ice closed, shutting up our lane, but its opposite sides continued for several hours to move past each other, rubbing off all projections, crushing, and forcing out of water masses four feet thick: although 120 yards distant, this pressure shook the ship and cracked the intervening ice.

I went out with a lantern to see the nip,—it certainly was awe-inspiring; no one in his senses could avoid reflecting upon the inevitable fate of a ship if exposed to such fearful pressure. It is now the time of spring tides.

19th.—All yesterday the lane remained open, in the evening it closed with but slight pressure; yet as the opposing fields of ice continued to move in opposite directions, all jagged points were brushed off, and the débris thus formed between their edges presented a heaving surface of ice-masses,—an ice river. On the separation of the floes, mass after mass forced itself up to the surface, until at length all the submerged ice had risen, except such as had been forced quite under their edges. One seldom meets with a cleanly fractured floe-edge, they are usually fringed with crushed-up ice or newly-formed sludge.

23rd.—Seals and dovekies are now common; the latter have already made considerable advances towards their summer plumage.

Yesterday there was a very heavy S.E. gale; it blew so furiously, and the snow-drift was so dense, that we could neither hear nor see what was going on twenty yards off; at night the ship, becoming suddenly detached from the ice, heeled over to the storm; until the cause was ascertained we thought the ice had broken up, and pressed against the ship. It was not so; but when the weather moderated we found that there had been heavy pressure upon the edge of the floes,—so much indeed, that the lane of water was now within 70 yards of the 'Fox;' and that ice 4½ feet thick had been crushed during the storm for a distance of about 50 yards.

25th.—Position, 69° 16' N., 58° 50' W. Strong N.W. winds lately, the ship rocking to the breeze, and rubbing her poor sides against the ice, producing a creaking sound which is far from pleasant. More ice-squeezing, and a further inroad upon our barrier; it has yielded slightly, nipping the ship, inclining her to port, and lifting her stern about a foot. Occasional groanings of the timbers within, and surgings of the ice without.

Our boats, provisions, sledges, and knapsacks, are ready for a hasty departure,—beyond this we can do nothing; as long as our friendly barrier lasts we need not fear, but who can tell the moment it may be demolished, and the ship exposed to instant destruction! I am scribbling within a foot of the sternpost—in fact there is a notch in my table to receive it; and I sympathise with its constant groanings; the ice allows it no rest.

27th.—Strong N.W. gale with a return of cold weather. We have drifted 39 miles in the last forty-eight hours! The lane is open; the whole pack appears to have plenty of room to drift, and, I am happy to add, is taking advantage of it,—so much so that the smaller pieces floating freely in the lane can hardly go at the same pace. Our remaining winter companion, the iceberg, was in sight a few days ago, far away to the N.W.; it may be still visible from aloft, but these March gales cut so keenly, that the crow's-nest is but seldom visited.

31st.—Another N.W. gale; it is also spring tides, and this conjunction makes one fearful of ice movement and pressure; but it seems as if the pack had more room to move in, as it does not close much. Seals are often shot, bear tracks are common, and narwhals are frequently seen migrating northward. The bears must prefer the night-time for wandering about, else we could not help seeing them; we often find their tracks within a few hundred yards of the ship.

Although the last, yet this is the coldest day of the month—thermometer down to $-27°$. The mean temperature for March has been unusually high, $-3°$; whilst Lieutenant De Haven's was $-17°$. Notwithstanding that heavy S.E. gales have three times driven us backward, yet we have advanced 100 miles further down Davis' Strait.

6th April.—Position, 67° 18' N., 58° 17' W. To-day we enjoy fine weather, the more so since it comes after a tremendous northerly gale of forty-eight hours' duration. Two days ago the friendly old floe, so long our bulwark of defence, was cracked; the lane of water thus formed soon widened to 60 yards, passed within 30 yards of the 'Fox,' and cut off three of our boats. Yesterday morning another crack detached the remaining 30 yards from us, and as it widened the ship swung across the opening; as quickly as we could effect it the ship was again placed alongside the ice and within a projecting point : had it closed only a few feet whilst she lay across the lane, the consequences must have been most serious. Even to effect this slight change of position we were fully occupied for four hours; for the gale blew furiously, and thermometer stood at 12° below zero, and the cold was very much felt; our hawsers were frozen so stiff as to be quite unmanageable, and we were obliged to use the chain cables to warp the ship into safety.

Throughout yesterday the wind continued extremely strong and keen,—fortunately the ice remained perfectly still: our funnels refused to draw up the smoke; so that between the suffocation, the cold, and anxiety lest the ice should move, our Easter Monday was sufficiently miserable. The half of our poor dogs were cut off from the ship by the lane, and continued to howl dismally until late, when the new ice over the lane was strong enough to bear them, and they came across to us.

To-day we have recovered the boats, shot four seals, seen two whales, and much water to the eastward; we are in latitude 67° 18′ N., and highly delighted with the rapidity of our southern drift.

10*th.—Position*, 66° 45′ N., 58° 20′ W. Yesterday evening the setting sun rendered visible the western land, probably Cape Dyer. We have drifted 70 miles in the last week, and are only 18 miles from De Haven's position of escape; but as we are two months earlier, we must expect to be carried farther south.

Lieutenant De Haven, in command of the United States exploring vessels 'Advance' and 'Rescue,' having become beset in Wellington Channel on 13th September, 1850, drifted with the ice until set free near this on 5th June, 1851.

12*th.*—This morning we drifted ingloriously out of the arctic regions, but with very different feelings from those with which we crossed the arctic circle eight months ago. However, we have not done with them yet; directly the ice lets us go, we will (D.V.) re-enter the frigid zone, and "try again," with, I trust, better success.

A gull and a few terns appeared to-day; these are the first of our summer visitors. The temperature improves; yesterday at one o'clock it was $+19°$ in the shade, $+15°$ in the crow's-nest 70 feet high, and $+51°$ against a black surface exposed to the sun.

16*th*.—Last night a bear came to the ship, was wounded, but escaped; to-day the tracks were followed up for three miles, the bear found, and again wounded—finally the unlucky beast was shot in the water seven miles from the ship; it was lost in consequence of the rapid drifting of the ice, which ran over the floating carcase.

To-night a dense fog-bank rests upon the water to the southward; its upper edge is illuminated by aurora, showing a faint tremulous light.

17*th*.—*Position*, 65° 28' N., 58° 24' W. Another northerly gale; holding fast to the ice with three hawsers; snow-drift limits the view to a couple of miles, so all to the eastward appears water, and to the westward ice.

Last night the ice opened considerably; to secure the ship occupied us for six hours: several of the dogs were again cut off; as the ice they were on was rapidly drifting away, I sent a boat to recover them; it was a difficult and hazardous business, but at length the boat and dogs returned in safety, to my great relief, for it was both dark and late.

18*th*.—Yesterday morning, when I wrote up my journal, I was hoping to hold on quietly to the floe-edge until the wind moderated, when with clear weather we could take advantage of the openings and make some progress towards the clear sea. But the storm increased, and the floe-edge broke away, setting us adrift. Our expulsion from "winter quarters" was a rude one.

Amid the wild commotion of the shattered floes, and clouds of piercing snowdrift, much anxious time was unavoidably spent in fetching off our boats and dogs, five of the latter, unfortunately, would not allow themselves to be caught.

With all possible haste the rudder was shipped, sail set, and before three o'clock the ship was running fast to the eastward.

During the night the ice closed, at daylight this morning scarcely any water was visible, and we were again beset after having sailed about 18 miles.

With the exception of a couple of icebergs, all the ice in sight is not more than two days old, and mainly owes its origin and rapid growth to the immense quantity of snow blown off the pack.

It still blows hard, and thermometer stands at 11°. A sudden opening of the ice this forenoon allowed us to run a few miles southward, and then it closed again.

20th.—*Position* 64° 22' N., 58° 45' W. We have been carried rapidly past the position where the arctic discovery ship 'Resolute' was picked up in September, 1855, whither she had drifted from 74° 41' N., and 101° W., the spot where she was abandoned in May, 1854.

Yesterday three bears, a fulmar petrel, and a snow bunting were seen; this hardy little bird is usually amongst the earliest of our summer visitors, but there is a still smaller bird—the red-pole—which has been found as far north as latitude 74°. How so frail a creature can take such an extensive flight, and cross even more than 100 miles of ocean, it is difficult to conceive. To-day a fine bear came within 150 yards, and was shot by our sportsmen; as they were standing round it afterwards upon the ice, a small seal, the only one seen for several days, popped up its head as if to exult over its fallen enemy—it was of course instantly shot: we have learnt to esteem very highly seal's liver fried with bacon for breakfast.

It seems hardly right to call polar bears *land* animals;

they *abound* here,—110 geographical miles from the nearest land,—upon very loose broken-up ice, which is steadily drifting into the Atlantic at the rate of 12 or 14 miles daily; to remain upon it would insure their destruction were they not nearly amphibious; they hunt by scent, and are constantly running across and against the wind, which prevails from the northward, so that the same instinct which directs their search for prey, also serves the important purpose of guiding them in the direction of the land and more solid ice.

I remarked that the upper part of both Bruin's fore-paws were rubbed quite bare: Petersen explains that to surprise the seal a bear crouches down with his fore-paws doubled underneath, and pushes himself noiselessly forward with his hinder legs until within a few yards, when he springs upon the unsuspecting victim, whether in the water or upon the ice. The Greenlanders are fond of bear's flesh, but never eat either the heart or liver, and say that these parts cause sickness. No instance is known of Greenland bears attacking men, except when wounded or provoked; they never disturb the Esquimaux graves, although they seldom fail to rob a câche of seal's flesh, which is a similar construction of loose stones above ground.

Petersen also tells me that a native of Upernivik, one dark winter's day, was out visiting his seal-nets. He found a seal entangled, and, whilst kneeling down over it upon the ice to get it clear, he received a slap on the back—from his companion as he supposed; but a second and heavier blow made him look smartly round. He was horror-stricken to see a peculiarly grim old bear instead of his comrade! Without deigning further notice of the man, Bruin tore the seal out of the net and commenced his supper. He was not interrupted, nor did the man await the conclusion of the meal.

The Greenlander's Supper appropriated by a Bear.

23rd.—Position 63° 41′ N., 58° 59′ W. I had long ago resolved, if we escaped before the 15th, or the 20th April at the latest, to go to Newfoundland to refresh the crew and to refit, even if no damage from the ice should be sustained. In order to do so it would have been necessary for us to visit a Greenland port for a supply of water. We could not have calculated upon much assistance from our engines upon such a voyage, Mr. Brand alone being capable of working the engines, so that ten or twelve hours daily is all the steaming that could have been expected.

But we are still ice-locked, so I purpose going to Holsteinborg in preference to a more southern port, as there we may expect to get reindeer and a small supply of stores suitable to our wants. The whalers sometimes reach Disco in March, Upernivik in May, and the North Water early in June. Unless we should be at once set free, we shall not have time to spare for a Newfoundland voyage.

24th.—Another anxious week has passed. Latterly we have experienced south-westerly currents, similar to those which Parry describes when beset here in June, 1819. To-day we have had a strong S.E. breeze, with snow and dark weather. The wind had greatly moderated when the swell reached us about eight o'clock this evening. It is now ten o'clock; the long ocean swell already lifts its crest five feet above the hollow of the sea, causing its thick covering of icy fragments to dash against each other and against us with unpleasant violence. It is however very beautiful to look upon, the dear old familiar ocean-swell! it has long been a stranger to us, and is welcome in our solitude. If the 'Fox' was as solid as her neighbours, I am quite sure she would enter into this ice-tournament with all their apparent heartiness, instead of audibly making known her sufferings to us. Every considerable surface of ice has been broken into many smaller ones; with feelings of exultation

I watched the process from aloft. A floe-piece near us, of 100 yards in diameter, was speedily cracked so as to resemble a sort of labyrinth, or, still more, a field-spider's web. In the course of half-an-hour the family resemblance of the fragments was totally lost; they had so battered each other, and struggled out of their original regularity. The rolling sea can no longer be checked; "the pack has taken upon itself the functions of an ocean," as Dr. Kane graphically expresses it.

26th.—Position 63° 47' N., 56° 36' W. At sea! How am I to describe the events of the last two days? It has pleased God to accord to us a deliverance in which His merciful protection contrasts—how strongly!—with our own utter helplessness; as if the successive mercies vouchsafed to us during our long long winter and mysterious ice-drift had been concentrated and repeated in a single act. Thus forcibly does His great goodness come home to the mind!

I am in no humour for writing, being still tired, worn, and perhaps a little sea-sick; at least I have a headache, caused by the rolling of the ship and rattling noise of everything.

On Saturday night, the 24th, I went on deck to spend the greater part of it in watching, and to determine what to do. The swell greatly increased; it had evidently been approaching for hours before it reached us, since it rose in proportion as the ice was broken up into smaller pieces. In a short time but few of them were equal in size to the ship's deck; most of them not half so large. I knew that near the pack-edge the sea would be very heavy and dangerous; but the wind was now fair, and, having auxiliary steam-power, I resolved to push out of the ice if possible.

Shortly after midnight the ship was under sail, slowly boring her way to the eastward; at two o'clock on Sunday morning commenced steaming, the wind having failed. By eight o'clock we had advanced considerably to the eastward, and the swell had become dangerously high, the waves rising ten feet above the trough of the sea. The shocks of the ice against the ship were alarmingly heavy; it became necessary to steer exactly head-on to swell. We slowly passed a small iceberg 60 or 70 feet high; impelled by the swell it crashed onward through the pack, leaving a water-space in its wake, small in extent, yet sufficient to allow the seas to break against its cliffs, and throw the spray in heavy showers quite over its summit.

The anxious day wore on without much change. Gradually the swell increased, and rolled along more swiftly, becoming in fact a heavy and regular sea, rather than a swell. The ice often lay so closely packed that we could hardly force ahead, although the fair wind had again freshened up. Much heavy hummocky ice and large berg-pieces lay dispersed through the pack; a single thump from any of them would have been instant destruction. By five o'clock the ice became more loose, and clear spaces of water could be seen ahead. We went faster, received fewer though still more severe shocks, until at length we had room to steer clear of the heaviest pieces; and at eight o'clock we emerged from the villainous "pack," and were running fast through straggling pieces into a clear sea. The engines were stopped, and Mr. Brand permitted to rest after eighteen hours' duty, for we now have no one else capable of driving the engines.

Throughout the day I trembled for the safety of the rudder, and screw; deprived of the one or the other, even for half-an-hour, I think our fate would have been sealed; to have steered in any other direction than *against* the swell would have exposed, and probably sacrificed both.

Our bow is very strongly fortified, well plated externally with iron, and so very sharp that the ice-masses, repeatedly hurled against the ship by the swell as she rose to meet it, were thus robbed of their destructive force; they struck us obliquely, yet caused the vessel to shake violently, the bells to ring, and almost knocked us off our legs. On many occasions the engines were stopped dead by ice choking the screw; once it was some minutes before it could be got to revolve again. Anxious moments those!

After yesterday's experience I can understand how men's hair have turned grey in a few hours. Had self-reliance been my only support and hope, it is not impossible that I might have illustrated the fact. Under the circumstances I did my best to insure our safety, looked as stoical as possible, and inwardly trusted that God would favour our exertions. What a release ours has been, not only from eight months' imprisonment, but from the perils of that one day! Had our little vessel been destroyed after the ice broke up, there remained no hope for us. But we have been brought safely through, and are all inexpressibly grateful, I hope, and believe.

I grieve to think of poor Lady Franklin and our friends at home. Severely as we have felt the failure of our first season's operations, yet the ordeal is now over with us: not so with her and them,—they have still to experience that bitter disappointment.

Our distance within the pack-edge, where we first made sail yesterday, was 22 miles. Before we got clear of the ice the height of the waves was $13\frac{1}{2}$ feet; after passing through the last of it there was no increase, but the sea was more confused; in fact, within the ice all minor disturbances were quelled or merged into a regular succession of fast-following waves. The ship and her machinery behaved most admirably in the struggle; should I ever have to pass through such an ice-covered heaving ocean again, let me secure a passage in the 'Fox.'

During our 250 days in the ice-pack of Baffin's Bay and Davis' Strait, we were drifted 1194 geographical or 1385 statute miles, and this is the longest drift I know of. Our winter may be considered as having been rather mild but very windy.

As long ago as 2nd January I noted in this diary, that our movement seemed due almost exclusively to the wind; in the Appendix will be found some interesting remarks on the effect of wind in producing ice movement.

We are now steering for Holsteinborg where I intend to refit, and to refresh the crew : it has the reputation of being the best place on the coast for reindeer.

CHAPTER VII.

A holiday in Greenland — A lady blue with cold — The loves of Greenlanders — Close shaving — Meet the whalers — Information of whalers — Disco — Danish Hospitality — Sail from Disco — Coaling — Kindness of the whalers — Danish establishments in Greenland.

Wednesday night, April 28*th.*—AT anchor off the settlement of Holsteinborg, and moored close in to its very rocks! How black they look, and what a welcome feeling of security they convey to us, so recently escaped from a long continuance of icy peril!! We have been visited by the Danish residents—the chief trader or governor, the priest, and two others: their latest European intelligence is not more recent than our own, but the Danish ship is hourly expected; she usually leaves Copenhagen about the middle of March.

The winter here has been just the reverse of our experience; it has been severe in point of temperature, but with very little wind; the land lies buried in snow, and as yet there is no thaw; it is too early for the cod-fishery, and not a single reindeer has been killed throughout the winter! Eider-ducks, looms, and dovekies are abundant, as well as hares and ptarmigan.

29*th.*—A bright and lovely day. Our poor, half-famished dogs have been landed near the carcasses of four whales, so they must be supremely happy. I visited the Governor to-day, and found his little wooden house as scrupulously clean and neat as the houses of the Danish residents in Greenland invariably are. The only ornaments about the room were portraits of his unfortunate wife and two children: they embarked at Copenhagen last year to rejoin him, and the ill-fated vessel has never since been heard of. Poor Governor Elberg is in ill health, and talks of returning home —by *home* he means Denmark, the land of his birth, and where once he had a home.

30*th*.—This is a grand Danish holiday; the inhabitants are all dressed in their Sunday clothes—at least, all who have got a change of garments,—and there is both morning and evening service in the small wooden church. As the Governor could not be persuaded to unlock the door of the dance-house, our men returned on board early; yesterday evening they were all on shore, and, with the Esquimaux, were wedged into this one large room: to be squeezed in a crowd of human beings is positive enjoyment after a winter's isolation such as ours has been. Old Harvey constituted himself master of the ceremonies, and with his flute led the orchestra; it consisted of one other flute and a fiddle: he managed to perch himself above all the rest, at one end of the room, and played with such vigour that our bluejackets and the Esquimaux ladies danced away most furiously for hours. These ladies can dance in the least possible space, their costume being particularly well adapted for the purpose, partaking, as it does, much more of the "Bloomer" than the "Crinoline."

Christian looks immensely happy: his countrymen regard him as a man whose fortune is made, and the women gaze with admiration upon his neat sailor's dress, his good-natured, full, round face, and huge fat, shining cheeks; Mr. Petersen is in great request to interpret between the English, Danes, and Esquimaux.

7*th May*.—I intended sailing for Disco this morning, but wind and weather were adverse. We have obtained but little here except water, a tolerable supply of rock cod, some ptarmigan, hares, wildfowl, and a few items of stores. The Governor *now* thinks the Danish ship must have been directed to visit Godhaab before coming here. We have left letters to go home in her, and they ought to be in England by the end of June.

I visited to-day a small lake at the foot of Mount Cunningham; it is said to occupy the centre of an extinct volcano, but I saw nothing to bear out the assertion. This is the only part of Greenland where earthquakes are felt. The Governor told me of an unusually severe shock which occurred a winter or two ago. He was sitting in his room and reading at the time, when he heard a loud noise like the discharge of a cannon; immediately afterwards a tremulous motion was felt, some glasses upon the table commenced to dance about, and papers lying upon the window-sill fell down: after a few seconds it ceased. He thinks the motion originated at the lake, as it was not felt by some people living beyond it, and that it passed from N.E. to S.W.

This rocky mountainous scenery is magnificent; but a little more animal life—reindeer, for instance—would make it far more pleasing in our eyes. The last twelvemonth's produce of this district amounts only to 500 reindeer skins, instead of 3000, as in ordinary years. The prevailing rock is syenitic granite. This settlement was first formed in 1772, it now contains about 200 souls; the present clergyman was born in it, and has succeeded his father in the priestly office; his wife is the only European female in the colony. Being told that fuel was extremely scarce in the Danish houses, and that "the priest's wife was blue with the cold," I sent on shore a present of some coals.

On Sunday afternoon, hearing the church bell tolling, I went on shore. It proved to be only a christening. The little dusky infant received a long string of European names; there was a small description of barrel-organ, to the sound of which the congregation joined in, keeping up a loud monotonous chant. Most of the young people had hymn-books in their hands, printed in the Esquimaux language.

Ravens seem very abundant; also large grey falcons: perhaps the dead whales may have attracted an unusual number.

Poor Christian has not only fallen desperately in love, but has engaged himself to the object of his affections, a pretty Esquimaux girl. He asked me to-day to give her a passage up to Godhavn, as he wished to leave her in charge of his mother until his return there with us next year, when his engagement for the voyage would be fulfilled. Having heard a rumour of a young woman awaiting his return with anxiety at Godhavn, I taxed him with it, but he replied with great simplicity that "he had never promised her, and would not marry her, as his friends objected to the match." What are the good Greenlanders coming to? I recommended that he should leave his betrothed in her own home, with her mother and family. His asking a passage for her, in order to leave her with his mother, is strong proof of the sincerity of his engagement, not only to his lady-love, but to the 'Fox' also.

Governor Elberg has promised to get me some fossil fish, to be found only in North Strom Fiord: they are interesting, as being of unknown geological date.

The fur of the arctic hare is beautifully soft and white; it is sometimes spun, and knitted into the nicest ladies' gloves possible. I was not able to procure more than one pair, and the poor woman who made them could not conceal her delight at receiving for them a shilling and a few biscuits.

Holsteinborg may be a charming spot in summer, but it has a northern aspect, and is now almost buried with snow. It is called "Wylie Fiord" by our whalers, and is, I believe, the only place on the coast suitable for laying a ship upon the ground to undergo repairs; the rise and fall at spring tides is 10 feet. We cannot land at all times of tide, for a very sufficient reason: at high-water-mark a broad fringe of ice margins the shore to which it is firmly frozen, and is convenient to step on to from a boat; but at low-water this "ice-foot" is several feet above one's head, and moreover the rocks now exposed are worn smooth and slippery by the constant attrition of ice.

The harbour is so small that the 'Fox' is moored by hawsers to the rocks on each side, and yet the water is so deep that our anchor lies in 17 fathoms. They tell me that oysters abound here, but I am not quite clear that they do not mean scallops.

10th.—On the morning of the 8th we left Holsteinborg with a pleasant land wind and bright weather. When 15 miles off shore we were stopped by ice formed during the last two nights, the thermometer having fallen to 12°; out in the offing the weather was gloomy and cold, and strong northerly winds were blowing. On closing the land again, we regained the offshore wind, and bright weather.

Keeping close alongshore, and threading our way through a vast deal of pack and numerous icebergs, we caught sight of Disco about noon to-day, and by the evening were within an hour's sail of Godhavn, when we were again stopped by a broad belt of ice stretching along the coast; this was a bitter disappointment, more particularly as a gale of wind with heavy sea was fast rising, and snow beginning to fall thickly; there was nothing for it, however, but to stand off under easy sail for the night.

12th.—At anchor at the Whalefish Islands. On the evening of the 10th we stood off from the inhospitable barrier of ice, prepared to meet the storm; snow fell so thickly that we could hardly see the icebergs in time to avoid them. We supposed ourselves to be well to leeward of the Whalefish Islands, but were deceived by the tides; suddenly a small, low islet was seen on the lee bow; not being able to pass to windward, we were obliged to wear ship, and, in doing so, she passed within her own length of destruction—for we were certainly within a few yards of the rocks! The islet was covered with snow, and, but for some very few dark points of rock showing through, it could not be distinguished from ice. On the 11th the weather improved, and in the evening we came to our present anchorage. From a hill we can watch an opportunity to enter Godhavn. Notwithstanding the blowing weather, some natives came about five miles off to us; the water washed over their little *kayaks*, and kept the occupants' sealskin dresses streaming with wet up to their shoulders; this part of their dress seems rather part of the kayak, as it is attached to it round the hole in which the *kayaker* sits, so that no water can enter. It is wonderful to see how closely a man can assimilate his habits to those of a fish.

The Danish cooper in charge of this out-station tells us there are thirteen English whalers already out, and some of them have been up to the north end of Disco; two vessels are in sight. The world, it appears, is at peace. Petersen was at one time in charge of this station; he is now seeking out his old acquaintances.

14th.—Summer has suddenly burst upon us—thermometer up to 40°; moreover, we are enjoying English newspapers, and have dined off roast beef and vegetables!

Two days ago I sent a note off to a whaler by a kayak, requesting her captain to lend me some newspapers; the note reached Captain J. Walker, of the 'Jane,' and yesterday his ship, accompanied by the 'Heroine,' Captain J. Simpson, approached us, and they both came in to call upon me, each of them bringing the very acceptable present of some newspapers, besides a quarter of beef, with vegetables. Nothing could exceed their sincere good feeling and kindness; they offered to supply me with anything their ships could afford. The account they give of last season is as follows: the whalers reached Devil's Point, near Melville Bay, as early as 21st May; southerly winds then set in, and blew incessantly for six weeks, during all which time they were closely beset, and the ships 'Gipsy' and 'Undaunted' were crushed. When able to move, the fleet returned southward along the pack-edge, which was everywhere found to be impenetrable; they sailed southward of Disco, and about the middle of July the earliest ships rounded the southern extremity of the middle ice in lat. $68\frac{1}{2}°$, and found no difficulty in their further passage to Pond's Bay. Captain Walker says ships could not have reached Lancaster Sound, as there was much ice north of Pond's Bay which he thought extended quite across to Melville Bay.

The position of the ice last season was considered to be most unusual; the long prevalence of southerly winds appeared to have separated the tail of the pack from the main body, the former lying against the west land about Cape Searle, whilst the latter was forced northward and pressed closely into Melville Bay; the ships sailed freely between these two great divisions, and found the west water unusually extensive.

Had I been able to collect a sufficient number of sledge-dogs at Godhavn last year, it was my intention to have sailed across to the west side if possible, instead of pursuing the usual route through Melville Bay; but the opinions of the captains of the lost whalers were in favour of a "Melville Bay" passage, and the necessity for obtaining dogs left me no choice as to whether I should proceed west, or north to Proven and Upernivik; I have already recorded what were my opinions *at the time*, so need only observe now, that, although I failed, I believe my decision was justified by all former experience, even independently of the circumstances which obliged me to adopt it. Nevertheless it is mortifying to find that ships had reached as far as Pond's Bay, and with but little difficulty. Sir Edward Parry, upon his third voyage, did not reach the west water until very late in the season, although some of the whalers met with better success by following up another route.

There is nothing more uncertain than ice-navigation, dependent as it is upon winds, temperatures, and currents: one can only calculate upon "the chances," and how nearly we succeeded we have already seen. In the preceding year (1856) some of the whalers got through Melville Bay, as early as the 15th June, only a few days after the commencement of the summer's thaw. Captain Walker tells me there are many years in which the whalers can pass up the western shore late in the season, but not always so far as Pond's Bay; of Melville Bay after the 10th or 15th July they know nothing, but the voyages of discovery afford us ample details; whilst of the southern route almost nothing has been made publicly known.

There are many intelligent whaling captains who possess much valuable knowledge of these lands and seas, and even in the *terra incognita* of Frobisher's Straits whalers have wintered, whilst our charts scarcely afford even a vague idea of the configuration of these extensive islands. The so-called "Home Bay" has been penetrated for fifty miles and is supposed to be a strait leading to Fox's Furthest. Scott's Inlet is also said to be a strait leading into a western arm of the same sea. A surveying vessel would be usefully employed for a couple of summers in tracing the general outline of these possessions of Her Majesty, more particularly as they are rather thickly inhabited by Esquimaux most eager to barter their produce for rifles, saws, files, knives, needles, and such like articles. Good coal has been found upon Durbin Island (near Cape Searle), in a convenient little cove upon its southern side; and as the old sailing whalers are fast being replaced by steamers, this place may become of great importance to them.

Amongst the many stray questions put to our kind visitors, "the fashions" were not forgotten, and, strange to relate, crinoline has actually quadrupled the price of whalebone within the last few years.

The sooner the poor whales memorialize the Empress for a change of fashion the better!

We are refitting, shooting, and devouring quantities of excellent mussels; eider ducks are very abundant, but extremely shy. Poor puss has been killed; tempted on deck by the unusually warm weather, she was pounced upon by the dogs.

17*th*.—Yesterday our attempt to enter the port of Godhavn failed, it is still filled with ice. This evening Young and I examined a narrow rocky cove—Upernivik Bay of the natives; finding it suitable for our purpose, the ship was brought in and moored to the rocks. We were received with much kindness by our friends Mr. and Mrs. Olrik, and were presented with a file of late English papers. A considerable supply of beer was ordered to be brewed for us.

I found Mrs. Olrik without a fire in her sitting room, it was unnecessary; the windows looked to the south, and the sun shone brightly in upon a profusion of geraniums and European flowers, at once reminding one of home, and refreshing the senses by their perfume and beauty; the merry voices of the children were also a most pleasing novelty. Mr. Olrik says the past winter has not been in any way remarkable, except for the prevalence of strong winds; April and the early part of May have been unusually cold.

24*th*.—We did honour to Her Majesty's birthday by

dressing the 'Fox' in all her flags, and regaling her crew with plum pudding and grog. The ice having moved off, we have come into the harbour of Godhavn, as being more convenient and safe. The day has been a busy one; we have completed our small purchases and closed our letters; I have added another Esquimaux lad to our crew, taking with him his rifle, kayak, and sledge. This evening there has been a brisk interchange of presents between us and our Danish friends. I have been given an eider-down coverlet by the Governor, a pair of fur boots by Mr. Andersen, and by Mrs. Olrik, some delicious preserves of Greenland cranberries, a tin of preserved ptarmigan, and a jar of pickled whaleskin; my table is decked with European flowers, including roses, mignonette, and violets.

With good reason shall we remember Godhavn; we have certainly been treated as especial favourites.

26*th*.—Left Godhavn early yesterday morning, and anchored this afternoon in our old position off the Coal Cliffs in Waigat Strait; a party of seal-hunters from Atanekerdluk came off to us, and their hunting having terminated successfully, they will assist us in coaling. From these men I obtained much information about this part of the coast; within a range of 20 miles upon the Disco shore there are four distinct coaling places; but at this early season two of them are deeply covered with snow. There is also very good coal at the S.E. end of Hare Island, where it can easily be obtained. The ice in this strait broke up as long ago as the 3rd April; it has all drifted out to the *northward*, and only a few icebergs now remain.

On the Greenland shore of the strait is the now celebrated fossilized forest of Atanekerdluk,—a brief notice of it will be found in the Appendix; the extraordinary interest attaching to it is due to the fact, that here about one hundred species of plants have been found, that flourished at quite a recent geological period, and required an English climate for their support.

The annual temperature of England may be taken at 49°; that of Iceland, where no trees will grow, at 39°; but of Greenland, under the 70th parallel where these trees grew, it is only 19°.

These miocene fossils, beeches, oaks, magnolias, and evergreens; the ammonites of Prince Patrick's Island in Lat. 77°; the widely spread coal plants; the stems of pine trees, still capable of being used as fuel, and found not only in the Arctic Archipelago, but in New Siberia; also the fossil firs and poplars of Spitzbergen in Lat. 79°; these all shew that there was a time when arctic lands enjoyed, at least a temperate climate; and we look to the astronomer for a solution of this mystery. Meanwhile the safest hypothesis to adopt is, I believe, that there has been a change in the earth's axis of rotation, which astronomy, as an exact science, is not yet old enough to detect. There is, however, nothing new under the sun—even here we find ourselves anticipated by an old Chinese tradition, that long ages ago the Pole star suddenly dipped down towards the horizon!

28th.—Again hastening northward; the business of coaling was very speedily and satisfactorily completed, but the quality of the coal is very inferior. Upon the green slopes our sportsmen found nothing but a few ptarmigan and a hare.

Shortly after running close past the deserted settlement of Noursak, we arrived off a small bay, and were startled by finding the water had suddenly changed from transparent blue to a thick muddy colour, but there was no change in its depth; we were crossing the stream of "Makkaks Elvin," or Clay River, which empties itself into the bay after running through a broad and extensive valley, said to abound with reindeer. This river has its origin in lakes and glaciers in the interior, and the discolouration of the water is probably the chief cause of success in white-whale fishing, which is carried on here in the autumn, as those timid animals will not permit boats to approach them in clear water.

This evening we are crossing Omenak's Fiord, and the land-wind, which here and all along the coast northwards blows from the N.E., has come off to us.

31*st.*—Lying fast to an iceberg off Upernivik.

The whalers are all within a dozen miles of us, unable to penetrate further north. The season appears forward, and the ice much decayed; but southerly winds prevail, retarding its disruption and removal. Captain Parker, of the 'Emma,' tells me he does not expect to make a north passage this year, and as his experience extends over a period of at least thirty years, I give his reason; it is simply this,—that as during the months of February, March, and April northerly winds prevailed to an unusual degree, therefore southerly winds may now be expected to continue; if he prove a prophet, it will be to our serious hindrance at this critical season. Governor Fliescher says the winter has been mild; there has been but little wind, and that chiefly from the southward.

4th June.—We have received much kindness from our friends Captains Parker and J. Simpson, as well as from others of the whaling fleet; the former has generously supplied us with many things we were rather short of, not only in ship's stores, but provisions and coals, and in return I have of course furnished him with a receipt for his owners. Captain Simpson has most handsomely presented the 'Fox' with a sail and yards, which, after some slight alterations, will enable us to add a main topsail to our spread of canvas. For the two days we lay at the iceberg, alongside of the 'Emma,' I made furious attacks upon Captain Parker's beefsteaks and porter; we amply availed ourselves of his hearty welcome. By the arrival of the fine steam whaler 'Tay,' from Scotland, we have received papers up to 17th April.

This morning we slowly steamed away from Upernivik, threading our way betwixt islands and ice, for about 30 miles, and now await further ice movement before it will be possible to proceed. These are called the Women Islands, so named by the celebrated arctic explorer John Davis, who visited them in Queen Elizabeth's reign; he found here only a few old women, their frightened lords and more active juniors having effected their escape.

Upon one of these islands a stone was picked up some 30 years ago, bearing a Runic inscription; it was sent home to Copenhagen as a most interesting relic of the early Scandinavian voyagers; but nothing was on it except the names of those men "who cleared this place" (or formed a settlement), and the date, 1135. In all probability their sojourn was extremely short, perhaps only for a single summer. The Esquimaux did not made their appearance for nearly two centuries later.

After Egede's settlement at Godhaab in 1721, the Danish trading establishments gradually extended along the coast, even to Upernivik; but it appears to have been soon abandoned. During Napoleon's wars all the Danish posts were withdrawn, as the British fleet effectually cut off communication with Europe; but after peace was restored in 1815, the trading posts were again resorted to, and a new settlement formed near the ruins of the old one at Upernivik; it enjoys pre-eminence as the most northern abode of civilized man.

Perilous Position of the 'Fox,' near Buchan Island, 7th June, 1858

CHAPTER VIII.

'Fox' nearly wrecked — Afloat, and push ahead — Arctic hair-breadth escapes — Nearly caught in the pack — Shooting little auks — The arctic highlanders — Cape York — Crimson snow — Struggling to the westward — Reach the West-land — Off the entrance of Lancaster Sound.

June 8th.—YESTERDAY morning we passed close outside Buchan Island; it is small but lofty, its north side is almost precipitous, yet, notwithstanding this strong indication of deep water, a reef of rocks lies about a mile off it. I happened to be aloft with the look-out-man at half-past eight o'clock as we were steaming through a narrow lead in the ice, when I saw a rock close ahead; it was capped with ice, therefore was hardly distinguishable from the floating masses around; the engines were stopped and reversed, but there was neither time nor room to avoid the reef, which now extended upon each side of us, and upon which the ship's bow stuck fast whilst her stern remained in 36 feet water; the tide had just commenced to fall, and all our efforts to haul off from the rocks were ineffectual. The floes lay within 30 yards of us upon each side. I feared their drifting down upon the ship and turning her over; but fortunately it was perfectly calm, and as the tide fell, points of the reef held them fast. The ship continued to fall over to starboard; at dead low water her inclination was 35°; the water covered the starboard gunwale from the mainmast aft; and reached almost up to the after hatchway; at this time the slightest shake must have caused her to fall over upon her side, when she would instantly have filled and sunk! The dogs, after repeated ineffectual attempts to lie upon the deck, quietly coiled themselves up upon such parts of the lee gunwale as remained above water and went to sleep.

To me the moments seemed lengthened out beyond anything I could have imagined; but at length the water began to rise, and the ship to resume her upright position. Boats, anchors, hawsers, &c., were got on board again with the utmost alacrity, and the ship floated off unhurt after having been eleven hours upon the reef. We had grounded during the day tide and were floated off by the night tide, which upon this coast occasions a much greater rise and fall,—so far we were favoured, but the poor little 'Fox' had a very narrow escape; as for ourselves, there was not the slightest cause for apprehension, three steam whalers being within signal distance.

To-day we are steaming along after the three vessels which passed us last evening and disappeared round Cape Shackleton during the night. The contrast between our prospects yesterday and to-day fills one with delight,—to be afloat and advancing unobstructedly once more, is indeed charming.

11th.—On the afternoon of the 8th we joined the steamers 'Tay,' Captain Deuchars; 'Chase,' Captain Gravill, sen.; and 'Diana,' Captain Gravill, jun. After repeated ice-detentions, we have reached Duck Island. Captain Deuchars says there is every prospect of an early north passage. We have had several conversations about the Pond's Bay natives, and their reports of ships, wrecks, and Europeans; but there appears to be not only great difficulty, but also uncertainty, in arriving at their meaning; to form an idea of the time elapsed since an event, or the distance to the spot where it occurred, is a still harder task. I look forward to our visit at Pond's Bay with greatly increased interest.

In August, 1855, when Captain Deuchars was crossing

through the middle ice, in latitude 70°, he found part of a steamer's topmast embedded in heavy ice; he also saw the moulded form of a ship's side, and thinks the latter must have sunk; the portion of the topmast visible was sawed off and taken to England. In the following month, and three degrees further South, the 'Resolute' was picked up. Now as Her Majesty's Ships 'Resolute' and 'Intrepid' were frozen up close together when we abandoned them in May, 1854, I conclude that the traces which Captain Deuchars discovered were those of my old ship, the 'Intrepid.' About two or three years ago Captain Deuchars lost his ship, the 'Princess Charlotte,' in Melville Bay. It was a beautiful morning; they had almost reached the North Water, and were anticipating a very successful voyage; the steward had just reported breakfast ready, when Captain Deuchars, seeing the floes closing together ahead of the ship, remained on deck to see her pass safely between them; but they closed too quickly; the vessel was *almost* through, when the points of ice caught her sides abreast of the mizenmast, and passing through, held the wreck up for a few minutes, barely long enough for the crew to escape and save their boats. Poor Deuchars thus suddenly lost not only his breakfast but his ship; within *ten minutes* her royal yards disappeared beneath the surface. How closely danger besets the arctic cruiser, yet how insidiously; everything looks so bright, so calm, so still, that it requires positive experience to convince one that ice only a very few inches, perhaps only three or four inches, *above water*,[1] perfectly level, and moving extremely slow, could possibly endanger a strong vessel! The 'Princess Charlotte' was a very fine, strong ship, and her captain one of the most experienced arctic seamen: he now commands the finest whaler in the fleet.

[1] Only about one-seventh of the whole thickness of sea ice is floated above water.

14th.—We have only advanced a few miles to the northward. The steamer 'Innuit' has joined our small steam squadron. Captain Sutter left Scotland only a month ago: he has very kindly and promptly sent us a present of newspapers and potatoes. Captain Deuchars has also been good enough to supply us with some potatoes and porter, perhaps the most serviceable present he could have made us after our long subsistence upon salted and preserved meats.

19th.—Once more alone in Melville Bay. The 'Innuit' and 'Chase' steamed much too fast for us, and the last of the four vessels, the 'Tay,' parted from us in a thick fog yesterday. We have come close along the edge of the fixed ice, passing about 6 miles outside of the Sabine Islands, and are advancing as opportunities offer. This morning the man who was stationed to watch a nip about a quarter of a mile ahead of the ship, came running back, pursued by three bears—a mother with her half-grown cubs. I suppose they followed him chiefly because he ran from them; at all events they were very close up when he reached the ship. Another bear was seen about the same time, but none of them came within shot. Rotchies (or little auks) are very abundant. Seals are occasionally shot. I ate some boiled seal to-day, and found it good : this is the first time I have eaten positive *blubber;* all scruples respecting it henceforth vanish.

25th.—The land-ice broke away inshore of the 'Fox' on the 19th or 20th, and we found ourselves drifting southward amongst extensive fields of ice. Sad experience has already shown us how powerless our small craft is under such circumstances. But after many attempts we regained the edge of the fast ice this morning, and steamed merrily along it towards Bushnan Island. When within a few miles a nip brought us to a standstill: here five or six icebergs, apparently aground, lie encompassed by land ice; one of them juts out and has caught the point of an immense field of ice;

there is some slight movement in the latter, but not enough to let us pass through.

Twelve or eighteen miles to the south there is a cluster of bergs, in all probability aground upon our " 70 fathom bank " of last September. The ice-field appears to rest against them, as both to the east and west there is much clear water. Exactly at this spot Captain Penny was similarly detained by a nip in August, 1850. Although progress is denied to us at present, yet it is an unspeakable relief to have got out of the drifting ice.

I have passed very many anxious days in Melville Bay, but hardly any of them weighed so heavily upon me as yesterday. Such a lovely day, so clear and bright, a sky intensely blue, and every distant object remarkably distinct; it was a day above all days to string one's nerves for unusual action; and the longed-for broad *land-water* was there—within a third of a mile—gently rippled by a pleasant fair breeze. But the nip—the *intervening nip*,—it worked sufficiently with wind and tide to keep one in suspense; it *nearly* opened at high water, but closed again with the ebb tide. I thought of the week already spent in struggling amongst drifting floes, and was haunted by visions of everything horrible—gales, fogs, ice-crushing, &c. Nor was it consoling to reflect that all the whaling ships might have actually slipped past us. In fact a prolonged condition of *unrest*, of intense mental and physical strain, had worked me up into a state of extreme anxiety at being so repeatedly baffled in all my efforts by the varying, yet continual perplexities of our position.[1] The only difference in favour of our prospects over those of the past year consists in our having arrived

[1] To those having responsibility, Melville Bay navigation admits of *no rest;* the unquiet ice ever threatens, whilst constant daylight not only seems to warn one against yielding to repose, but banishes for a time the desire for natural rest.

here two months earlier; but the importance of this difference is incalculable.

The opportunities afforded by the delays to which we have been subjected were turned, however, to some account. Nearly one thousand rotchies were shot; they are excellent eating, their average weight is four ounces and a half, but when prepared for the table they probably do not yield more than three ounces each. A young bear imprudently swam up to the ship, and was shot,—his skin fell to the sportsman, and carcase to the dogs. Several others have been seen : we watched one fellow surprise a seal upon the ice, and carry it about in his mouth as a cat does a mouse.

27th.—Lying fast to the ice off the Crimson Cliffs, of Sir John Ross. Yesterday we succeeded in passing through the nip, and by evening reached Cape York. Seeing natives running out upon the land-ice, the ship was made fast for an hour in order to communicate with them. A party of eight men came on board : they immediately recognised Petersen for they lived at Etah in Smith's Sound when he was there in the American expedition. They asked for Dr. Kane, and told us Hans was married and living in Whale Sound. They all said he was most anxious to return to Greenland, but had neither sledge-dogs nor kayak ; hunger had compelled him to eat the sealskin which covered the framework of the latter. Petersen gave them messages for Hans from his Greenland friends, and advice that he should fix his residence here, where he might see the whalers and perhaps be taken back to Greenland. The natives did not seem to be badly off for anything except dogs, some distemper having carried off most of these indispensable animals, I was therefore unable to procure any from them. These people spent last winter here; they seemed to be healthy, well-clad, and happy little fellows. One of them is brother-in-law to Erasmus York, who voluntarily came to England in the 'Assistance' in

Esquimaux near Cape York watching the approach of the 'Fox;' also Christian in his kayak.

1851. This man is an *angekok*, or magician; he has a still flatter face than the rest of his countrymen, but appears more thoughtful and intelligent.

Petersen pointed out to me a stout old fellow, with a tolerable sprinkling of beard and moustache. This worthy perpetrated the only murder which has taken place for several years in the tribe : he disliked his victim and stood in need of his dogs, therefore he killed the owner and appropriated his property ! Such motives and passions usually govern the "unsophisticated children of nature;" yet, as savages, the Esquimaux may be considered exceedingly harmless.

Of late years these arctic highlanders have become alarmed by the rapid diminution of their numbers through famine and disease, and have been less violent towards each other in their feuds and quarrels.

The appearance of the men, as they danced and rolled about in frantic delight at our approach, was wild and strange, and their costumes uniform and picturesque. Their long, coarse, black hair hung loosely over the sealskin frock, which in its turn overlapped their loose shaggy bearskin breeches, and these again came down over the tops of their sealskin boots. Most of them carried a spear formed out of the horn of a narwhal. They watched the rapid evolutions of Christian in his kayak with intense interest, for they do not possess any themselves, and their knowledge of them is only traditional. My first interview with these northern Esquimaux was in 1852, when commanding H.M.S. 'Intrepid'; then, as now, the men came off on the land ice to us; they appeared to me to be very little people, with large flat faces and a sprinkling of beard and moustache, apparently in sound health and perfectly happy. A party of us walked to the land to visit their abodes, and the female population; one vociferous old hag met us at the beach, and seemed to be introducing us to all the rest, and gave us a detailed account of their relationships and accomplishments. There were three tents only; words can scarcely describe the filth and wretchedness of such abodes; the sealskins composing the tents, and the skins of various sorts which served for beds, and blankets, were scarcely half dressed, and emitted an intolerable effluvium, whilst the ground in every direction was strewed with bones and decaying animal matter. The dresses of the women were covered with blubber and soot, their faces and necks black and greasy, and eyes bleared, from constantly superintending the slow process of cooking in a stone vessel over a smoky blubber lamp. Several fresh sealskins were stretched upon the earth, and pegged down with small bones, whilst the carcases, not required for present use, were covered over with large stones to preserve them from the dogs. Not twenty yards from the tents stood the ruin of a winter hut; I looked in through a crevice and saw that the ordinary flooring of flat stones was nearly covered with ice, and, from the quantity of scraps and bones lying about, it seemed to have become the occasional habitation of the dogs;—but there was also a human skeleton, and near to it that of a dog. In times of distress, when unable to bury the dead, the hut is usually abandoned, as appears to have been the case in this instance.

It would be difficult to find a more repulsive and humiliating spectacle than I have here briefly described.

The dogs were very fine, large, wolfish in appearance, and with much of the carriage and the quick, intelligent, restless eyes peculiar to beasts of prey.

These degraded people are effectually cut off from civilization, and from the more southern inhabitants of Greenland by the enormous and impassable glaciers of Melville Bay; the distance from Cape York to Upernivik, the nearest inhabited land to the southward, is about 250 miles. At Godhavn I received a request from the Royal Danish Greenland Company, through the Inspector of North Greenland, to convey from their isolated locality these arctic highlanders (numbering in all 120 souls), to the Danish settlements in Greenland; and had the object and circumstances of my voyage permitted me to turn aside for this purpose, it would have afforded me very sincere satisfaction to have carried out so humane a project.

It is indeed hard to realize their state of existence; they have no vegetable food whatever, neither wood nor metal, no canoes, not even a bow; and yet they exist in a mean annual temperature of 34° below the freezing point, further north than any other known people, and where the sun is absent for one third of the year!

Having distributed presents of knives and needles, and explained to them that we did so because they had behaved well to the white people (as we learn from Dr. Kane's narrative of their treatment of him and his crew), we pursued our voyage, not doubting but that we should soon reach the North Water, an extensive sea through which we could sail uninterruptedly to Pond's Bay.

During the night we advanced through loose ice; but fog and a rising S.E. gale delayed us, and to-day the pack has pressed in against the land, so that our wings are most unexpectedly clipped. A walrus was shot through the head by a Minié bullet; none other will penetrate such a massive skull: unfortunately for my collection of specimens and for the dogs, the animal sank.

2nd July.—For five days we have been almost beset amongst loose ice and grounded bergs; the winds were generally from the S.E. and accompanied by fog. To avoid being squeezed we had constantly to shift our position; once we were caught and rather severely nipped; the ship was heeled over about ten degrees and lifted a couple of feet: the ice was three feet thick, but broke readily under her weight. Unfortunately there was not time to unship the rudder, so it suffered very severely. Upon a previous occasion the screw-shaft was bent and a portion of the screw broken off.

We landed to obtain a good view of the sea in the offing; from the hills we could see nothing but pack to seaward. There was no land ice; we stepped out of the boat upon a narrow icefoot which fringed the coast; immediately above it we trod over a velvet sward of soft bright-green moss; the turf beneath was of considerable depth. Here and there under this noble range of cliffs, which are composed of primary rock, there exists much vegetation for so high a latitude. From the fact of thick layers of turf descending quite down to the sea, it is evident that the land has been gradually sinking. Steep slopes of rocky *débris*, which screen the bases of the most precipitous cliffs, form secure nurseries for the little auk; these localities were literally alive with them; they popped in and out of every crevice, or sat in groups of dozens upon every large rock. I have nowhere seen such countless myriads of birds. The *rotchie*, or little auk, lays its single egg upon the bare rock, far within a crevice beyond the reach of fox, owl, or burgomaster gull. We shot a couple of hundred during our short stay on shore, and, by removing the stones, gathered several dozens of their eggs.

The huge predatory gulls, long ago named "Burgomasters" by the Dutch seamen (because they lord it over their neighbours, and appropriate everything good to themselves), have established themselves in the cliffs, where their nests are generally inaccessible: we were a month too late for their eggs; the young birds were as large as spring chickens. Of course we obtained specimens of the red snow, but had to seek rather diligently for it; its colour was a dirty red, very like the stain of port wine: very few patches of it were found.

Final liberation from the Melville Bay ice, 2nd July, 1858.

Last night a westerly wind blew freshly and dispersed the ice outside of us, so much so that this evening we have got out into almost clear water. Farewell, Greenland,—hurrah for the west!

5th.—After getting free from the ice off the Crimson Cliffs, we soon lost sight of the last fragment, and steered for Pond's Bay. And now we all set to work in zealous haste to write our last letters for England, to go by the whalers, which we hoped soon to meet at Pond's Bay.

After running 60 miles the ice reappeared, and we sailed through a vast deal of it, but it became more closely packed, and a thick fog detained us for a day.

When the weather became clear, the main pack was seen to the W., S., and S.E.; in the hope of rounding its northern extreme we ran along it to the N.W. To-day it has led us to the N. and N.E., so that this evening Wolstenholme Sound is in sight. To the N. the pack appears impenetrable, and there is a strong ice-blink over it. All the ice we have lately sailed through is loose, and much decayed; it seems but recently to have broken away from the land, is not water-washed, neither has it been exposed to a swell, the fractured edges remaining sharp.

6th.—*Position,* 75° 17′ N., 73° 35′ W. Midnight. Last evening I persevered to the N. until every hope of progress in that direction vanished. To the W. the pack appeared tolerably loose; the wind was fresh at E.S.E., so I determined once more to push into it, and endeavour to battle our way through; I hoped it would prove to be merely a belt of 30 or 40 miles in width. We found the ice to lie for the most part in streams at right angles to the wind, and therefore much more open than it had appeared: there was seldom any difficulty in winding through it from one water space to another. The wind greatly increased, bringing much rain, but fortunately no fog;—the dread of this hung over me like a nightmare,—for our progress entirely depended upon the vigilance of the look-out kept in the crow's-nest. By noon we had made good 60 miles. Throughout the day the wind gradually moderated; the rain gave place to snow, which in its turn was succeeded by mist. The evening was fine and clear; but still we find the ice is all around. Just before midnight the termination of our lead was discovered, whilst the ice through which we had passed was closing together, and a dense fog came rolling down. Under these circumstances the ship was made fast as near to the nip as safety permitted, to await some favourable change.

10th.—Position, 75° 26′ N., 76° 58′ W. All the 7th we remained in our small basin, there being no outlet from it, and but little water anywhere visible. To pass away the dull hours and get rid of unwelcome reflections upon the similarity of our present position and that in August last, I commenced an attack upon all the feathered denizens of the pack—they seemed so provokingly *contented* with it—but they soon became wary, and deserted our vicinity, so I shot only a dozen fulmar petrels, three ivory gulls, two looms,[1] and a *lestris parasiticus;* some of them were useful as specimens, and such as were not destined for our table were given to the dogs. Although Cobourg Island was 45 miles distant from us, its lofty rounded outlines were very distinct, and much covered with snow. On the 8th we squeezed through nips for 4 or 5 miles, and on the 9th, reaching a large space of water, steamed towards Cobourg Island until again stopped by the pack at an early hour this morning, when within 5 or 6 leagues of it. The reader will now find it convenient to turn from the sketch-map in the Preface

---

[1] These birds are called "willocks" at home; they are the "Uria Brunnichii" of naturalists.

which he has hitherto used, to the large and accurate one at the end of the book.

This evening we are endeavouring to steam in towards the West-land, and fancy we can trace with the crow's-nest telescope a practicable route through the intervening ice-mazes to a faint streak of water along the shore. This sort of navigation is not only anxious, but wearying. To me it seems as if several months instead of only eight days had elapsed since we left Cape York. We are constantly wondering what our whaling friends are about, and where they are.

14th.—The faint streak of water seen on the night of the 10th proved to be an extensive sheet to leeward of Cobourg Island. We reached it next morning. Jones' Sound appeared open, and a slight swell reached us from it, but all along the shore there was close pack. Although but little water was visible to the southward, we persevered in that direction, and, as the ice was rapidly moving offshore under the combined influence of wind and tide, we were only occasionally detained.

Two hundred and forty-two years ago to a day, I believe, William Baffin sailed *without hindrance* along this coast and discovered Lancaster Sound. What a very different season he must have experienced!

Passing near Cape Horsburgh we approached De Ros Islet at midnight.[1] The air being very calm and still, the

---

[1] The whaler 'Queen,' of Peterhead, spent the winter of 1865-6 in a small harbour, lat. 74° 44' N., and long. 80° W., about four leagues south-westward of De Ros Islet, and between Point Beatrice and Hope's Monument. A channel was discovered between Bank's Bay and Hyde Bay, thus making an Island of what appears on our charts as a continuous coast line. About 20 foxes, 3 lemmings, a wolf, and 150 ptarmigan, besides some reindeer's antlers, and the skeleton of a musk ox, were seen on the land; and upon the ice or sea coast, 30 bears, and 70 or 80 walruses. No Esquimaux were met with, although their

shouting of some natives was heard, although we could scarcely distinguish them upon the land ice. The ship was made fast, and the shouting party, consisting of three men, three women, and two children, eagerly came on board. Only four individuals remained on shore.

The old chief Kal-lek is remarkable amongst Esquimaux for having a bald head. He inquired by name for his friend Captain Inglefield. The above three families have spent the last two years upon this coast, between Cape Horsburgh and Croker Bay. Their knowledge does not extend further in either direction. They are natives of more southern lands, and crossed the ice in Lancaster Sound with dog-sledges. Since the visit of the 'Phœnix' in '54 they have seen no ships, nor have any wrecks drifted upon their shores. They seemed very fat and healthy, but complained that all the reindeer had gone away, and asked if *we* could tell where they had gone to. Our presents of wood, knives, and needles were eagerly received. They assured us that Lancaster Sound was still frozen over, and that all the sea was covered with pack. After half an hour's delay we steamed onward, and on reaching a larger space of water our hopes (somewhat depressed by the native intelligence) began to revive. But we soon found that our clear water terminated near Cape Warrender. Lancaster Sound, although not frozen over, was crammed full of floes and icebergs. The wind increased to a strong gale from the

---

traces were abundant, the people seen having returned to the south of Lancaster Sound. North-east winds prevailed almost constantly, and perhaps in some degree aided the strong tides in keeping a considerable space of open water in the offing throughout the whole winter. The voyage proved unsuccessful, as no whales were taken; they had the additional mortification of seeing the Dundee whaling ships steam past them on the 22nd of June, and of remaining imprisoned in their harbour by the ice, until the 4th August. I am indebted to Dr. Ed. P. Philpots of Leamington, who was the surgeon of the ship, for this interesting information.

east, and pressed in more ice. At length the ship was with difficulty made fast to a strip of land ice, a few miles westward of Point Osborn. Gradually the gale subsided, but not until the pack was close in against the land. The tides kept sweeping it to and fro, to our great discomfort. The land is composed of gneiss, and the gravelly shore is low. A few ducks only have been shot, and traces of reindeer and hares seen. Our Melville Bay friends, the rotchies, are very rare visitors upon this side of Baffin's Bay.

Part of a ship's timber has been found upon the beach; it measures 7 inches by 8 inches, is of American oak, and, although sound, has long been exposed to the weather.

CHAPTER IX.

Off Cape Warrender — Sight the whalers again — Enter Pond's Bay — Communicate with Esquimaux — Ascend Pond's Inlet — Esquimaux information — Arctic summer abode — An arctic village — No intelligence of Franklin's ships — Arctic trading — Geographical information of natives — Information of Rae's visit — Improvidence of Esquimaux — Travels of Esquimaux.

16th July.—To borrow a whaling phrase, we are "dodging about in a hole of water" off Cape Warrender. I recognise the little bay just to the west of the cape where Parry landed in September, 1824. The "immense mass of snow and ice containing strata of muddy-looking soil" is there still, and, I should think, had considerably increased. Here his party shot three reindeer out of a small herd. We have narrowly scanned the steep hill-sides with our glasses, but without discovering any such inducement to land.

None of the cairns of former expeditions are visible upon Cape Warrender; the natives have probably removed them. Dense pack prevents us from approaching Port Dundas or crossing to the southern shore. We find these vexatious delays by no means conducive to sleep. The mind is busy with a sort of magic-lantern representation of the past, the present, and the future, and resists for weary hours the necessary repose.

17th.—Last night's calm has allowed the pack to expand so much, that to-day we have steamed through it until within three miles of the noble cliffs of Cape Hay; and now we are drifting eastward with the ice precisely as did the

'Enterprise' and 'Investigator' in September, '49. Upon that occasion we were set free off Pond's Bay. There is a very extensive *loomery*[1] at Cape Hay; we regret the circumstances which prevent our levying a tax upon it. Here, if anywhere, I expected to find a clear sea, but east winds have prevailed for twenty days out of the last twenty-five, and this accounts for the present state of the sea; the next succession of west winds will probably effect a prodigious clearance of ice.

21st.—Position, 73° 58' N., 78° 25' W. The 'Tay' was seen to-day in loose ice, and much farther off the land. She gradually steamed through it to the southward, and by night was almost out of sight. Her appearance surprised us, as we supposed she must have reached Pond's Bay long ago. Ten hours' struggling with steam and sails at the most favourable intervals has only advanced us five miles. The weather is remarkably warm, bright, and pleasant. A very large bear came within 150 yards, and was shot by Petersen, the Minié bullet passing through his body. This beast measured 8 ft. 3 in. in length; his fat carcase was hoisted on board with great satisfaction, as our dogs' food was nearly expended.

24th.—Last night the ice became slack enough to afford some prospect of release, so we charged the nips vigorously, and steamed away through devious openings towards Cape Fanshawe. For several hours but little progress was made, but this morning the ice became more open; clear water was seen ahead, and reached by noon. Although it is calm, I prefer waiting for a breeze to expending more coals. We are only ten miles from Possession Bay. The air is so very clear that the land appears quite close to us. All that is not mountainous is well cleared of snow. There is immense

---

[1] A name given to the breeding cliffs of the looms, or willocks, and where they assemble each summer in countless myriads.

refraction. Only a single iceberg in sight. The sea-water is light green, as remarked by Parry in 1819.

26th.—A vessel was seen yesterday morning; the day continuing calm, we steamed through some loose ice, and joined her off Cape Walter Bathurst in the evening. It proved to be the 'Diana'; she parted from us on the 16th of June in Melville Bay, has everywhere been obstructed by the pack, as we have been, and only reached Cape Warrender three days before us. From thence to Possession Bay she met with *no obstruction*. The subsequent east winds brought in all the ice which has so much retarded us.

The 'Diana' has already captured twelve whales. Taking the hint from Capt. Gravill, we have made fast to a loose floe, and are drifting very nearly a mile an hour to the southward along the edge of very formidable land-ice, which is seven or eight miles broad. All to seaward of us is packed ice. The old whaling seamen of the 'Diana' are astounded at the unusual and unaccountable abundance of ice which everywhere fills up Baffin's Bay. All the 'Diana's' steaming-coals, her spare spars, wood, and even a boat, were burnt in the protracted struggle through the middle ice.

27th.—After putting our letter-bag on board the 'Diana' this morning we steamed on for Pond's Bay, and at noon made fast near Button Point to the land ice, which still extends across it.

For four hours Petersen and I have been bargaining with an old woman and a boy, not for the sake of their seal-skins, but in order to keep them in good humour whilst we extracted information from them. They said they knew nothing of ships or white people ever having been within this inlet, nor of any wrecked ships. They knew of the depot of provisions left at Navy Board Inlet by the 'North Star,' but had none of them. The woman has traced on paper the shores of the inlet as far as her knowledge extends, and has given me the name of every point. She says the ice will break up with the first fresh wind. These two individuals are alone here. They remained on purpose to barter with the whalers, and cannot now rejoin their friends, who are only 25 miles up the inlet, because the ice is unsafe to travel over, and the land precipitous and impracticable.

This afternoon the 'Tay' stood in towards us, and Captain Deuchars kindly sent his boat on board with an offer to take charge of our letters. The 'Tay' reached this coast only a few days ago, having met with the same difficulties which we experienced. The 'Innuit' was last seen nearly a month ago beset off Jones' Sound. The remaining steamer, the 'Chase,' has not been seen or heard of.

29th.—The old woman's denial of all knowledge of wrecks or cast-away men was very unsatisfactory. I determined to visit her countrymen at their summer village of Kaparōktolik, which she described as being only a short day's journey up the inlet.

Petersen and one man accompanied me. We started yesterday morning with a sledge and a Halkett boat. Although the ice over which we purposed travelling broke away from the land soon after setting out, yet we managed to get half-way to the village before encamping. This morning we learnt the truth of the old woman's account. A range of precipitous cliffs rising from the sea cut us off by land from Kaparōktolik, so we were obliged to return to the ship. Our walk afforded the opportunity of examining some native encampments and câches. We found innumerable scraps of seal-skins, bird-skins, walrus and other bones, whalebone, blubber, and a small sledge. The latter was very old, and composed of pieces of wood and of large bones ingeniously secured together with strips of whalebone. Five preserved-meat tins were found; some of them retaining their original coating of red paint. Doubtless these were part of the spoils from Navy Board Inlet depot. The total absence of fresh wood or iron was strongly in favour of the old woman's veracity. Since yesterday, ice, about 16 miles in extent, has broken up in the inlet, and is drifting out into Baffin's Bay.

During my absence our shooting parties have twice visited a *loomery* upon Cape Graham Moore, and each time have brought on board 300 looms.

The most favourite dish of the three former expeditions was loom soup. So long as we had the necessary ingredients, the following receipt of our excellent steward, James Gore, was strictly followed. It suited well for divers, ducks, and all sea-birds, especially those with dark flesh; and it would in many instances be useful in rendering very palatable this description of wholesome food, which otherwise would be rejected. We considered our loom soup incomparable; more like hare soup than any other, but richer, darker, and better adapted to our climate, our appetites, and consequently to our tastes:—

LOOM SOUP.

Take 8 looms, skin and take off the two white lumps near the tail; clean and split them into pieces; wash them well, also the livers. Put them into a large saucepan, and cover them well with water, and boil for four or five hours.

An hour before serving up, put in ½ lb. of bacon cut up small; season with pepper and salt, 2 tablespoonfuls of Harvey sauce, a little Cayenne pepper, half a wineglass of lemon juice, a teaspoonful of ground allspice, and a few cloves; thicken with 4 tablespoonfuls of flour mixed in cold water, then stirred gradually into the soup.

Add ½ pint of wine, after which let it boil for a few minutes.

The result will be 4 quarts of rich soup.

Only a very few birds were seen during our walk over the rich mossy slopes to-day. I saw a pair of Canadian brown cranes, the first of the species I have ever seen so far north. Sir Robert M'Clure found them on Bank's Land.

The lands enjoying a southern aspect, even to the summits of hills 700 or 800 feet in height, were tinged with green; but these hills were protected by a still loftier range to the north. Upon many well-sheltered slopes we found much rich grass. All the little plants were in full flower; some of them familiar to us at home, such as the buttercup, sorrel, and dandelion. I have never found the latter to the north of 69° before.

The old woman is much less excited to-day; she says there came a wreck upon the coast when she was a little girl; it lies a day's journey and a half (about 45 miles) to the north; and came there without masts and very much crushed; the little which now remains is almost buried in the sand. A piece of this wreck was found near her *abode* —she has neither hut nor tent, but a sort of lair constructed of a few stones and a seal-skin spread over them, so that she can crawl underneath. This fragment is part of a floor timber, English oak, 7½ inches thick; it has been brought on board.

30*th*.—A gale of wind and deluge of rain have detained the ship until this evening; we are now steaming up the inlet, having the old lady and the boy on board as our pilots; they are delighted at the prospect of rejoining their friends, from whom they were effectually cut off until the return of winter should freeze a safe pathway for them; they had, however, abundance of looms stored up *en câche* for their subsistence. She has drawn me another chart, much more neatly than the former, but so like it as to prove that her geographical knowledge, and not her powers of invention, has been taxed. She is a widow; her daughter is married, and lives at a place called Igloolik, which is six or seven days' journey from here,—three days up the inlet, then about three days overland to the southward, and then a day over the ice.

Thinking it not quite impossible that this Igloolik might be the place where Parry wintered in 1822–3, I told Petersen to ask whether ships had ever been there? She answered, "Yes, a ship stopped there all one winter; but it is a long time ago." All she could distinctly recollect having been told about it was that one of the crew died, and was buried there, and his name was Al-lah or El-leh. On referring to Parry's 'Narrative,' I found that the icemate, Mr. Elder, died at Igloolik. This is a very remarkable confirmation of the locality,—for there are several places called Igloolik. She also told us it was an island, and near a strait between two seas. The Esquimaux take considerable pains to learn and remember names; this woman knows the names of several of the whaling captains, and the old chief at De Ros Islet remembered Captain Inglefield's name, and tried hard to pronounce mine.

She now told us of another wreck upon the coast, but many days' journey to the south of Pond's Bay; it came there before her first child was born. Her age is not less than forty-five.

August 4*th*.—Our Esquimaux friends have departed from us with every demonstration of friendship, to return to their village. We have had free communication with them for four days—not only through Mr. Petersen, but also through our two Greenlanders; the result is that they have no knowledge whatever of either the missing or the abandoned searching ships. Neither wrecked people nor wrecked ships have reached their shores. They seemed to be much in want of wood; most of what they have consists of staves of casks, probably from the Navy Board Inlet depot.

In their bartering with us, saws were most eagerly sought for in exchange for narwhals' horns; they are used by them in cutting up the long strips of the bones of whales with which they shoe the runners of their sledges, also the ivory and bone used to protect the more exposed parts of their kayaks and the edges of their paddles from the ice.

Files were also in great demand, and I found were required to convert pieces of iron-hoop into arrow and spear heads. If any suspicion existed of their having a secret supply of wood such as a wreck or even a boat would afford, it was removed by their refusing to barter the most trifling things for axes or hatchets.

But I must relate the events of the last few days as they occurred. When 17 miles within the inlet we reached the unbroken ice and made the ship fast. Here the *strait*—originally named Pond's *Bay*, and more recently Eclipse *Sound*—appears to be most contracted, its width not exceeding 7 or 8 miles. Both its shores are very bold and lofty, often forming noble precipices. The prevailing rock is grey gneiss, generally dipping at an angle of 35° to the west.

Early on the 1st of August I set out for the native village with Hobson, Petersen, two men, and the two natives from Button Point. Eight miles of wet and weary ice-travelling, which occupied as many hours, terminated our journey; the surface of the ice was everywhere deeply channelled, and abundantly flooded by the summer's thaw : we were almost constantly launching our small boat over the slippery ridges which separated pools or channellings, through which it was generally necessary to wade.

After toiling round the base of a precipice, we came rather suddenly in view of a small semicircular bay; the cliffs on either side were 800 or 900 feet high, remarkably forbidding and desolate; the mouth of a valley or wide mountain gorge opens out into its head. Here, in the depth of the bay, upon a low flat strip of land, stood seven tents,—the summer village of Kaparöktolik. I never saw a locality more characteristic of the Esquimaux than that which they have here selected for their abode;—it is wildly picturesque in the true arctic application of the term.

Although August had arrived, and the summer had been a warm one, the bay was still frozen over; and if there was an ice-covered *sea* in front, there was also abundance of ice-covered *land* in the rear—a glacier occupied the whole valley behind, and to within 300 yards of the chosen spot!

The glacier's height appeared to be from 150 to 200 feet; its sea-face extending across the valley,—a probable width of 300 or 400 yards,—was quite perpendicular, and fully 100 feet high. All last winter's snow had thawed away from off it and exposed a surface not free from earth and stones, fissured by innumerable small rivulets, which threw themselves over the glacier cliffs in pretty cascades, or shot far out in strong jets from their deeply serried channels in its face; whilst other streamlets near the base burst out through sub-glacial tunnels of their own forming.

A strange people to confine themselves to such a mere strip of beach! Upon each side they have towering rocky hills rising so abruptly from the sea that to pass along their bases or ascend over their summits is equally impossible; whilst a threatening glacier immediately behind bears onward a sufficient amount of rock and earth from the mountains, whence it issues, to convince even the unreflecting savage of its progressive motion.

The land is devoid of game, although lemmings and ermines are tolerably numerous; it only supplies the moss which the natives burn with blubber in their lamps, and the dry grass which they put in their boots; even the soft stone, *lapis ollaris*, out of which their lamps and cooking vessels are made, and the iron pyrites with which they strike fire, are obtained by barter from the people inhabiting the land to the west of Navy Board Inlet. But the sea compensates for every deficiency. The assembled population

Village and Glacier of Kaparoktolik, 4th August, 1858.

amounted to only 25 souls: 9 men, the rest women and children.

All of them evinced extreme delight at seeing us; as we approached the huts the women and children held up their arms in the air and shouted "Pilletay" (give me), incessantly; the men were more quiet and dignified, yet lost no opportunity, either when we declined to barter or when they had performed any little service, to repeat "Pilletay" in a beseeching tone of voice.

We walked everywhere about the tents and entered some of them, carefully examining every chip or piece of metal; our visit was quite unexpected. They had only two sledges; both were made of 2½-inch oak-planks, devoid of bolt-holes or treenails, and having but very few nail-holes. These sledges had evidently been constructed for several years, the parts not exposed to friction were covered with green fungus; one of them measured 14 feet long, the other about 9 feet; we were told the wood came from a wreck to the southward of Pond's Bay. Most of the sledge crossbars were ordinary staves of casks. Amongst the poles and large bones which supported the tents we noticed a painted fir oar. Some pieces of iron hoop and a few preserved-meat tins—one of which was stamped "Goldner,"—completed their stock of European articles.

Petersen questioned all the men *separately* as to their knowledge of ships or wrecks; but their accounts only served to confirm the old woman's story. None of them had ever heard of ships or wrecks anywhere to the westward. Both individually and collectively we got them to draw charts of the various coasts known to them, and to mark upon them the positions of the wrecks. The two chiefs, Nōo-luk and Ā-wăh-lah, soon made themselves known to me, and, when we desired to go to sleep, sent away the people who were eagerly pressing round our tent. All these natives were better-looking, cleaner, and more robust than I expected to find them.

Ā-wăh-lah has been to Igloolik; one of his wives, for each chief has *two*, has a brother living there. I spread a large roll of paper upon a rock, and got him to draw the route overland, and also round by the coast to it; this novel proceeding attracted the whole population about us; Ā-wăh-lah constantly referred to others when his memory failed him; at length it was completed to the satisfaction of all parties. When I gave him the knife I had promised as his reward, and added another for his wives, he sprang up on the rock, flourished the knives in his hands, shouted, and danced with extravagant demonstrations of joy. He is a very fine specimen of his race, powerful, impulsive, full of energy and animal spirits, and moreover an admirable mimic. The men were all about the same height, 5 feet 5 in.; they eagerly answered our questions, and imparted to us all their geographical knowledge, although at first they hesitated when we asked them about Navy Board Inlet, in consequence of the depot placed there having been plundered; but we soon found that they were easily tired under cross-examination, and often said they knew no more; it was necessary to humour them.

According to their account the depot was discovered and robbed by people living farther west. This is probably true, as so few relics were to be seen here, which would not be the case if such active fellows as Ā-wăh-lah and Nōo-luk had received the first information of its proximity. These people of Kaparōktolik are the only inhabitants of the land lying eastward of Navy Board Inlet, and live entirely upon its *southern* shore. In a similar manner, it is only the *southern* coast of the land to the west of Navy Board Inlet that is inhabited. After distributing presents to all the women and children, and making a few trifling purchases from the men, we returned next day to the ship.

During my absence more ice had broken away, involving the ship and almost forcing her on shore. It required every exertion to save her. For two hours she continued in imminent danger, and was only saved by the warping and ice-blasting, by which at last she got clear of the drifting masses, *four minutes* only before they were crushed up against the rocks!

Four Esquimaux came off to the ship in their kayaks, bringing whalebone, narwhals' horns, &c. to barter. Next to handsaws and files, they attached the greatest value to knives and large needles. These men remained on board for nearly two days, and drew several charts for us. Nōo-luk explained that seven or eight days' journey to the southward there are *two* wrecks a short day's journey apart. The southern is in an inlet or strait which contains several islands, but there his knowledge of the coast terminates. The man A-ra-neet said he visited these wrecks five winters ago. All of them agreed that it is a very long time since the wrecks arrived upon the coast; and Nōo-luk, who appears to be about forty-five years of age, showed us how tall he was at the time.

In the 'Narrative of Parry's Second Voyage,' at p. 437, mention is made of the arrival at Igloolik of a sledge constructed of ship timber and staves of casks; also of two ships that had been driven on shore, and the crews of which went away in boats. In August, 1821, nearly two years previous to the arrival of this report through the Esquimaux to Igloolik, the whalers 'Dexterity' and 'Aurora' were wrecked upon the west coast of Davis' Strait, in lat. 72°, 70 or 80 miles southward of Pond's Bay. The old man, Ow-wang-noot, drew the coast-line northwards from Cape Graham Moore to Navy Board Inlet, and pointed out the position of the northern wreck a few miles east of Cape Hay. Had it been conspicuous, we must have seen it when we slowly drifted along that coast.[1]

These people usually winter in snow-huts at Green Point, a mile or two within the northern entrance of Pond's Bay. They hunt the seal and narwhal, but when the sea becomes too open they retire to Kaparōktolik ; and when the remaining ice breaks up—usually about the middle of August—a further migration takes place across the inlet to the S.W., where reindeer abound, and large salmon are numerous in the rivers. Every winter they communicate with the Igloolik people. Two winters ago (1856–7) some people who live far beyond Igloolik, in a country called A-ka-nee (probably the Ak-koo-lee of Parry), brought from there the information of white people having come in two boats, and passed a winter in snow-huts at a place called by the following names :— A-mee-lee-oke, A-wee-lik, Net-tee-lik.

Our friends pointed to our whale-boat, and said the boats of the white people were like it, but larger. These whites had tents inside their snow huts; they killed and ate reindeer and narwhal, and smoked pipes; they bought dresses from the natives; none died; in summer they all went away, taking with them two natives, a father and his son. We could not ascertain the name of the white chief, nor the interval of time since they wintered amongst the Esquimaux, as our friends could not recollect these particulars.[2]

The name of the locality, A-wee-lik (spelt as written down at the moment), may be considered identical with " Ay-wee-lik," the name of the land about Repulse Bay in the chart of the Esquimaux woman, Iligliuk (Parry's 'Second Voyage,' p. 197).

[1] The remains of this wreck have since been visited by an English whaler, thus confirming the Esquimaux report.
[2] Dr. Rae wintered at Repulse Bay in *stone* huts in 1846–7. Again wintered there in *snow* huts in 1853–4.

We were of course greatly surprised to find that Dr. Rae's visit to Repulse Bay was known to this distant tribe; and also disappointed to find they had heard nothing of Franklin's Back River parties through the same channel of communication. They were anxiously and repeatedly questioned, but evidently had not heard of any other white people to the westward, nor of their having perished there.

Ow-wang-noot lived at Igloolik in his early days, and made a chart of the lands adjacent, but said he was so young at the time that "it seemed like a dream to him." He was acquainted with Ee-noo-lōō-apik, the Esquimaux who once accompanied Captain Penny to Aberdeen, and told us he had died, lately I think, at a place to the southward called Kri-merk-sū-malek, but that his sister still lives at Igloolik.

Although they told us the Igloolik people were worse off for wood than they were themselves, yet it was evident that here also it is very scarce. We could not spare them light poles or oars such as they were most desirous to obtain for harpoon and lance staves and tent-poles; and they would willingly have bartered their kayaks to us for rifles (having already obtained some from the whaling-ships), but that they had no other means of getting back to their homes, nor wood to make the light framework of others.

They collect whalebone and narwhals' horns in sufficient quantity to carry on a small barter with the whalers. Ā-wăh-lah showed us about thirty horns in his tent, and said he had many more at other stations. A few years ago, when first this bartering sprang up, an Esquimaux took such a fancy to a fiddle that he offered a large quantity of whalebone in exchange for it. The bargain was soon made, and subsequently this whalebone was sold for upwards of a hundred pounds! Each successive year, when the same ship returns to Pond's Bay, this native comes on board to visit his friends, and goes on shore with many presents in remembrance of the memorable transaction. It is much better for him thus to receive annual gifts than to have received a large quantity at first, as the improvidence of these men surpasses belief.

Of the "rod of iron about four feet long, supposed to have been at one time galvanised," which was brought home in 1856 by Captain Patterson, and forwarded to the Admiralty, I could obtain no information. The natives were shown galvanised iron, and said they had never seen any before; if their countrymen had any, it must have come from the whalers; none like it was found in the wrecks. Rod-iron is very valuable to Esquimaux for spears and lances, and narwhals' horns very tempting to the seamen, not only as valuable curiosities, but the ivory is worth half a crown a pound; and I have but little doubt that many of the things said to have been stolen by the natives were fraudulently bartered away by the sailors. That there was no galvanised iron on board any of the Government searching-ships, nor in the missing expedition which sailed from England as far back as 1845, I am almost certain. But is it *certain* that this iron rod was galvanised? The natives gave Captain Patterson to understand that they got it from the wreck to the north.

In July, 1854, Captain Deuchars was at Pond's Bay, and many natives visited his ship, coming over the ice on twelve or fourteen sledges made of ship's planking. Now at this time Sir Edward Belcher's ships were still frozen up in Barrow Strait. My own impression is that the natives whom Captain Deuchars communicated with in 1854 were visitors at Pond's Bay—certainly from the *southward*—and probably attracted by the barter recently grown up at that whaling rendezvous. Having discovered the use of the saws obtained by barter from our whalers, they had successfully applied them to the stout planking of the old wrecks, which they could not have stripped off with any tools previously in their possession.

That the various tribes, or rather groups of families, occasionally visit each other, sometimes for change of hunting-grounds, but more frequently for barter, is well known. Captain Parker told me that a native whom he had met one summer at Durbin Island, came on board his ship at Pond's Bay the following year. The distance between the two places, as travelled by this man in a single winter, is scarcely short of 500 miles; and the information given us of Rae's wintering at Repulse Bay, information which must have travelled here in two winters, shows that these natives communicate at still greater distances.

Did other wrecks exist nearer at hand, our Pond's Bay friends would be much better supplied with wood. If the Esquimaux knew of any within 300, 400, or even 500 miles, the Pond's Bay natives would at least have heard of them, and could have had no reason for concealing it from us.

CHAPTER X.

Leave Pond's Bay — A gale in Lancaster Sound — The Beechey Island depot — An arctic monument — Reflections at Beechey Island — Proceed up Barrow's Strait — Peel Sound — Port Leopold — Prince Regent's Inlet — Bellot Strait — Flood-tide from the west — Unsuccessful efforts — Fox's Hole — No water to the west — Precautionary measures — Fourth attempt to pass through.

6th Aug.—CONTINUED calms have delayed us. This evening we steamed from Pond's Bay northward, although our coals have been sadly reduced by the almost constant necessity for steam-power since leaving the Waigat. The three steam-whalers have gone southward; none others have arrived. They appear to us to be leaving the whales behind them; we saw many whilst up the strait, and at the edge of the remaining ice. The natives said that these animals arrive in early spring, and do not pass through the strait into any other sea beyond; that they themselves would remain as long as the ice remained, but when it all broke up, they would return into Baffin's Bay and go southward.

Monday evening, 9th.—On the night of the 6th a pleasant fair breeze sprang up, and enabled us to dispense with the engine. An immense bear was shot; he measured 8 feet 7 inches in length, and is destined for the museum of the Royal Dublin Society. On the 7th the wind gradually freshened and frustrated my intention of examining the wreck spoken of near Cape Hay; at night it increased to a very heavy gale. Although past Navy Board Inlet, very little ice had yet been met with. The weather, and fear of ice to leeward, obliged us to heave the vessel to, under main trysail and fore staysail. The squalls were extremely violent and seas unusually high.

All Sunday, the 8th, the gale continued, although not with such extreme force; the deep rolling of the ship, and moaning of the half-drowned dogs amidst the pelting sleet and rain, was anything but agreeable. Notwithstanding that I had been up all the previous night, I felt too anxious, to sleep; the wind blew directly up Barrow Strait, drifting us about two miles an hour. Occasionally we drifted to leeward of masses of ice, reminding us that if any of the dense pack which covered this sea only three weeks ago remained to leeward of us, we must be rapidly setting down upon its weather edge. The only expedient in such a case is to endeavour to run into it—once well within its outer margin, a ship is comparatively safe—the danger lies in the attempt to penetrate; to escape out of the pack afterwards, is also a doubtful matter.

In the evening we were glad to see the land, and find ourselves off the north shore near Cape Bullen, for the violent motion of the ship and very weak horizontal magnetic force had rendered our compasses useless. This morning (the 9th) the gale broke, and the sea began to subside rapidly; by noon it was almost calm, but a thick gloom prevailed, ominous, it might be, of more mischief. All along the land there is ice, but broken up into harmless atoms. We have carried away a maingaff and a jibstay, but have come remarkably well through such a gale with only this damage.

11*th*.—Before noon to-day we anchored inside Cape Riley, and immediately commenced preparations for embarking coals. I visited Beechey Island house, and found the door open; it must have been blown in by an easterly gale long ago, for much ice had accumulated immediately inside it. Most of the biscuit in bags was damaged, but everything else was in perfect order. Upon the north and west sides of the house, where a wall had been constructed, there was a vast accumulation of ice, in which the lower tier of casks between the two was embedded, and its surface thawed into pools. Neither casks nor walls should have been allowed to stand near the house. The southern and eastern sides were clear and perfectly dry. The ' Mary ' decked boat, and two 30-foot lifeboats, were in excellent order, and their paint appeared fresh; but oars and bare wood were bleached white.

The gutta-percha boat was useless when left here, and remains in the same state. Two small sledge travelling boats were damaged; one of them had been blown over and over along the beach until finally arrested by the other. The bears and foxes do not appear to have touched anything. I have taken on board all letters left here for Franklin's or Collinson's expeditions, and also a 20-foot sledge-boat for our own travelling purposes.

Last night we steamed very close round Cape Hurd in a dense fog, and crept along the land as our only guide : we were thus led into Rigby Bay, and discovered a shoal off its entrance by grounding upon it. After a quarter of an hour we floated off unhurt.

In lowering a boat to pursue a bear, Robert Hampton fell overboard; fortunately he could swim, and was very soon picked up, but the intense cold of the water had almost paralyzed his limbs. The bear was shot and taken on board.

Sunday, 15*th*, 9 P.M.—Our coaling was completed yesterday, and the ship brought over and anchored off the house in Erebus Bay. A small proportion of provisions and winter clothing has been embarked to complete our deficiencies ;

the ice has been scraped out of the house and its roof thoroughly repaired, a record deposited, and door securely closed.

At Godhavn I found a marble tablet which had been sent out by Lady Franklin, in the American expedition of 1855 under Captain H. J. Hartstein, U.S.N., for the purpose of being erected at Beechey Island. Circumstances prevented his executing this kindly service, and it fell to my lot to convey it to the site originally intended. The tablet was constructed in New York under the direction of Mr. Grinnell at the request of Lady Franklin, in order that the only opportunity which then offered of sending it to the arctic regions might not be lost. I placed the monument upon the raised flagged square in the centre of which stands the cenotaph recording the names of those who perished in the Government expedition under Sir Edward Belcher. Here also is placed a small tablet, sent out by John Barrow, Esq., to the memory of Lieutenant Bellot. I could not have selected for Lady Franklin's memorial a more appropriate or conspicuous site. The inscription runs as follows :—

TO THE MEMORY OF
FRANKLIN,
CROZIER, FITZJAMES,

AND ALL THEIR
GALLANT BROTHER OFFICERS AND FAITHFUL
COMPANIONS WHO HAVE SUFFERED AND PERISHED
IN THE CAUSE OF SCIENCE AND
THE SERVICE OF THEIR COUNTRY.

THIS TABLET
IS ERECTED NEAR THE SPOT WHERE
THEY PASSED THEIR FIRST ARCTIC
WINTER, AND WHENCE THEY ISSUED
FORTH TO CONQUER DIFFICULTIES OR

TO DIE.
IT COMMEMORATES THE GRIEF OF THEIR
ADMIRING COUNTRYMEN AND FRIENDS,
AND THE ANGUISH, SUBDUED BY FAITH,
OF HER WHO HAS LOST, IN THE HEROIC
LEADER OF THE EXPEDITION, THE MOST
DEVOTED AND AFFECTIONATE OF
HUSBANDS.

"*AND SO HE BRINGETH THEM UNTO THE
HAVEN WHERE THEY WOULD BE.*"
1855.

This Tablet having been left at Disco by the American Expedition, which was unable to reach Beechey Island, in 1855, was put on board the Discovery Yacht Fox, and is now set up here by Captain M'Clintock, R.N., commanding the final expedition of search for ascertaining the fate of Sir John Franklin and his companions. 1858.

The Three Graves, and Depot House, Beechey Island.

We are now ready to proceed upon our voyage from Beechey Island, and there is no ice in sight; but having worked almost unceasingly since our arrival up to the present hour, the men require a night's rest. Nearly forty tons of fuel have been embarked.

The total absence of ice in Barrow Strait is astonishing. No less so are the changes and chances of this singular navigation. Twelve days later than this in 1850, when I belonged to Her Majesty's ship 'Assistance,' with considerable difficulty we came within sight of Beechey Island: a cairn on its summit attracted notice; Captain Ommanney managed to land, and discovered the *first traces* of the missing expedition. Next day the United States schooner 'Rescue' arrived; the day after, Captain Penny joined us, and subsequently Captain Austin, Sir John Ross, and Captain Forsyth—in all, ten vessels were assembled here.

This day six years, when in command of the 'Intrepid,' we sailed from here for Melville Island in company with the 'Resolute.' Again I was here and frozen up in the 'North Star' at this date in 1854, and doubts were entertained of the *possibility* of *escape*.

To-day it is only a fortnight since I set out for the native village in Pond's Inlet, under guidance of an old woman; whilst I was so engaged our little vessel had a most providential escape from being crushed against the cliffs. This day week was spent in contending with a furious gale, during which the ship had nearly been driven to leeward and dashed to pieces by the sea-beaten pack. It is to be hoped the poor 'Fox' has many more lives to spare, as it is only now that the real interest of her voyage commences.

Monday night, 16*th Aug.*—Sailed from Beechey Island this morning, and this evening we landed at Cape Hotham. A small depot of provisions and three boats were left here by former expeditions; of the depot all has been destroyed with the exception of two casks landed in 1850. The boats were sound, but several of their oars, which had been secured upright as marks, lest they should be hidden by snow, were found broken down by bears—those inquisitive animals having a decided antipathy to anything "stuck up"—such a position being both unusual and unnatural in this bleak country. Fragments of the depot and the broken oars were tossed about in every direction. Numerous records were found; to the most recent a few lines were added, stating that we had removed the two whale-boats—one to be left at Port Leopold, the other to replace our own crushed by the ice.

17*th.*—Last night battling against a strong foul wind with *sea*, in rain and fog. To-day much loose ice is seen southward of Griffith's Island. The weather improved this afternoon, and we shot gallantly past Limestone Island, and are

Departure from Beechey Island, 16th August, 1858.

now steering down Peel Sound : all of us in a state of wild excitement—a mingling of anxious hopes and fears !

18*th*.—For 25 miles last evening we ran unobstructedly down Peel Sound, but then came in sight of unbroken ice extending across it from shore to shore! It was much decayed, and of one year's growth only; yet, as the strait continues to contract for 60 miles further, and it appeared to me to afford so little hope of becoming navigable in the short remainder of the season, I immediately turned about for Bellot Strait, as affording better prospect of a passage into the western sea discovered by Sir James Ross from Four River Point in 1849. Our disappointment at the interruption of our progress was as severe as it was sudden. We did not linger in hope of a change, but steered out again into the broad waters of Barrow Strait. However, should Bellot Strait prove hopeless, I intend to return hither to make one more effort before the close of the season.

We are now approaching Port Leopold, where it is necessary to stop for a few hours to examine the state of the steam launch, provisions, and stores, left there in 1849, for adverse circumstances may oblige me to fall back upon it as a point of support.

19*th*.—At anchor in Port Leopold ; it is perfectly clear of ice ; we arrived here in the night. How astonishingly bare the land looks ; it is more barren than Beechey Island, whilst the rock contains far fewer fossils ! On this day nine years ago the harbour and sea continued covered with ice, and the ships ('Enterprise' and 'Investigator') were unable to escape. At some period since then, the ice has been pressed in upon the low shingle point; it has forced the launch up before it, and left her broadside on to the beach, with both bows stove in, and in want of considerable repairs, but the means are all at hand for executing them. We tried to haul her further up, but she was firmly imbedded in the frozen ground. Many things appear to have been covered with the loose shingle, bags of coal and coke just appearing through it scarcely above high-water mark. Amongst the missing articles is the steam-engine.

Although the flagstaff upon the summit of North East Cape is still standing, the one erected upon this point and almost the whole of the framing of the house lies prostrate. The provisions appeared to be sound, but were not generally examined. The whale-boat we removed from Cape Hotham was landed here, and a record of our proceedings added to the many which have accumulated here during the last ten years. Some coke and a few things useful to us and merely decaying here were taken on board, and by evening we were again speeding onward with augmented resources, and the confidence inspired by a secure depot in our rear; buoyed up moreover by the joyful anticipation of soon reaching the goal of our long-deferred hopes.

20*th, noon.*—Exactly off Fury Point. There is one large iceberg far off in the S.E.; no other ice in sight! I would have landed at Fury Beach to examine the remaining supplies there, but a snow shower prevented our distinguishing anything, and a strong tide carried us past before we were aware of it.

This morning, as one of the officers was scrutinising this desperately barren land, and reflecting that in a few weeks the whole sea would be frozen over, old Harvey stepped up to him and remarked that "everything was looking *werry* prosperous;" but Harvey only looked *ahead*, and he saw no *ice* there. He had no doubt a vivid recollection of intense hardships undergone in the long sledging-parties of the expeditions under Austin and Belcher, when he was a few years younger, and well knew that every mile now sailed towards the unexplored area would save us two miles of sledge-dragging—a mile out and a mile home.

We *feel* that the crisis of our voyage is near at hand. Does Bellot *Strait* really exist? Poor Bellot himself doubted it, and Kennedy, his commander, could not positively assert that it did. And if there be a strait, is it free from ice?

A depot of provisions is being got ready to be landed, should it be practicable for us to push through and proceed to the southward.

21*st.*—On approaching Brentford Bay last evening, *packed ice was seen streaming out of it*,[1] also much ice in the S.E. The northern point of entrance was landed upon by Sir John Ross in 1829, and named Possession Point; we rounded it closely, and could distinguish a few stones piled up upon a large rock near its highest part—this is his cairn. As we passed westward between the point and Browne's Island, through a channel a mile in width, a close pack was discovered a few miles ahead; and it being past ten o'clock, and almost dark, the ship was anchored in a convenient bay three or four miles within Possession Point. Here our depot is to be landed, therefore we shall name this for the present *Depot Bay;* a very narrow isthmus between its head and Hazard Inlet unites the low limestone peninsula, of which Possession Point is the extreme, to the mainland.

To-day an unsparing use of steam and canvas forced the ship eight miles further west; we were then about halfway through Bellot Strait! Its western capes are lofty bluffs, such as may be distinguished fifty miles distant in clear weather; between them there was a clear broad channel, but five or six miles of close heavy pack intervened—the sole obstacle to our progress. Of course this pack will

---

[1] When sailing past here in 1829, Sir James C. Ross observed heavy packed ice, differing from such as would be formed in the sheltered depth of a bay, streaming out of it; he therefore inferred the existence of a channel. Relying mainly on his judgment, I came with confidence to seek one: and this sight was an intense relief, for it convinced me that the strait did exist.

speedily disperse;—it is no wonder that we should feel elated at such a glorious prospect, and content to abide our time in the security of Depot Bay. A feeling of tranquillity —of earnest, hearty satisfaction—has come over us. There is no appearance amongst us of anything boastful; we have all experienced too keenly the vicissitudes of arctic voyaging to admit of such a feeling.

At the turn of tide we perceived that we were being carried, together with the pack, back to the eastward; every moment our velocity was increased, and presently we were dismayed at seeing grounded ice near us, but were very quickly swept past it at the rate of nearly six miles an hour, though within 200 yards of the rocks, and of instant destruction! As soon as we possibly could, we got clear of the packed ice, and left it to be wildly hurled about by various whirlpools and rushes of the tide, until finally carried out into Brentford Bay. The ice-masses were large, and dashed violently against each other, and the rocks lay at some distance off the southern shore; we had a fortunate escape from such dangerous company. After anchoring again in Depot Bay, a large stock of provisions and a record of our proceedings were landed, as there seems every probability of advancing into the western sea in a very few days.

The appearance of Bellot Strait is precisely that of a Greenland fiord; it is about 20 miles long and scarcely a mile wide in the narrowest part, and there its depth within a quarter of a mile of the north shore, was ascertained to be 400 feet. Its granitic shores are bold and lofty, with a very respectable sprinkling of vegetation for lat. 72°. Some of the hill-ranges rise to about 1500 or 1600 feet above the sea.

The low land eastward of Depot Bay is composed of limestone, destitute alike of fossils and vegetation. The granite commences upon the west shore of Depot Bay, and

Stranded mass of heavy floe ice.

is at once bold and rugged. Many seals have been seen; a young bear was shot, and Walker took a photograph of him as he lay upon our deck, the dogs timidly creeping near to lick up the blood.

The great rapidity of the tides in Bellot Strait fully accounts for the spaces of open water seen by Mr. Kennedy[1] when he travelled through, early in April. The strait runs very nearly east and west, but its eastern entrance is well masked by Long Island; when half-way through, both seas are visible. As in Greenland, the night tides are much higher than the day tides; last night it was high water at about half-past eleven; as nearly as we can estimate, the tide runs through to the west, from two hours before high water until four hours after it; that is, the flood-tide comes from the west. Such is also the case in Hecla and Fury Strait; in both places the tide from the west is much the strongest. I am not sufficiently informed to discuss this subject fully, but I infer the existence of a channel between Victoria and Prince of Wales' Land. The rise and fall is much less upon the western side of the Isthmus of Boothia than upon the east, and it likewise decreases, we know, in Barrow Strait, as we advance westward.

23rd.—Yesterday Bellot Strait was again examined, but the five miles of close pack occupied precisely the same position as if heaped together by contending tides; considerable augmentations were moreover seen drifting in from the western sea. Finding nothing could be effected in Bellot Strait, we sought in vain for the more southern channel which should exist to form Levesque Island: we did, however, find a beautiful harbour, and are now securely anchored in its north-west arm; I have named it after the gentleman whose supposed island I find is a part of the

[1] Mr. Kennedy discovered this important passage when in command of the 'Prince Albert' in 1851.

Boothian Peninsula, and consequently of the American continent. The south-western angle of Brentford Bay is still covered with unbroken ice.

This evening we all landed to explore our new ground. Young and Petersen shot some brent geese; Walker saw two deer, but he was botanising, and had no gun; others were seen by some of the men, and followed, but without success.

I enjoyed a delightfully refreshing ramble, a mile or two inland, through a gently ascending valley, then two miles along the narrow margin of a pretty little lake between mountains, beyond which lay a much larger one, four or five miles in diameter; this farther lake was only partially divested of its winter ice. Here there was enough of vegetation to tint the craggy hill-sides and to make the sheltered hollows absolutely green, therefore the scenery was beautiful as well as grand; deer-tracks and the footprints of wild fowl were everywhere numerous along the water-side. I saw two decayed skulls of musk oxen, and circles of stones by the little lake, doubtless at some remote period the summer residence of wandering Esquimaux: hence I infer that fish abound in the lake, and that this valley is a favourite deer-pass.

But the contemplation of these objects, although agreeable, was not the object of my solitary ramble: I came on shore to enjoy calm and earnest reflection, on the progress and the prospects of our campaign. We hoped very soon to enter an unknown sea: discoveries would be made, various contingencies arise, and we must be prepared to meet them.

Yesterday Petersen shot an immense bearded seal; it sank, but floated up an hour afterwards. This animal measured 8 feet long, and weighed about 500 lbs. We prefer its flesh to that of the small seals, and its blubber will afford a valuable addition to our stock of lamp oil for the coming winter.

25th.—In Depot Bay. We remained but twenty-four hours in Levesque Harbour; a change of wind led us to hope for a removal of the ice in Bellot Strait, therefore I determined to make another attempt.

When off the table-land, where the depth is not more than from 6 to 10 fathoms, and the tides run strongest, the ship hardly moved over the ground, although going 6½ knots through the water ! Thus delayed, darkness overtook us, and we anchored at midnight in a small indentation of the north shore, christened by the men *Fox's Hole*, rather more than half-way through the strait.

For several hours we had been coquetting with huge rampant ice-masses that wildly surged about in the tideway, or we dashed through boiling eddies, and sometimes almost grazed the tall cliffs ; we were therefore naturally glad of a couple or three hours' rest, even in such a very unsafe position. At early dawn we again proceeded west, but for three miles only ; the pack again stopped us, and we could perceive that the western sea was covered with ice ; the east wind, which could alone remove it, now gave place to a hard-hearted westerly one.

All the strait to the eastward of us, and the eastern sea, as far as could be seen from the hill-tops, is perfectly free from ice, whereas in the direction we wish to proceed there is nothing but packed ice, or water which cannot be reached. Bitterly disappointed we are, of course ; yet there is reasonable ground for hope ; grim winter will not ratify the obstinate proceedings of the western ice, for nearly four weeks.

Last evening's *amusement* was most exciting, nor was it without its peculiar perils. With cunning and activity worthy of her name, our little craft warily avoided a tilting-match with the stout blue masses which whirled about, as if with wilful impetuosity, through the narrow channel; some of them were so large as to ground even in 6 or 7 fathoms water. Many were drawn into the eddies, and, acquiring considerable velocity in a contrary direction, suddenly broke bounds, charging out into the stream and entering into mighty conflict with their fellows. After such a frolic the masses would revolve peaceably or unite with the pack, and await quietly their certain dissolution; may the day of that wished-for dissolution be near at hand! Nothing but strong hope of success induced me to encounter such dangerous opposition. I not only hoped, but almost felt, that we deserved to succeed.

Two plans were now occupying my thoughts, both of them resulting from the conviction that we should probably be compelled to winter to the eastward of Bellot Strait: the most important of these plans is that of finding some series of valleys, chain of lakes, or continuous low land, practicable as an overland sledge-route to the western coast, along which we may transport depots of provisions this autumn; for it is certain that the strong tides will prevent Bellot Strait being frozen over till winter is far advanced, and its surface will afford us no means of passing westward with our sledges.

The other plan, and that which we are now about to execute—whilst the sea continues navigable—is to land a small depot of provisions 60 or 70 miles to the southward, and down Prince Regent's Inlet, in order to facilitate communication with the Boothian Esquimaux either this autumn or in early spring.

And this precautionary step seems the more necessary, as I do not think it prudent to trust altogether to the yet undiscovered west coast of Boothia for a sledge-route towards King William's Island. Therefore quitting "Fox's Hole," and resting for one night in Depot Bay, we sailed from thence on the 26th. A fine breeze carried us rapidly southward along the coast of Regent Inlet. There was but little obstruction, though occasionally it was necessary to pass through a stream of loose ice. We saw little of any kind, compared to the experiences of Sir John Ross.

About dusk (nine o'clock) much loose ice to the southward prevented our making any attempt at further progress; we therefore anchored off the coast—in Stillwell Bay I think—about 45 miles from Depot Bay. Here the depot, consisting of 120 rations, was landed. I observe that it has only been on penetrating into Brentford Bay that we have found the primary rocks washed by the sea; the coast-line both north and south, as far as, and beyond, our present position, is a low shore of pale limestone, destitute of fossils; we can however see granitic hill-ranges far in the interior.

On the 27th we commenced beating back to the northward, tacking between the land and the ice which lay about 15 miles off shore. Towards night the wind greatly increased, and the ship, under reefed sails, plunged violently into the short, swift, high seas; we also felt quite as uneasy and restless as the ship, in our great anxiety to get back and ascertain what changes were likely to be effected by the gale.

28*th*.—To-night the weather is more pleasant; the keen and contrary wind has given place to a gentle fair breeze, the swell has almost subsided, no ice has been seen to-day, and the night is therefore unusually dark and mild—temperature 31°. I can hardly fancy that the sea which gently rocks us is not the ocean, and the soft air the breath, of our own temperate region. The delusion is charming!

30*th*.—Yesterday, after anchoring in Depot Bay, I walked over to Possession Point, to visit Ross's cairn. I found a few stones piled up on two large boulders, and under each a halfpenny, one of which I pocketed. Upon the ground lay the fragments of a bottle which once contained the record, and near it a staff about 4 feet long. Having calculated upon finding the bottle sound, I was obliged to make an impromptu record-case of its long neck, into which I thrust my brief document, and consigned it to the safe custody of a small heap of stones, the staff being erected over it.

It was dark before I got on board again. The strait had been reconnoitred from the hills, and was reported to be perfectly clear of ice. This morning we made a *fourth* attempt to pass through; but Bellot Strait was by no means clear; the same obstruction existed which defeated our last attempt, and in precisely the same place. Returning eastward, we entered a narrow arm of the sea, nearly a couple of miles to the west of Depot Bay, and anchored in a small creek, perfectly sheltered and land-locked, at the foot of a sugar-loaf hill, subsequently named after our surgeon, Mount Walker. The temperature is falling; last night it stood at 24°.

Bellot Strait, 1st September, 1858.

CHAPTER XI.

Proceed westward in a boat — Unpromising state of the western sea — Struggles in Bellot Strait — Falcons, good arctic fare — The resources of Boothia Felix — Future sledge travelling — Heavy gales — Hobson's party start — Winter quarters — Bellot Strait — Advanced depot established — Observatories — Intense cold — Autumn travellers — Ravens — Narrow escape — Wolves.

BEING most anxious to know the real state of the ice in the western sea—upon which our hopes so entirely depend—I intend starting this evening by boat, as far through Bellot Strait as the ice will permit, then land and ascend the hills overlooking the western coast.

1st Sept.—My boat party consisted of four men and the Doctor, who came with me for the novelty of the cruise, bringing his camera to fasten upon anything picturesque. We landed near Half-way Island, and pitched our tent for the night. Early next morning I commenced the rather formidable undertaking of ascending the hills, for it is not possible to pass under the cliffs, and at last I gained the summit of the loftiest, overlooking Cape Bird at a distance of 3 or 4 miles, and affording a splendid view to the westward, as well as glimpses between the hills, of the blue eastern sea. Long and anxiously did I survey the western sea, ice, and lands, and could not but feel that in all probability we should not be permitted to pass beyond our present position.

To the northward Four River Point-- Sir James Ross's

farthest in 1849—was at once recognised; rather more than nine years ago I stood upon it with him, and gazed almost as anxiously in *this* direction! My present view confirmed the impression then received, of a wide channel leading southward. The outline of the western land is very distant; it is of considerable but uniform elevation, and slopes gradually down to the strait, which is between 30 and 40 miles wide. This western land appears to be limestone, and without off-lying islands. Our side of the strait or sea, on the contrary, is primary rock, and fringed with islets and rocks; its southern extreme bears S.S.W., and is probably 30 miles distant.

Now for the ice. Although broken up, it lies against this shore in immense fields: there is but little water or room for ice-movement. Along the west shore I can distinguish long faint streaks of water. There is no appearance of disruption about Four River Point or in the contracted part of Peel Strait—we have nothing to hope for in that quarter; neither is there any evidence of current or pressure; the ice appears much decayed, but, as I am surveying it from a height of about 1600 feet, I may be deceived.

The strong contrast between the eastern and western seas and lands is very unfavourable to the latter.

Apart from the ice, I was fortunate however, in discovering a long narrow lake—subsequently named after Macgregor Laird Esq., an ardent supporter of the Franklin search—occupying a valley which lies between a small inlet south of Cape Bird, and Hazard Inlet—in fact, a sort of echo of Bellot Strait—and I look upon it as our sledge-route for the autumn, since it appears probable we shall winter in our present position.

This is a *surprisingly rough* country to scramble over; one never ceases to wonder how such huge blocks of rock can have got into so many strange positions. I noticed two masses in particular, each of them perched upon three smaller ones. The rock is gneiss; there is also much granite, and even upon the hill-tops pieces of limestone are occasionally met with.

My walk occupied eleven hours and although I everywhere saw traces of animals, the only living thing seen was a grey falcon. During my absence from the tent the men rambled all over the hills, but saw no game, our encampment was therefore shifted to a better position near the eastern termination of the table-land. This morning we explored the neighbouring valleys; saw three deer, and shot one, returning on board the 'Fox' in time for dinner.

Many deer had been seen not far from the ship, and Hobson had shot a bearded seal. I have organised another boat party; Young will start with it to-morrow morning to seek a sledge-route from the southern angle of Brentford Bay to the western sea.

5*th*.—Young returned this morning; he reports the southwest angle of the bay not to run in so far as we expected, and to be environed by very high land, impracticable for sledges.

Our Esquimaux, Samuel, shot a fawn to-day.

Strong northerly winds have latterly prevailed; Bellot Strait is at last quite clear of ice; to-morrow morning, therefore, we shall make our *fifth* attempt to get the 'Fox' through.

6*th*.—Steamed through the clear waters of Bellot Strait this morning, and made fast to the ice across its western outlet at a distance of two miles from the shore, and close to a small islet, which we have already dubbed *Pemmican Rock*, having landed upon it a large supply of that substantial traveller's fare, with other provisions for our future sledging-parties. This ice is in large stout fields, of more than one winter's growth, apparently immovable in consequence of the numerous islets and rocks which rise through and hold it fast. If the weather permits, we shall remain here for a few days and watch the effect of winds and tides upon it; that the ship will get any farther seems improbable.

10th.—I have explored the small inlet near Cape Bird, which we have named *False Strait*, from its striking resemblance to the true one, and find it is only separated from the long lake by half a mile of low land; the lake we have ascertained to be about 12 miles long, and from it valleys extend eastward and southward, so that we are sure of a good sledge route—an important matter, as the hills rise to 1600 feet above the sea.

Cape Bird is 500 feet high; from its summit we carefully observe the ice. This granite coast presents a jagged appearance; it is deeply indented and studded with islets. The ice in the western sea is much more broken up than it was upon the 31st ultimo; there is no longer any fixed ice except within the grasp of the islets. The "western sea" here mentioned is a continuation of Peel Sound. It has been navigated by Franklin only, and by him proved to be a strait. I have deemed it due to that distinguished man to designate it "Sir John Franklin Strait."

Birds and animals have become very scarce; three seals have been shot, and a bear seen. To-morrow we shall return to our harbour, and endeavour to procure a few more reindeer before they migrate southward.

12th.—Yesterday we anchored within the entrance of our creek, being a more convenient position than up at its head. We are already in our wintering position, and, having scarcely any occupation, one day seems most remarkably like another. Although the fondly cherished hope of pushing farther in our ship can no longer be entertained, yet as long as the season continues navigable, it is our duty to be in readiness to avail ourselves of any opportunity, however improbable, of being able to do so.

Once firmly frozen in, our autumn travelling will commence, and afford welcome occupation. Almost all on board have guns; ammunition is supplied, and a sailor with a musket is a very contented and zealous sportsman, if not always a successful one; it is a powerful incentive to exercise. To-day the ramblers saw only two hares, an ermine, and an owl. Some peregrine falcons have lately been shot; Petersen declares they are "*the best beef in the country, and the young birds tender and white as chicken!*"

A few days ago a large cask of biscuit was opened, and a living mouse discovered therein; it was small, but mature in years. The cask, a strong watertight one, was packed on shore at Aberdeen in June, 1857, and remained ever since unopened; there was no hole by which the mouse could have got in or out, besides it is the only one ever seen on board. Ship's biscuit is certainly *dry feeding;* but who dares assert, after the experience of our mouse, that it is not wonderfully nutritious?

15*th*.—Two nights ago a comet was observed just beneath the constellation of the Great Bear; a series of measurements was commenced for determining its path. Yesterday I walked for eight hours through the most promising valleys, but did not see a living creature; yet there is a very fair show of vegetation, much more so than at Melville Island, where game is abundant. To the east there is not a speck of ice, excepting only a huge iceberg, probably the same we saw off Fury Point, a very unusual visitor from Baffin's Bay, whence it must have been driven by those long-continued east winds of painful memory in June and July. Eight year's experience in these seas gives this day's date as the average for the limit of the navigable season.

Hobson and two men encamped out for three days in order to scour the country; they have seen only one hare and one lemming. Walker geologises; amongst other things he finds much iron pyrites. The dredge has been used, but with very little success. The thermometer ranges between 20° and 30°. Fresh water pools are frozen over, sea ice forms in every sheltered angle of the creeks. There is no snow upon the land, and this makes it more difficult to find game, as we can neither track nor distinguish them so easily.

I have determined upon naming this beautiful little anchorage *Port Kennedy*, after my predecessor, the discoverer of Bellot Strait, of which it is decidedly *the* port. This is an agreeable duty, and nowhere could Mr. Kennedy's name be more appropriately affixed than in close proximity with his interesting discovery. And now having acknowledged his prior discovery, I venture to confer our little vessel's name upon the islets which protect its entrance.

The island upon which Mr. Kennedy and Lieutenant Bellot encamped was Long Island, about three miles farther to the south-east.

17*th.*—Of late we have been preparing provisions and equipments for our travelling parties. My scheme of sledge search comprehends three separate routes, each of the three parties being composed of four men, a dog sledge and driver; Hobson, Young, and I will lead them.

My journey will be to the Great Fish River, examining the shores of King William's Land in going and returning; Petersen will be with me.

Hobson will explore the western coast of Boothia as far as the magnetic pole, this autumn I hope, and from Gateshead Island westward next spring.

Young will trace the shore of Prince of Wales' Land from Lieutenant Browne's farthest, to the southwestward to Osborn's farthest, if possible, and also examine between Four River Point and Cape Bird.

Our probable absence will be sixty or seventy days, commencing from about the 20th March.

Greenland dog-sledge.

In this way I trust we shall complete the Franklin search and the geographical discovery of arctic America, both left unfinished by the former expeditions; and in so doing we can hardly fail to obtain some trace, some relic, or, it may be, important records of those whose mysterious fate it is the great object of our labours to discover. But previous to setting forth upon these important journeys, I must communicate with the Boothians, if possible, either upon the west or east coast, in November or February. Sir John Ross's 'Narrative' informs us that they sometimes winter as far north upon the east coast as the Agnew River; and we know that upon the west, at the magnetic pole, their abandoned snow huts were occupied in June by Sir James Ross.

19th.—Yesterday we steamed once more through Bellot Strait, and took up our former position at the ice-edge, off its western entrance; the ice, hemmed in by islets, has not moved.

From the summit of Cape Bird I had a very extensive view this morning; there is now much water in the offing, only separated from us by the belt of islet-girt ice *scarcely four miles in width!* My conviction is that a strong east wind would remove this remaining barrier; it is not yet too late. The water runs parallel to this coast, and is four or five miles broad; beyond it there is ice, but it appears to be all broken up.

Yesterday Young went upon a dog-sledge to the nearest south-western island, distant 7 or 8 miles. He reports the intervening ice cracked and weak in some places, but practicable for loaded sledges; the far side of the island is washed by a clear sea, and a bear which he shot plunged into it, and, drifting away, was lost; Young is in favour of carrying out the depot provisions to or beyond this island by boat; but as the temperature fell to 18° last night, and new ice forms whenever it is calm, I prefer the safer, although more laborious mode, of sledging; accordingly to-day our dogs carried out to it two sledge-loads of the provisions intended for the use of our parties hereafter.

22nd.—All the provisions have now been carried out to the nearest island, which I shall temporarily name *Separation*,[1] as there our spring parties will divide; and a portion intended for Hobson's party and my own has been carried on to the next island 7 or 8 miles farther. Our travelling boat and a small reserve depot have been placed upon Pemmican Rock, so already something has been done. Animal life is very scarce; a few seals, an occasional gull, and three brown falcons, are the only creatures we have seen for several days past. Last evening at eight o'clock a very vivid flash of lightning was observed; its appearance in these latitudes is very rare; once only have I seen it before—in September, 1850.

25th, Saturday night.—Furious gales from N. and S.W., but our barrier of coast ice remains undiminished. This morning Hobson set off upon a journey of fourteen or fifteen days' duration, with seven men and fourteen dogs; he is to advance the depots along shore to the south, and, if successful, will reach latitude 71°.

The temperature is mild (+17°), but it is snowy and disagreeable weather; there is already enough snow upon the old ice to make walking laborious, and the land has also assumed its wintry complexion.

28th.—The ship was kept available for prosecuting her voyage up to the *latest hour;* it was only yesterday that we left the western ice, and in consequence of the vast accumulation of young ice in Bellot Strait we had considerable difficulty in reaching the *entrance* of Port Kennedy: all within was so firmly frozen over that after three hours'

---

[1] Subsequently named after my excellent friend A. Arcedeckne, Esq., commodore of the Royal London Yacht Club.

steaming and working we penetrated only 100 yards; however, we are in an excellent position, although our wintering place will be farther out by a quarter of a mile than I intended.

To-day we are unbending sails and laying up the engines —uncertainty no longer exists—here we are compelled to remain; and if we have not been as successful in our voyaging as a month ago we had good reason to expect, we may still hope that Fortune will smile upon our more humble, yet more arduous, pedestrian explorations—" Hope on, hope ever." In the meantime the sudden transition, from mental and physical wear and tear, of no ordinary description, to the absolute security and quiet of winter quarters, is an immense relief.

2nd Oct.—Mr. Petersen has shot two very fine bucks; one is a magnificent fellow, weighing 354 lbs. (minus the paunch). Several deer have been seen; they come from the N. along the slopes of the eastern hills. An ermine came on board a few nights ago and kept the dogs in a violent state of excitement, being much too wary to come out from under the boat to be caught by them; at length one of the men secured it. This beautiful little animal does not appear to be full grown; its extreme length is 13 inches. Two others came off to the ship, and to our great amusement eluded the men who gave chase, by darting into the soft snow—which is now a foot deep—and reappearing several yards off.

It is remarkable that although the Greenlanders know the musk ox and wolf by name, yet these animals do not exist in Greenland; neither do the ermine nor lemming, so common here and even upon the west shore of Baffin's Bay; there is also a fifth animal, the wolverine, unknown in Greenland, though found in Boothia, but not, I believe, further to the north.

The lemming is a little creature about twice the size of the short-tailed field-mouse, which it also resembles in its habits. They have been found all over the arctic regions westward of Baffin's Bay wherever vegetation exists; but where it is extremely scanty, as along the shores of Barrow Strait, and in North Somerset, they are very rare. Melville Island and Prince Patrick's Land are well stocked with them. They are strange fearless little things; even when freshly caught and put on the dinner-table, they would run about, visit every one's plate, and nibble biscuit quite unconcernedly. We have kept them on board for weeks, during which time some of them exhibited the nasty habit of devouring their own offspring.

It is not uncommon to meet their tracks on the ice several miles off shore crossing from one island to another. Sir Edward Parry found the skeleton of one upon the ice, in latitude $81\frac{3}{4}°$ N., and sixty miles from the nearest known land!

Almost all animated nature preys upon them: bear, wolf, fox, ermine, birds of prey, the *lestris parasiticus*, and the larger gulls. The burgomaster has frequently been seen to pounce down upon the lemming, and carry him up to his resting place in the cliffs.

In his sledge journal, Young mentions shooting some of these gulls for supper, and finding whole lemmings in their stomachs. This was in early spring before the thaw, when probably no other food was available for them. At this season, the warmth of the returning sun probably tempted the unlucky lemmings out of their burrows beneath the snow.

The weather is too mild to satisfy us; we wish for severe frost to seal us up securely, and make the ice strong enough to bear the sledge-loads of provisions, &c., which are to be landed for the purpose of making more room in the ship.

6th.—A herd of a dozen reindeer crossed the harbour to-day. Last night Hobson and his companions returned, all well. They were stopped by the sea washing against the cliffs in latitude $71\frac{1}{2}°$, and to that point they have advanced the depots. Although the weather has been stormy here, they have been able to travel every day. They found the coast still fringed with islets, and deeply indented; upon every point, moss-grown circles of stones indicated the abodes of Esquimaux in times long since gone by.

One night they muzzled a dog, as she was in the habit of gnawing her harness : in this defenceless state, unable even to bark and arouse the men, her *amiable* sisterhood attacked her so fiercely that she died next day.

In honour of so important and successful a commencement of our travelling as that accomplished by Hobson, we had a feast of good venison, plum pudding, and grog. It is quite evident that no more travelling can be accomplished until the ice forms a pathway along shore; in this, as in some other respects, we anxiously await the advance of the season. The weather is mild; Bellot Strait is almost covered with ice, which drifts freely with every tide. Reindeer are seen almost daily; they too are awaiting the freezing over of the sea to continue their southern travels. Our harbour-ice is weak and covered a foot deep with a sludgy compound of snow and water.

8th.—Yesterday an ermine was caught in a trap; hitherto these most active little skirmishers have successfully robbed our fox-traps of their baits as fast as they could be renewed. To-day Peterson shot another reindeer; it weighs 130 lbs.; many others were seen, also a wolf. Sometimes a few ptarmigan are met with, but hares very rarely.

12th.—Fine weather generally prevails. We have landed about 100 casks, all our boats, and much lumber, so we shall have abundance of room on board. I enjoyed a long and exhilarating ramble upon snow-shoes to-day; without them I could not have gone over half the distance—the snow lies so deep and soft—but I saw only one reindeer.

14th.—One of our magnetic observatories has been built; it stands upon the ice, 210 yards S. (magnetic) from the ship, and is built of ice sawed into blocks—there not being any suitable snow; it is just large enough to hold the declinometer for hourly observations, to be noted throughout the winter. The housings have been put over the ship already, as Hobson will leave us again in a few days to advance his depot and my own to the vicinity of the magnetic pole if possible. I would also send Young upon a similar duty, but the western sea cannot have frozen over yet.

19th.—All the 17th a N.W. gale blew with fearful violence; yesterday it abated, but not sufficiently to allow our party to start. This morning Hobson got away with his nine men and ten dogs; his absence may be from eighteen to twenty days. Autumn travelling is most disagreeable; there is so much wind and snow, the latter being soft, deep, and often wet; the sun is almost always obscured by mist, and is powerless for warmth or drying purposes, and the temperature is very variable. Moreover there are now only eight hours of misty daylight. To-day the morning was fine, and temperature $+8°$. Having completed the preliminary observations of the times of horizontal and vertical vibrations, also of the magnetic intensity, I set up to-day the declinometer, and commenced the hourly series of observations on the diurnal variation. I trust it may continue unbroken until we all set out upon our spring travels in March. A hare has been shot, but no other animals seen. The arctic expeditions have found hares everywhere except at Port Leopold, where there is no vegetation at all. They love steep rocky slopes having a southern aspect, and in such favourable situations as many as a dozen may some-

Interior of the Magnetic Observatory.

times be seen together: failing this they sometimes betake themselves to the hummocks of ice, to doze in shelter from the wind; I have also found long burrows made by them in the snow. They are large, and bring forth five or six at a birth.

29*th*.—It generally blows a gale of wind here; the only advantage in return for so much discomfort is that the snow is the more quickly packed hard. As we have only three working men and an Esquimaux left on board for ship's duties, I was assisted a few days ago by the Doctor, the Engineer, and the Interpreter in building another observatory, intended for special monthly magnetic observations. This edifice is constructed of snow. Whenever we have a calm night, we can hear the crushing sound of the drift-ice in Bellot Strait, which continues open to within 500 yards of the Fox Islands, and emits dark chilling clouds of hateful, abominable mist.

The last two days have been very fine and calm: the men visited their fox and ermine traps, which are secreted amongst the rocks in a most mysterious manner—one ermine only has been taken. Seven or eight reindeer and some ptarmigan were seen; two of the latter and a hare were shot. We have commenced brewing sugar beer.

2*nd Nov.*—Very dull times. No amount of ingenuity could make a diary worth the paper it is written on. An occasional raven flies past, a couple more ptarmigan have been shot; another N.W. gale is blowing, with temperature down to $-12°$.

Of all our feathered visitors, the raven alone scorns to change either his colour or his clime. Sometimes in midwinter, when the frost is intense and no sound heard save the crunching of snow under foot, you are startled by a loud, deep, sonorous croak, and find yourself closely reconnoitred by a raven! The gloomy bird sails slowly past, and even the clear starlight is sufficient to render visible to you an ice-ring round his throat, his own breath frosted on his black feathers.

We seldom were so wanton as to shoot a raven, but when we did so, we generally found it to be minus some of the joints of its toes, the results of frost-bites.

All over the arctic regions they have been found: the same bird which still hovers over the sweltering plains of Jericho, and lodges in the rocky hill-side which overhangs the brook Cherith; the same wonderful bird which the early Vikings, we are told, took with them upon their voyages, somewhat in the double capacity of mariner's compass and chief pilot—their extraordinary powers of sight and smell enabling them to discover land at incredible distances.

Were it not for the frost-bitten toes, one might fairly doubt whether ravens are sensible of the rigours of this climate, which they endure apparently without any adequate protection.

6th, Saturday night.—The N.W. gale blew without intermission for seventy hours, the temperature being about $-15°$: we hoped that our absent shipmates might be housed safely in snow huts. This afternoon all doubts respecting them were dispelled by their arrival in good health, but they evidently have suffered from cold and exposure during their absence of nineteen days. For the first six days they journeyed outward successfully; on that night they encamped upon the ice; it was at spring tide, a N.E. gale sprang up, and, blowing off shore, detached the ice and drifted them off.

As soon as they discovered that the ice was drifting off shore with them, they packed their sledges, harnessed the dogs, and passed the long and fearful night in anxious watching for some chance to escape. When the ice got a little distance off shore, it broke up under the influence of the wind and sea, until the piece they were upon was scarce

20 yards in diameter; impelled by the storm—they knew not whither, for the night was dark, and snow fell thickly—it drifted across the mouth of a wide inlet,[1] nearly to the opposite shore. The gale was quickly followed by a calm, and an intense frost which in a single night formed ice sufficiently strong to bear them in safety to the land, although it bent fearfully beneath their weight. They suffered much from the exposure, but their escape was indeed providential.

The depots were eventually established in latitude $71\frac{1}{4}°$; beyond this Lieutenant Hobson did not attempt to advance, not only because their remaining provisions would not have warranted a longer absence, but because the open sea was seen to beat against the next headland. They have lived in tents only, and have not experienced the heavy gales so frequent here, and which probably are mainly due to our position in Bellot Strait, which performs the part of a funnel for both winds and tides between the two seas.

That the western sea should still remain open argues a vast space southward for the escape of the ice; our western parties are thus prevented from carrying across their depot. We must only be stirring earlier in the spring. I am truly thankful for the safe return of our travellers—all this toil and exposure of ten persons and ten dogs has only advanced the depots 30 miles farther, *i. e.* from 50 to 80 miles distant from the ship.

Hardly a particle of snow remains upon the harbour-ice, the recent gales having swept it away; and the porch of my snow-hut has been fretted away to a mere cobweb by the attrition of the snowdrift; the Doctor and I rebuilt it to-day. Three reindeer and a wolf have been seen.

---

[1] Named after the late Lord Wrottesley, in remembrance of the support given by him to the expedition, his advocacy of it in the House of Lords, and of the facilities granted me by the Royal Society—of which he was President—for the pursuit of scientific observations.

Wolves are sparingly distributed over all arctic lands wherever reindeer exist, excepting only Greenland, Iceland, and Spitzbergen, where, happily for the latter, they are unknown; this may be partly due to their want of courage and instinct to venture out upon the ice and cross wide straits, as even the tiny lemming does. Their fur becomes white in winter and brown in summer.

For several months a wolf lived about our ships in Wellington Channel; as his appearance was duly entered in the log-book, it was found that he made excursions from one to the other, being one day near the 'Assistance,' and next day fifty-two geographical miles off, at the 'North Star.'

They have been seen attempting to surprise seals upon the ice; but their chief dependance is upon the reindeer. A pack of ten of them have been observed manœuvring about a herd until they succeeded in cutting off a straggler; their next stratagem was to surround it, and then, gradually and without alarming it, close in until sufficiently near for a simultaneous rush, when instantly it was torn to pieces, and in a few seconds scarcely a fragment of it remained.

I believe that wolfish propensities attain their perfection under the pressing necessities of this climate. Our arctic species is gaunt, meagre, and insatiable of course, a cowardly, slouching, yet untiring beast, that one feels it a virtue to hate; and he is cunning to a degree that confounded all our devices for his capture. As to coming upon him unawares, an officer[1] has told me that one took up his residence in a cleft in the rocks near the ship, and there he would *sleep* for hours, out of bullet range, but near enough for an observer with a telescope to discover, that on the slightest noise on board he would erect his ears. No one ever got within shot of that wolf!

[1] Dr. Philpots, of the 'Queen,' of Peterhead.

CHAPTER XII.

Death of our engineer—Scarcity of game—The cold unusually trying—Jolly, under adverse circumstances—Petersen's information—Return of the sun of 1859—Early spring sledge parties—Unusual severity of the winter—Severe hardships of early sledging—The western shores of Boothia—Meet the Esquimaux—Intelligence of Franklin's ships—Return to the 'Fox'—Allen Young returns.

Nov. 7th, Sunday evening.—BRIEF as is the interval since my last entry, yet how pregnant with warning, and to one of our small company how fatal! Yesterday Mr. Brand, our engineer, was out shooting as usual, and in robust health; in the evening Hobson sat with him for a little time. Mr. Brand turned the conversation upon our position and employments last year; he called to remembrance poor Robert Scott, then in sound health, and the fact of his having carried our "Guy Fawkes" round the ship on the preceding day twelvemonth, and added mournfully, " Poor fellow! no one knows whose turn it may be to go next." He finished his evening pipe, and shut his cabin door shortly after nine o'clock. This morning, at seven o'clock, his servant found him lying upon the deck, a corpse, having been several hours dead. Apoplexy appears to have been the cause. He was a steady, serious man, under forty years of age, and leaves a widow and three or four children; what their circumstances are, I am not aware.

10th.—This morning the remains of Mr. Brand, enclosed in a neat coffin, were buried in a grave on shore. A suitable headboard and inscription will be placed over it. From all that I have gathered, it appears that his mind had been somewhat gloomy for the last few days, dwelling much upon poor Scott's sudden death. Whether he really saw three reindeer on Saturday, watched their movements, and fired his Minié rifle at them when 700 yards distant, or whether it was the creation of a disordered brain, none can tell. On his first return on board he said he had seen deer *tracks* only.

We are now without either engineer or engine-driver : we have only two stokers, and they know nothing about the machinery. Our numbers are reduced to twenty-four, including our interpreter and two Greenland Esquimaux.

15*th*.—We have enjoyed ten days of moderate winds and calms, but the temperature has fallen as low as −31°. This causes frost-cracks in the ice *across* the harbour ; they will freeze over, and others will form, and gape, and freeze at intervals, so that by next spring we shall probably be moved several feet off shore.

Mists have obscured the sun of late, and now it does not rise at all. We are indifferent ; its departure has become to us a matter of course. The usual winter covering of snow has been spread upon deck rather more than a foot thick. Its utility in preventing the escape of heat became at once strikingly apparent. Nothing has been seen but a few ptarmigan and one reindeer, which trotted off from the land towards the ship. Our bullets missed him, and the dogs unfortunately caught sight and chased him away. I do not think any dogs could overtake a reindeer in this rough country ; the rocks would speedily lame them, and the snow, in many places, is quite deep enough to fatigue them greatly, whereas it offers but slight impediment to the deer, furnished as he is with long legs and spreading hoofs.

29*th*.—Animals have become very scarce. A few ptarmigan and willow-grouse have been seen, and three shot. Two days ago I saw two reindeer. The eastern sea is frozen over, and our old acquaintance the iceberg in Prince Regent's Inlet is still visible on a clear day. We brew sugar-beer; and we set nets for seals, but catch none, although the nets have been made and set in favourable positions under the ice by the Greenlanders; hence we suppose the seals also have migrated elsewhere; if so, the Esquimaux could not winter here. We have no regular school this winter, but five of the men study navigation every evening under the guidance of Young. Hobson and I are doing all we can to make the ship dry, warm, and comfortable: our large snow porches over the hatchways are a great improvement.

5th Dec.—Cold, windy weather, with chilling mists from the open water in Bellot Strait. We can seldom leave the shelter of the ship for a walk on shore, and, when we do, rarely see even a ptarmigan. Although these birds are summer visitors only, yet some few remain throughout the winter. They make holes in the snow and even burrow under it to gain shelter from the icy blast.

In the month of January two ptarmigan were shot at Melville Island, and were both in excellent condition; the largest weighed two pounds and a half, its crop contained two ounces and a half of slender willow-shoots, many of them as thick as a crow-quill and three-fourths of an inch in length. This fine bird, when prepared for cooking, weighed a pound and a quarter.

12th.—Very cold weather; thermometer down to $-41°$, and the breeze comes to us loaded with mist from the open water, causing the air to feel colder than it otherwise would. Bellot Strait has become a nuisance, not only from this cause, but from the strong winds — purely local — which seldom cease to blow through it.

The seal nets have produced nothing; and as there are no seals, we no longer wonder at not seeing bears. Three foxes have been trapped and a hare seen. Our canine force numbers twenty-four serviceable dogs and six puppies; but these, I fear, will not be strong enough for sledging by March.

The monotony of our lives is vastly increased by want of occupation, and confinement by severe gales to the ship, for five days out of every seven. Those who have spent an arctic winter in a government expedition will please to remember, when they read this admission, how differently we are circumstanced; only twenty-four souls, including Petersen the Dane, and the two Esquimaux, confined in one small vessel. We are, of course, unable to get up *bals masqués*, or theatres, newspaper, skittle-alley, or ice billiard-table as was ingeniously devised on board the 'Enterprise;' and this being our second winter, we know all each other's stories by rote, in fact we take a malicious pleasure in *correcting* each other when telling them. Captain Collinson's skittle-alley and billiard-room were splendid edifices—snow walls and ice windows—genuine crystal palaces.

But if our dulness and monotony is intense, it will also be brief, for we shall recommence sledging as soon as there is sufficient light (early in February), which will be about two months sooner than has been usual hitherto.

The general health is good, but there is a natural craving for fresh meat and fresh vegetables—in great measure, perhaps, because they cannot be obtained; but a well-filled letter bag would be more welcome than anything I know of.

26th.—Upon four days only during the last fourteen has the weather permitted us to take walks on shore. I allude to the wind as the obstacle to our exercise; for low temperature, when the air is still, is no bar to any reasonable amount of it. Three or four coveys of ptarmigan have been seen, and of these I shot one brace. The cold increases: thermometer has fallen to $-47\frac{1}{2}°$, although blowing a moderate gale at the time, and the atmosphere dense with mist.

Our Christmas has been spent with a degree of loyalty to the good old English custom at once spirited and refreshing. All the good things which could possibly be collected together appeared upon the snow-white deal tables of the men, as the officers and myself (by invitation) walked round the lower deck. Venison, beer, and a fresh stock of clay pipes, appeared to be the most prized luxuries; but the variety and abundance of the eatables, tastefully laid out, was such as might well support the delusion which all seemed desirous of imposing upon themselves—that they were in a land of plenty—in fact, *all but* at home! We contributed a large cheese and some preserves, and candles superseded the ordinary smoky lamps. With so many comforts, and the existence of so much genuine good feeling, their evening was a joyous one, enlivened also by songs and music.

Whilst all was order and merriment within the ship, the scene without was widely different. A fierce north-wester howled loudly through the rigging, the snowdrift rustled swiftly past, no star appeared through the oppressive gloom, and the thermometer varied between 76° and 80° *below the freezing point*. At one time it was impossible to visit the magnetic observatory, although only 210 yards distant, and with a rope stretched along, breast high, upon poles the whole way. The officers discharged this duty for the quartermasters of the watches during the day and night.

1st Jan. 1859.—This being *Saturday night* as well as *New Year's Day*, "Sweethearts and Wives" were remembered with even more than the ordinary feeling. New year's eve was celebrated with all the joyfulness which ardent hope can inspire: and we *have* reasonable ground for *strong hope*. At midnight the expiration of the old year and commencement of the new one was announced to me by *the band*—flutes, accordion, and gong—striking up at my door. Some songs were sung, and the performance concluded with "God save the Queen:" the few who could find space in our mess-room sang the chorus; but this by no means satisfied all the others who were without and unable to show themselves to the officers, so they echoed the chorus, and the effect was very gratifying to our feelings, if not to our ears. Our new year's day has been commemorated with all the substantials of Christmas fare, but without so much display—less tailoring in pastry, not quite so much clipping of dough into roses, and anchors, and nondescript animals, &c. &c. One of the pleasing little incidents which attracted my attention on Christmas Day was the unusual display of daguerreotypes, portraits of wives or mothers, children or sisters, and a few of sweethearts: almost all the crew are married.

The past week has been cold and stormy; it now blows strong, and the temperature is $-44°$.

On the 29th a few fresh tracks of animals and a ptarmigan were seen; yesterday I saw three ptarmigan. December proved to be an unusually cold month, its mean temperature being $-33°$; and it was rendered more than ordinarily dark and gloomy by continual mists from Bellot Strait. This open water adds seriously to the drawbacks of a spot already sufficiently cheerless, gameless, and "wind-loved."

9th.—Another week of uniform temperature, $-40°$, and confinement to the ship by strong winds; the atmosphere is loaded with enveloping mists which impart a raw and surprisingly keen edge to the chilling blasts, blasts that no human nose can endure without blanching, be its proportions what they may. It is wonderful how the dogs stand it, and without apparent inconvenience, unless their fur happen to be thin. They lie upon the snow under the lee of the ship, with no other protection from the weather.

It surprises a man when he finds, for the first time, that his tobacco pipe won't draw in consequence of the essential oil in the stem becoming frozen! and it still more astonishes him when, instead of smoke issuing from the funnels, he sees pendant icicles a foot or more in length attached to them! It is easily explained: all night long, whilst the fire is out, warm air charged with moisture escapes by the funnel, and the upper part of this copper tube, being as cold as the external air, is quickly lined with the frozen moisture of the escaping air.

Even the smoke during the day only partially thaws this frost, coating over the remainder with soot; thus layers of ice and of soot accumulate alternately, until the passage is so contracted that the smoke can no longer ascend. Then, instead of the chimney-sweeper, the blacksmith is sent for, the funnel taken down and its contents removed. Unless the cold is intense for some days together, the fire a very small one, and the funnel rather long, this does not occur. We are rarely troubled in this way, although our  daily expenditure of coals this winter, for all purposes, is only 88 lbs., and this supplies the galley fire and three warming stoves. I have seen the frozen contents of a stove pipe, made up of numerous concentric laminæ of ice and soot alternately, having so completely filled up the funnel as to leave only a hole of an inch in diameter through the centre of it.

To-day, the winds being light and temperature *up to* $-30°$, we enjoyed walks on shore, although the mist continued so dense as to limit our view to a couple of hundred yards.

I learn from Petersen that the natives of Smith's Sound are well acquainted with the continuation of its shores considerably beyond the farthest point reached by Kane's exploring parties, but unfortunately no one thought of getting them to delineate their local knowledge upon paper. They spoke much of a large island near the west coast called "Umingmak" (musk ox) Island, where there was much open water, abounding with walrus, and where some of their people formerly lived.[1]

Esquimaux exist upon the east coast of Greenland as far north as lat. 75°; how much farther north is not known. They are separated from the South Greenlanders by hundreds of miles of icebound coasts and impassable glaciers.

Centuries ago a milder climate *may* and probably *did* exist, and a corresponding modification of glacier and a sea less ice-encumbered might have rendered the migration of these poor people from the south to their present isolated abodes practicable; but to me it appears much more easy to suppose that they migrated eastward from the northern outlet of Smith's Sound.

The very little that we know of the east coast of Greenland, stretching northward from Cape Farewell in lat. 60° to 76°, and probably much farther, is derived from Scoresby's 'Journal of a Voyage to the Northern Whale Fishery,' in 1822; from the voyage of H.M.S. 'Griper,'[2] in 1823, when Captain Clavering, R.N., was accompanied by Captain Sabine, R.A., now General Sabine, the distinguished President of the Royal Society; and from the boat voyages of Captain Graah, of the Royal Danish Navy, in 1828–30.

To commence with the most northern voyage: Clavering's ship was unable to penetrate farther north than 75° 12′;

---

[1] Petersen conversed with two men who had themselves been up to Umingmak Island.

[2] See new 'Edinburgh Philosophical Journal,' July, 1830.

three weeks were devoted to magnetic and other observations at the Pendulum Islands, in 74° 32' N., where from an elevation of 1800 feet he noticed on one occasion clear water close along the mainland as far as could be seen, although loose ice intervened; the ice he describes as 20 or 30 feet thick, heavier than Davis' Strait ice, but not so massive as that to the westward of Melville Island. In writing to a friend, he says, "There is nothing in this voyage that proves we could not have gone farther north; and I think that so long as there is a continuance of land, perseverance will get along it, but the main must be kept on board." He met with a party of twelve Esquimaux in Gale Hamke's Bay, lat. 74° 3' N.; they wore sealskin dresses, possessed dogs, a kayak, and harpoon staves made of walrus tusk, tipped with iron which had not been smelted, appearing to be meteoric iron; they were living in a tent of skins supported on bones of whales and pieces of wood. Several graves, and other indications of their permanent residence, were met with. Foxes, hares, a bear, ptarmigan, and a few antlers of reindeer, were seen. No driftwood was found, and no southerly current detected.

Scoresby visited this coast between the latitudes of 70° and $72\frac{1}{2}°$; he found numerous graves, ruined winter huts, and other Esquimaux traces, but did not meet with people; he also obtained proofs of the existence of deer, hares, foxes, bears, walruses, seals, narwhals, and whales; shot a few ptarmigan, and captured the only lemming seen. Deep fiords penetrate far into the land, Scoresby's Sound extending westward for 90 miles, and appearing to continue still farther in that direction; in these fiords there was not a particle of ice, the heat on shore was unexpectedly great, and once (25th July) was most oppressive; vegetation was proportionably abundant.

It thus appears that there are natives and the ordinary

arctic animals as far towards the south as lat. 70°; but from hence to the northern extreme reached by Graah there is a distance of 550 miles, of which we are totally ignorant.

From Cape Farewell, Graah proceeded as far north as Aluik, in 64¼° N., where his farther progress was barred by ice; a few natives were there, but none of them lived farther north, and their traditional knowledge of the coast only extended six or eight journeys farther—probably 100 miles —to an impassable glacier of unknown extent; they knew nothing of the more northern Esquimaux, resembling in this respect the West Greenlanders, who did not know of the arctic highlanders to the north of Melville Bay previous to the late Sir John Ross's discovery of them in 1818; neither did they know of any land animal except the fox. It therefore does seem that some extraordinary barrier such as a 100 miles or more of glacier exists between the discoveries of Scoresby and of Graah, such as on the west coast so effectually isolates the Cape York Esquimaux from their countrymen 250 miles to the southward of them.

21st.—More pleasant weather since my last entry; and although last night the temperature fell to $-47°$ yet it has generally been mild; once it rose to $-14°$, but amply made amends by falling to $-38°$ within twelve hours. We have enjoyed much of the moon's presence for the last ten days, but now she is waning and hastening away to the south. Daylight increases in strength and duration, consequently we walk more, and see more, and the winter's gloom gives place to activity and cheerfulness. Several ptarmigan, three or four hares, a snowy owl, and a bear-track, have at various times been seen. Young has shot four ptarmigan, and I have shot a couple more and a hare, and the men have trapped two foxes.

On board the ship the preparations for travelling take precedence of all other occupations. These preparations may be summed up thus:—First, our personal apparel: making face-covers, light over-all dresses or *snow-repellers*, to keep out the penetrating drift-snow; altering and fitting

Travelling Costume.

mocassins and canvas boots, re-sewing everything, and testing the warmth and comfort of the suit by preparatory walks. Secondly, preparing the sledges, re-lashing them, and burnishing the steel shoeing of the runners; adapting and strengthening our small calico tents (mine, which serves for six persons, weighs only 18½ lbs., the poles included); making blanket sleeping-bags, and tent robes. And lastly, making bags of the lightest material to hold the provisions, cans for spirit-fuel and for rum, and packages of all sorts; also altering and testing our cooking utensils. In short, doing all things necessary to enable us to turn out upon the ice, to encamp upon it, and to march over it for months, from February until June or July, under a temperature which may be expected to range through 100°—from 50° below zero to 50° above it. How to accomplish this is a most deeply interesting problem, and one that taxes our utmost ingenuity.

26th.—Part of the sun's disc loomed above the horizon to-day, somewhat swollen and disfigured by the misty atmosphere, but looking benevolent withal. I happened to be diligently traversing the rocky hill-sides in the hope of finding some solitary hare dozing in fancied security, when the sun thus appeared in view, and I halted to feast my eyes upon the glorious sight, and to scan the features of our returning friend after an absence of seventy-three days. Hope and promise mingled in his bright beams. Again I moved upward, and with more elastic step; for now the sun of 1859 was shining upon all nature around me. On looking over the records of previous voyages I find that the average amount of refraction upon the horizon is about 45 minutes of arc, the temperature being −35°. Last year, when the sun reappeared on 28th January, there was 59 minutes of refraction, and the temperature at the time was −38°.

2nd February.—A lovely, calm, bright day, and beautifully clear, except over the water-space in Bellot Strait, where rests a densely black mist, very strongly resembling the West Indian rain-squall as it looms upon the distant horizon. The increasing sunlight is cheering, but void of heat, and the mercury is often frozen. A few more ptarmigan have been shot.

Our remaining serviceable dogs, twenty-two in number, have been divided with great care into three teams of seven each; the odd dog is added to my team, as my journey is expected to be the longest. The different sledge-parties will now feed up their dogs without limit, so that the utmost degree of work may be got out of them hereafter.

January has been slightly colder than December, mean temperature being $-33\frac{1}{2}°$, but there has been rather less wind.

8th.—All will be ready for the departure of Young and myself upon our respective journeys on the morning of the 14th.

Mr. Petersen and Alexander Thompson accompany me, with two dog-sledges, and fifteen dogs, dragging twenty-four days' provisions. My object is to communicate with the Boothians in the vicinity of the magnetic pole. Young takes his party of four men and his dog-sledge; he will carry forward provisions for his spring exploration of the shores of Prince of Wales' Land, between the extreme points reached by Lieutenant Osborn, and Lieutenant Browne, in 1851.

On the 3rd I walked for seven hours and a half, and saw two reindeer, but could not approach within shot. Young examined the water-space in the strait, and finds it washes both shores, but extends east and west only about one mile. The Doctor has seen a seal and a dovekie sporting in it.

For the last four days strong winds and intense cold have prevented us from rambling over the hills, besides which the minor preparations for travelling have given us more occupation on board.

James Pitcher has got a slight touch of scurvy; his gums are inflamed; and now it comes out that he dislikes preserved meats, and has not eaten any since he has been in the ship. He has lived upon salt meat and preserved vegetables, except for the very short periods in summer when birds could be obtained. He is rather a "used up" old fellow, too much so for our severe sledge-work, therefore is one of the few who will remain to take care of the ship.

That he should have retained his health for nineteen months, under the circumstances, speaks well for the wholesomeness and quality of our provisions, and the ventilation and cleanliness of the ship.

It may be interesting here to notice our dietary scale; it is hardly necessary to observe that there has been very little to vary it during all that time.

Briefly, it is a daily allowance of three-quarters of a pound of biscuit, or bread baked on board, on alternate days; three-quarters of a pound of salt beef, half a pound of preserved vegetables, half a pound of flour, and suet for a pudding; to be followed next day by three-quarters of a pound of salt pork, and pea soup; and on the third day by three-quarters of a pound of preserved meat, with a quarter of a pound of preserved potatoes.

Cranberries or preserved apples, and sugar, for a tart twice a week; and daily, an ounce of pickles, an ounce of lemon-juice, an eighth part of a pint of rum, also tea and chocolate.

We have not much time or space to devote to the growth of mustard and cress on board, so do but little in that way. In a former expedition we used to produce about thirty pounds of this agreeable antiscorbutic from six pounds of the seed in fourteen days, if kept at a temperature between 60° and 70°, and watered with lukewarm water frequently; in this way it was grown throughout the winter in wooden trays two feet long and one foot wide, and having two inches depth of earth in them. In summer the trays were placed in the most favourable situations on shore and covered with glass, when tolerable crops were also procured.

10*th*.—Extremely cold, with dense mists from the open water. Yesterday eight ptarmigan and a sooty fox were seen. We have consumed the last of our venison; it supplied us for three days. We are drinking out a cask of sugar beer, which is a very mild but agreeable beverage; we make it on board; our chief difficulty in manufacturing it is to prevent its temperature falling below 60°, when the process of fermentation would be checked; the cask is therefore kept close to the galley-fire, and at night, whilst the fire is out, it is covered with a pile of blankets. As this beer is a valuable antiscorbutic, is easily made, and much appreciated, I give its receipt.[1] I also give one for a still better beer; 700 gallons of it were made in H.M.S. 'Assistance,' one of the ships of the last expedition, during a single winter.[2]

Sunday night, 13*th*.—To-morrow morning, if fine, Young and I set off upon our travels. He has advanced a portion of his sledge-load to the west side of the water in Bellot Strait, having been obliged to carry it overland for about a mile in order to get there. I have explored the route to the long lake, and find we can reach it without crossing

---

[1] *Receipt for Sugar Beer.*—Boil 4 lbs. of hops in 30 gallons of water until they sink to the bottom; strain the liquor on to 45 lbs. of moist sugar, add 2 lbs. of mixed arrowroot, and strain off into a 30-gallon cask, and leave the bung out. When its temperature has fallen to 80°, add the yeast. It will ferment for 14 days, but its temperature must not be allowed to fall below 60°, and the froth thrown off must be received in a tub, and the cask frequently filled up with it. After the 14th day, add 2 lbs. of burnt sugar to colour it; two days after this bung it up, and if not disturbed, it will be fit for use in a fortnight, but would be improved by keeping a couple of months.

[2] *Receipt for Beer from Essence of Malt.*—120 lbs. of essence of malt, 4 lbs. of hops, 54 gallons of water, boiled together for two hours, and then strained into a 54-gallon cask, and kept near a fire, and at a temperature of about 70°. When its temperature has fallen to 90°, add ½ lb. of yeast in a state of fermentation, made by mixing dried yeast and sugar in hot water. Vigorous fermentation soon follows, and continues for 7 or 8 days. The froth thrown off to be received in a tub, and the cask constantly filled up with it. When fermentation ceases, the cask to be bunged up, removed, and a fortnight allowed to settle. This beer was then good, but would have improved by keeping. Three such casks were in constant use, one to issue from, one to settle, and one in a state of fermentation.

elevated or uncovered land. I saw two reindeer, and Young saw about twenty ptarmigan.

The mean temperature of February up to this date is $-33\cdot2°$, being an exact continuation of January. I confess to feeling some anxiety upon this point, as hitherto the winter has been unusually severe, and the journeys to be performed will occupy more than twenty days. Besides, we shall be earlier in motion than any of the previous travellers, unless we are to make an exception in favour of Mr. Kennedy's trip of thirty miles from Batty Bay to Fury Beach, between the 5th and 10th January, during which time the lowest temperature registered was only $-25°$. Should either Young or myself remain absent beyond the period for which we carry provisions, Hobson is to send a party in search of us. A sooty fox has been captured lately.

15th February.—A strong N.W. wind, with a temperature of $-40°$, confines us on board. One cannot face these winds, therefore it is fortunate that we did not start, the ship being much more comfortable than a snow-hut.

*   *   *   *   *   *

20th March.—Already I have been a week on board, and so difficult is it to settle down to anything like sedentary occupation, after a period of continued vigorous action, that even now I can scarcely sit still to scribble a brief outline of my trip to Cape Victoria.

On the morning of the 17th February the weather moderated sufficiently for us to set out; the temperature throughout the day varied between $-31°$ and $-42\frac{1}{2}°$. Leaving Young's party to pass on through the strait, I proceeded by way of Macgregor Laird Lake, which I found to be $10\frac{1}{2}$ geographical miles in length, with an average width of half a mile.

We built our snow-hut upon the west coast, near Pemmican Rock, after a march of 19 or 20 geographical miles. We always speak of *geographical* miles with reference to our marches; six geographical are equal to seven English miles.

On the following day the old N.W. wind sprang up with renewed vigour, and the thermometer fell to $-48°$; the cold was therefore *intense*.

On the third day most of our dogs went lame, in consequence of sore feet; the intense cold seems to be the principal, if not the only cause, having hardened the surface snow beyond what their feet can endure; it moreover so hardened the particles of snow that they resembled grains of sand, consequently the friction of the sledge-runners, and labour of the draft, were greatly increased. I was obliged to throw off a part of the provisions, still we could not make more than 15 or 18 miles daily. We, of course, walked, so that the dogs had only the remaining provisions and clothing to drag, yet several of them repeatedly fell down in fits.

For several days this severe weather continued, the mercury of my artificial horizon remaining frozen (its freezing-point is $-39°$); and our rum, at first thick like treacle, required thawing latterly, when the more fluid and stronger part had been used. We travelled each day until dusk, and then were occupied for a couple of hours in building our snow-hut. The four walls were run up until $5\frac{1}{2}$ feet high, inclining inwards as much as possible; over these our tent was laid to form a roof; we could not afford the time necessary to construct a dome of snow.

Our equipment consisted of a very small brown-holland tent, macintosh floor-cloth, and felt robes; besides this, each man had a bag of double blanketing, and a pair of fur boots, to sleep in. We wore mocassins over the pieces of blanket in which our feet were wrapped up, and, with the exception of a change of this foot-gear, carried no spare clothes. The daily routine was as follows:—I led the way; Petersen and Thompson followed, conducting their sledges; and in this manner we trudged on for eight or ten hours without halting, except when necessary to disentangle the dog-harness. When we halted for the night, Thompson and

I usually sawed out the blocks of compact snow and carried them to Petersen, who acted as the master-mason in building the snow hut: the hour and a half or two hours usually employed in erecting the edifice was the most disagreeable part of the day's labour, for, in addition to being already well tired and hungry, we became thoroughly chilled whilst standing about. When the hut was finished, the dogs were fed, and here the great difficulty was to insure the weaker ones their full share in the scramble for supper; then commenced the operation of unpacking the sledge, and carrying into our hut everything necessary for ourselves, such as provision and sleeping gear, as well as all boots, fur mittens, and even the sledge dog-harness, to prevent the dogs from eating them during our sleeping hours. The door was now blocked up with snow, the cooking-lamp lighted, foot-gear changed, diary written up, watches wound, sleeping bags wriggled into, pipes lighted, and the merits of the various dogs discussed, until supper was ready; the supper swallowed, the upper robe or coverlet was pulled over, and then to sleep.

Next morning came breakfast, a struggle to get into frozen mocassins, after which the sledges were packed, and another day's march commenced.

In these little huts we usually slept warm enough, although latterly, when our blankets and clothes became loaded with ice, we felt the cold severely. When our low doorway was carefully blocked up with snow, and the cooking-lamp alight, the temperature quickly rose, so that the walls became glazed, and our bedding thawed; but the cooking over, or the doorway partially opened, it as quickly fell again, so that it was impossible to sleep, or even to hold one's pannikin of tea, without putting our mitts on, so intense was the cold! The most enjoyable time in the twenty-four hours was shortly after the commencement of each day's march, when brisk exercise seldom failed to warm us up, and when fatigue and hunger had not yet made themselves felt.

On the 21st I visited our main depot laid out last October; it was safe, but unfortunately had been placed far into Wrottesley Inlet, and only 40 miles south of Bellot Strait.

On the 22nd an easterly gale prevented our marching, but we had the good fortune to shoot a bear, so consoled ourselves with fresh steaks, and the dogs with an ample feed of *unfrozen* flesh—a treat they had not enjoyed for many months.

We coasted along a granitic land, deeply indented and fringed with islands, and found it to be the general characteristic of the Boothian shore from Bellot Strait, until we had accomplished half the distance to the Magnetic Pole; limestone then appeared, and the remainder of our journey was performed along a low, straight shore, which afforded us much greater facility for sledging.

Throughout the whole distance we found a mixture of heavy old ice, and light ice of last autumn, in many places squeezed up into pack; but as we advanced southward, the old floes were less frequently seen.

On the 1st of March we halted to encamp at the supposed position of the Magnetic Pole—for no cairn remains to mark the spot. I had almost concluded that my journey would prove to be only labour in vain, because hitherto no traces of Esquimaux had been met with, and, in consequence of the reduced state of our provisions, and the wretched condition of the poor dogs—six out of the fifteen being quite useless—I could only advance one more march.

But we had done nothing more than look *ahead;* when we halted, and turned round, great indeed was my surprise and joy to see four men walking after us! Petersen and I immediately buckled on our revolvers, and advanced to meet them. The natives halted, made fast their dogs, laid down their spears, and received us without any evidence of surprise. They told us they had been out upon a seal hunt on the ice, and were returning home: we proposed to join them, and all were soon in motion again; but another hour brought sunset, and we learned that their village of eight snow huts was still a long way off, so we hired them, at the rate of a needle for each Esquimaux, to build us a hut, which they completed in an hour; it was 8 feet in diameter, 5½ feet high, and in it we all passed the night. Perhaps the records of architecture do not furnish another instance of a dwelling-house so cheaply constructed!

We gave them to understand that we were anxious to barter with them, and very cautiously approached the real object of our visit. A naval button upon one of their dresses afforded the opportunity; it came, they said, from some white people who were starved upon an island where there are salmon (that is, in a river); and that the iron of which their knives were made came from the same place. One of these men said he had been to the island to obtain wood and iron, but none of them had seen the white men. Another man had been to "Ei-wil-lik" (Repulse Bay), and counted on his fingers seven individuals of Dr. Rae's party whom he remembered having seen.

These Esquimaux had nothing to eat, and no other clothing than their ordinary double dresses of fur; they would not eat our biscuit or salt pork, but took a small quantity of bear's blubber and some water. They slept in a sitting posture, with their heads leaning forward on their breasts. Next morning we travelled about 10 miles farther, by which time we were close to Cape Victoria; beyond this I would not go, much as they wished to lead us on; we therefore landed, and they built us a commodious snow hut in half an hour; this done, we displayed to them our articles for barter—knives, files, needles, scissors, beads, &c. —expressed our desire to trade with them, and promised to purchase everything which belonged to the starved white men, if they would come to us on the morrow. Notwithstanding that the weather was now stormy and bitterly cold, two of the natives stripped off their outer coats of reindeer skin, and bartered them for a knife each.

Despite the gale which howled outside, we spent a comfortable night in our roomy hut.

Next morning the entire village population arrived, amounting to about forty-five souls, from aged people to infants in arms, and bartering commenced very briskly. First of all we purchased all the relics of the lost expedition, consisting of six silver spoons and forks, a silver medal, the property of Mr. A. M'Donald, assistant surgeon, part of a gold chain, several buttons, and knives made of the iron and wood of the wreck, also bows and arrows made out of materials obtained from the same source. Having secured these, we purchased a few frozen salmon, some seal's blubber and venison, but could not prevail upon them to part with more than one of their fine dogs. One of their sledges was made of two stout pieces of wood, which might have been a boat's keel.

All the old people recollected the visit of the 'Victory.' An old man told me his name was "Ooblooria :" I recollected that Sir James Ross had employed a man of that name as a guide, and reminded him of it; he was, in fact, the same individual, and he enquired after Sir James by his Esquimaux name of "Agglugga."

I enquired after the man who was furnished with a wooden leg by the carpenter of the 'Victory :' no direct answer was given, but his daughter was pointed out to me. Petersen explained to me that they do not like alluding in any way to the dead, and that, as my question was not answered, it was certain the man was no longer amongst the living.

None of these people had seen the whites : one man said he had seen their bones upon the island where they died, but some were buried. Petersen also understood him to say that the boat was crushed by the ice. Almost all of them had part of the plunder; they say they will be here when we return, and will trade more with us; also that we shall find natives upon Montreal Island at the time of our arriving there.

Next morning, 4th March, several natives came to us again. I bought a spear 6½ feet long from a man who told Petersen distinctly that a ship having three masts had been crushed by the ice out in the sea to the west of King William's Island, but that all the people landed safely; he was not one of those who were eye-witnesses of it; the ship sank, so nothing was obtained by the natives from her; all that they have got, he said, came from the island in the river. The spear staff appears to have been part of the gunwale of a light boat. One old man, "Oo-na-lee," made a rough sketch of the coast-line with his spear upon the snow, and said it was eight journeys to where the ship sank, pointing in the direction of Cape Felix. I can make nothing out of his rude chart.

The information we obtained bears out the principal statements of Dr. Rae, and also accounts for the disappearance of one of the ships; but it gives no clue to the whereabouts of the other, nor the direction whence the ships came. One thing has been ascertained by my journey—the crews did not at any time land upon the Boothian shore.

These Esquimaux were all well clothed in reindeer dresses, and looked clean; they appeared to have abundance of provisions, but scarcely a scrap of wood was seen with them which had not come from the lost expedition. Their sledges, with the exception of the one already spoken of, were wretched little affairs, consisting of two frozen rolls of sealskins coated with ice, and attached to each other by bones, which served as the crossbars. The men were stout, hearty fellows, and the women arrant thieves, but all were good-humoured and friendly. The women were decidedly plain; in fact, this term would have been flattering to most of them; yet there was a degree of vivacity and gentleness in the manners of some that soon reconciled us to these arctic specimens of the fair sex. They had fine eyes and teeth, as well as very small hands, and the young girls had a fresh rosy hue not often seen in combination with olive complexions.

Esquimaux mothers carry their infants on their backs within their large fur dresses, and where the babes can only be got at by pulling them out over the shoulder. Whilst intent upon my bargaining for silver spoons and forks belonging to Franklin's expedition, at the rate of a few needles or a knife for each relic, one pertinacious old dame after having obtained all she was likely to get from me for herself, pulled out her infant by the arm from its snug retreat in her fur robe, and quietly held the poor little creature, perfectly naked, before me in the breeze, the temperature at the time being 60° below freezing point! Petersen informed me that she was begging for a needle for her child. I need not say I gave her one as expeditiously as possible; yet before the infant was again put out of sight sufficient time elapsed to alarm me considerably for its safety in such a temperature. The natives, however, seemed to think nothing of what looked to me like cruel exposure of a naked baby.

We now returned to the ship with all the speed we were capable of; but stormy weather occasioned two days' delay, so that we did not arrive on board until the 14th March. Though considerably reduced in flesh, I and my companions were in excellent health, and blessed with insatiable appetites. On washing our faces, which had become perfectly black from the soot of our blubber lamp, sundry scars, relics of frost-bites, appeared; and the tips of our fingers, from constant frost-bites, had become as callous as if seared with hot iron.

In this journey of twenty-five days we travelled 360 geographical miles (420 English), and completed the discovery of the coast-line of continental America, thereby adding about 120 miles to our charts. The mean temperature throughout the journey was 30° below zero of Fahrenheit, or 62° below the freezing point of water.

On reaching the ship, I at once assembled my small crew, and told them of the information we had obtained, pointing out that there still remained one of the ships unaccounted for, and therefore it was necessary to carry out all our projected lines of search.

During this journey I acquired the arctic accomplishment of eating frozen bear's blubber, in delicate little slices on biscuit, and vastly preferred it to frozen pork. At the present moment I do not think I could even taste it, but the same privation and sense of starvation from *cold* rather than *hunger*, which induced me to eat it then, would doubtless enable me again to partake of it *very kindly*, if similarly "cooked with frost."

I shot a couple of foxes which came playing about the dogs; conscious of their superior speed, they were very impudent, snapping at the dogs' tails, and passing almost under their noses. I shot these foxes, intending to eat them; but the dogs anticipated me with respect to one; the other we feasted off at our mess-table; it proved insipid, but decidedly better to our tastes than preserved meat.

Young and his party had returned on board on the 3rd of March, having placed their depot upon the shore of Prince of Wales' Land, about 70 miles S.W. of the ship. Young found the ice in Bellot Strait so rough as to be impassable, and was obliged to adopt the lake route. Prince of Wales' Land was found to be composed of limestone; the shore was low, and fringed for a distance of ten miles to seaward with an ancient land-floe. The remaining width of the strait between this land (North Somerset) and Prince of Wales' Land was about 15 miles, and this space was composed of ice formed since September last; this was the water we looked at so anxiously last autumn from Cape Bird and Pemmican Rock. His party lived in their tent, protected from the wind by snow walls, and, like ourselves, escaped with a few trivial frost-bites. So far all was very satisfactory, the general health good, and the eagerness of my crew to commence travelling quite charming.

Young proposed carrying out another depot to the northwest, in order to explore well up Sir John Franklin Strait, and would have started on the 17th, but the weather was too severe. The day was spent in a fruitless search for three casks of sugar—a serious and unaccountable deficiency—but, as it was important to replace them with as little delay as possible, Young set off on the 18th, although it blew a N.W. gale at the time, with two men and eighteen dogs, for Fury Beach; failing to find the requisite quantity there, he will go on to Port Leopold.

Boothian Mother and Infant.

CHAPTER XIII.

Dr. Walker's sledge journey — Snow-blindness attacks Young's party Departure of all sledge-parties — Equipment of sledge-parties — Meet the same party of natives — Intelligence of the second ship — My depot robbed — Part company from Hobson — Matty Island — Deserted snow-huts — Native sledges — Land on King William's Land.

DOCTOR WALKER'S zeal for travelling was not to be restrained; I therefore gladly availed myself of his willingness to go with a party to Cape Airey and bring back the depot of provisions left there in August last. These trips will delay our spring journeys for a few days.

During my absence from the 'Fox' the weather was often stormy, and temperature unusually low; the mean for the month of February was $-36°$, showing it to be one of the coldest on record. When possible the men were allowed to go out shooting, and obtained fifty or sixty ptarmigan and a hare; a few foxes were taken in traps, and two reindeer were seen.

Yesterday two bears came near the ship, but were frightened away by the dogs. Hobson shot three ptarmigan. To-day I rambled over the hills, the weather being fine, and saw a hare.

29th.—Continued fine weather. A couple more foxes and a lemming in its *brown* (or summer) coat have been captured, and a hare and four ptarmigan shot. This fine bright weather seems to have awakened the lemmings and ermines; their tracks, which were very rarely seen during winter, are now tolerably numerous; foxes appear in greater numbers, probably following up the ptarmigan from the south. The thermometer ranges between zero and $-20°$; it has once been up to $+13°$. When exposed to a noon-day sun against the ship's side, it rises $50°$ higher. The earth-thermometer—placed 2 feet 2 inches beneath the surface—which gradually fell until the 10th of this month, has now begun to ascend; its minimum was $+\frac{1}{2}°$; much snow also lay over it, 6 feet deep at this season.

On the 25th Dr. Walker and his party returned, not having been able to find the depot. They found a barrel of flour upon the beach a few miles south of Brentford Bay; it appeared to have lain there for years, just inside a shingle projection, which kept off the ice pressure, so that it had not been forced up high upon the beach; the ice which bore it there—probably from Port Leopold—had disappeared, and the cask was frozen into the shingle. The heading has been brought on board, but the "scribing" upon it is very indistinct, and unintelligible to us. The flour is of the ordinary description used in the navy, and known as "seconds;" most of it was good, and a plain pudding made of it for our mess could not be distinguished from fresh flour. A specimen has been preserved with the view of identifying it with the Fury Beach or Port Leopold stores of flour; these stores were landed, the former in 1825 and the latter in 1848. With the exception of a solitary bear, the party saw no living creature. The shore along which they travelled was a very low shingly limestone.

Last evening I was delighted to see Young and his two dog-sledges heave in sight; he brought about 8 cwt. of sugar from Fury Beach, but not without much difficulty, owing to the roughness of the pack in Creswell Bay, and also to the breaking down of one of his sledges; to avoid this pack he found it necessary to travel nearly all round Creswell Bay.

Cape Garry he describes as a gradually curved extent of flat land, and not the decided cape it appears to be upon the chart; two reindeer were seen near it, and during the journey four bears; no other animals were met with. His labour has been very severe; one sledge broke down and all the sugar had to be piled upon the other: the consequence was that the sledge was so heavily loaded that it would only run freely after the dogs on smooth ice; and directly any hummocks were encountered, the dogs, with their usual instinct, not to drag a sledge unless it does run freely, would lie down, and oblige Captain Young and his two men to unload and carry the packages, over the obstacle, upon their own backs. After this, snow-blindness came on; Young and one of his men became blind as kittens; and the third man had to load, lead, and unload them, when these portages occurred. Young's Esquimaux dog-driver, Samuel, was quite blind when the party reached the ship. Two dogs, not choosing to allow themselves to be caught and put in harness, had been left behind at the last encampment.

This sugar formed part of the stores of H.M.S. 'Fury,' and was landed in 1825, when that ship was driven on shore and destroyed by the ice; there still remains at Fury Beach an immense stack of preserved vegetables and soups; the party supped off them and found them good. Young brought me back two specimen tins of "carrots plain" and "carrots and gravy." All small casks and packages were covered with snow; of the large ones which appeared through it, he saw thirty-four casks of flour, five of split peas, five of tobacco, and four of sugar. Only a very few tons of coals remained. There were two boats, a short four-oared gig and a large cutter; the former required nothing but caulking to make her serviceable, but the latter had a large portion of one bow and side cut out, as if for making, or repairing, flat sledges. No record was found.

We have now enough sugar to last us for seven or eight months, but by the survey of provisions which has just been completed, we find a deficiency of many other articles, including three casks of salt beef. Fortunately this is of no consequence, as we have abundance of both salted and preserved meat, but it shows the alarming extent to which a negligent steward may mislead one. This unfortunate man has now got scurvy; want of exercise and fresh air is the apparent cause, combined with irregular living; the spirits have hitherto been in his charge.

The bustle of preparation for the extended searching journeys has been exciting. Hobson's party and my own are now all prepared, and Young having returned, we purpose setting out on the 2nd April—God willing. Young's new sledge will be ready, and he will also start a few days after us. All our winter defences of snow—our porches, our deck-layer, and our external embankment—have been removed. Dr. Walker, of necessity, remains in charge of the ship, with two stewards, a cook, a carpenter, and a stoker. My party, as well as Hobson's, will be provisioned, including the depots, for an absence of about eighty-four days; but not being able to afford auxiliary or supporting sledge parties, much time will be occupied in transporting our depots farther out, in order that we may start with as much as we can possibly carry, from the Magnetic Pole, besides leaving there a depot for our return.

The declinometer was taken on board two days ago; hourly observations have been made with it for more than five months: we can no longer spare any one for this interesting duty.

* * * * * *

24th June.—One thing is certain, the wild sort of tent-life we lead in arctic exploration quite unfits one for such tame work as writing up a journal; my present attempt will illustrate the fact—yet with such ample materials what a deeply interesting volume might be written! Since I last opened this familiar old diary—the repository alike of dry facts and the most trivial incidents—winter has passed away, summer is far advanced, and the glorious sun is again returning southward. We, too, have endeavoured to move on with the times and seasons.

As for myself—I have visited Montreal Island, completed the exploration and circuit of King William's Island, passing on foot through the only feasible North-West Passage; but all this is as nothing to the interest attached to the FRANKLIN RECORDS picked up by Hobson, and now safe in my possession! The fate of the 'Erebus' and 'Terror,' and of their truly gallant but ill-fated crews, is *now* known to us. The sole object of our voyage has at length been completed, and we anxiously await the time when escape from these bleak regions will become practicable.

* * * * * *

The morning of April 2nd was inauspicious, but as the day advanced the weather improved, so that Hobson and I were able to set out upon our journeys; we each had a sledge drawn by four men, besides a dog-sledge, and dog-driver. Mr. Petersen having volunteered his services to drive my dogs—an offer too valuable to be declined—managed my dog-sledge throughout. Our five starveling puppies were harnessed, for the first time in their lives, to a small sledge which I drove myself, intending to sell them to the Esquimaux, if I could get them to drag their own supply of provisions so far. The procession looked imposing—it certainly was most deeply interesting; there were five sledges, twelve men, and seventeen dogs, the latter of all sizes and shapes. The ship hoisted the Royal Harwich Yacht flag, and our sledges displayed their gay silk banners; mine was a very beautiful one;

Starting of the Exploring Parties, 2nd April, 1859.

it bears the name of Lady Franklin in white letters upon a red ground, and is margined with white embroidery.

The equipment of my sledge-party and the weights of the several articles were as follows : those of Hobson and Young were almost precisely similar.

	lbs.
Two sledges and fittings complete … … … …	110
Tent, waterproof blanket, floorcloth, two sleeping-robes, and six blanket sleeping-bags … … …	90
Cooking-utensils, shovel, saw, snow-knife, and sundry small articles … … … … …	40
Sledge-gun and ammunition … … … … …	20
Magnetic and astronomical instruments … … …	60
Six knapsacks, containing spare clothing … …	60
Various tins and bags, in which provision and fuel were stored … … … … … … … …	50
Articles for barter … … … … … … …	40
Provisions … … … … … … … … …	930
Total … … … … … …	1400

The load for each man to drag was fixed at 200 lbs., and for each dog 100 lbs. Our provisions consisted mainly of pemmican, biscuit, and tea, with a small addition of boiled pork, rum, and some tobacco.

The men being untrained to the work, and sledges heavily laden, our march was fatiguing and slow. We encamped the first night upon the long lake. On the second day we reached the western sea, and upon the third, aided by our sledge sails—that is to say, our tents hoisted as sails, the tent poles serving as mast and yard—we advanced some miles beyond Arcedeckne Island.

The various depots carried out with so much difficulty and danger in the autumn were now gathered up as we advanced, until at length we were so loaded as to be compelled to proceed with one-half at a time, going three times over the same ground. For six days this tedious mode of progression was persevered in, by which time (15th April) we reached the low limestone shore in latitude 71° 7′ N., which continues thence in almost a straight line southward for 60 or 70 miles. We now commenced laying down provisions for our consumption upon the return journey; and the snow being unusually level, we were able to advance with the whole of our remaining provisions, amounting to nearly sixty days' allowance.

Hitherto the temperature continued low, often nearly 30° below zero, and at times with cutting north winds, bright sun, and intensely strong snow glare. Although we wore coloured spectacles, yet almost all suffered great inconvenience and considerable pain from inflamed eyes. Our faces were blistered, lips and hands cracked—never were men more disfigured by the combined effects of bright sun and bitterly cold winds; fortunately no serious frost-bites occurred, but frost-bitten faces and fingers were universal.

On 20th April, in latitude 70½° N., we met two families of natives, comprising twelve individuals; their snow huts were upon the ice three-quarters of a mile off shore, and their occupation was seal-hunting. They were the same people with whom I had communicated at Cape Victoria in February.

Old Oo-na-lee laid his hands on Petersen's shoulders to measure their width, and said, "He is fatter now:" true enough, the February temperature and sharp marching had caused us both at that time to shrink considerably.

Their snow huts were built in the annexed form, the common entrance and both passages being just sufficiently high to get in without having to crawl upon our hands and knees, and the widened parts serving as antechambers for articles which should remain frozen. A slab of ice in the roof admitted sufficient light. A snow bank or bench two feet high, and occupying half the area of each hut, was covered with reindeer skins, and formed the family place of repose. An angular snow bench served as the kitchen table, and

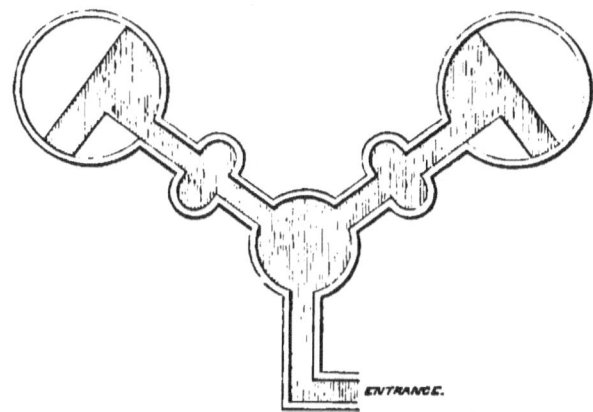

Plan of the Snow Huts.

immediately beside it sat the lady of the establishment attending the stone lamp which stood thereon, and the stone cooking vessel suspended over it. The lamp was a shallow open vessel, the fuel seal oil, and the wick dried moss. Her "tinder box" was a little seal-skin bag of soft dry moss, and with a lump of iron pyrites and a broken file she struck fire upon it. I purchased the file because it was marked with the Government broad arrow.

We saw two large snow shovels made of mahogany board, some long spear handles, a bow of English wood, two preserved meat tins, and a deal case which might have once contained a large telescope or a barometer; it measured 3 feet 1 inch in length by 9 inches wide and $3\frac{1}{2}$ inches deep; there was no lid, but part of the brass hinges remained.

I also purchased a knife which had some indistinct markings on it such as ship's cutlasses or swords usually have; the man told us it had been picked up on the shore near where a ship lay stranded; that it was then about the length of his arm, but his countryman who picked it up broke it into lengths to make knives.

After much anxious enquiry we learned that *two ships* had been seen by the natives of King William's Island; *one of them* was seen to sink in deep water, and nothing was obtained from her, a circumstance at which they expressed much regret; but *the other* was forced on shore by the ice, where they suppose she still remains, but is much broken. From this ship they have obtained most of their wood, &c.; Oot-loo-lik is the name of the place where she grounded.

Formerly many natives lived there, now very few remain. All the natives have obtained plenty of the wood.

The most of this information was given us by the young man who sold the knife. Old Oo-na-lee, who drew the rough chart for me in March, to show where the ship sank, now answered our questions respecting the one forced on shore; not a syllable about her did he mention on the former occasion, although we asked whether they knew of only one ship. I think he would willingly have kept us in ignorance of a wreck being upon their coasts, and that the young man unwittingly made it known to us.

The latter also told us that the body of a man was found on board the ship; that he must have been a very large man, and had long teeth: that is all he recollectad having been told, for he was quite a child at the time.

They both told us it was in the fall of the year—that is, August or September—when the ships were destroyed; that all the white people went away to the "large river," taking a boat or boats with them, and that in the following winter their bones were found there.

These two Esquimaux families had been up as far north as the Tasmania Group[1] in latitude $71\tfrac{1}{4}°$ N., and were

---

[1] These islands were so named by me, at the request of Lady Franklin, in grateful acknowledgment of many proofs of affectionate sympathy

returning to Něitchillěe, hunting seals by the way; those we met at Cape Victoria had already gone there. The nearest natives to us at present, they said, were residing at the island of Amitoke, ten days' journey distant from here. Can this Amitoke be Matty Island?

We purchased some seal's blubber and flesh, as well as their only two dogs; but next morning Oo-na-lee repented his bargain, or feigned to do so, but as he came back without the knife to exchange, we retained his dog; he tried to steal a tin vessel off one of the sledges, and perhaps it was for the purpose of regaining our favour that he made known to us, just as we were starting, that his countrymen had followed my homeward track in March, discovering my depot of blubber, articles of barter, and two revolvers, and carried them all off to Něitchillěe—by no means pleasant intelligence; their dogs must have enabled them to find the blubber by scenting it, for it was buried under 4 feet of snow, and strong winds had obliterated all traces upon the surface.

I was now glad we had purchased both the dogs of the men, as it would probably prevent their seeking for our depots to the northward; the knowledge of the insecurity of *all* depots amongst these people will keep us on our guard for the future. I regretted the loss of the pistols, as it left my party with no other arms than two guns.

Oo-na-lee told us when we first met him that one of his countrymen was very sick; not seeing a sick man in their huts, we forgot all about it until after starting, when Petersen interpreted to me Oo-na-lee's parting information, and told me how he described that the breech of the revolver turned round; it then occurred to me that one of the men

received from the colony of Van Dieman's Land, or Tasmania, over which her husband presided for several years, and, in particular, of the large contributions raised there in aid of her expeditions of search.

might have been wounded—they had discovered how to cock the locks, and the pistols were loaded and capped.

Oo-na-lee was well acquainted with the coast-line up to Bellot Strait, and had names for the different headlands, although he had never been so far north. He made many enquiries about the position of our ship, her size, and the number of men. Had he been able to travel so far with his wife and several young children, and without sledge or dogs, I think he certainly would have gone up to Port Kennedy; but we did not give him any encouragement to do so. His wife was one of the most importunate of the many women we saw at Cape Victoria in March. She was the woman who plucked out an infant by its arm from inside her dress, and exposed it regardless of temperature, $-30°$, and a fresh wind, as already related.

The information respecting *both* the missing ships was most important, and it remained for us to discover, if possible, the stranded ship.

Continuing our journey, we crossed a wide bay upon level ice, and the most perfectly smooth hard snow I ever saw; there must have been much open water here late last autumn. Seven or eight snow huts, recently abandoned, were found near the Magnetic Pole. During the 25th, 26th, and 27th we were confined to our tents by a very heavy south-east gale, with severe cold. During the gale it was very cold in our little tent, and the steam from our pemmican and tea, together with the moisture of our breath, condensed in considerable quantity on the inside, so that each flap caused a shower of fine snow to fall over us, penetrating and wetting our blanket bags. Early on the 28th we reached Cape Victoria; here Hobson and I separated. He marched direct for Cape Felix, King William's Land, whilst I kept a more southerly course. Not daring to leave depots upon this coast, we carried on our whole supply, intending to deposit a small portion upon the Clarence Islands.

Hobson was unwell when we parted, complaining of stiffness and pain in his legs; neither of us then suspected the cause. I gave him directions to search the west coast of King William's Island for the stranded ship and for records, and to act upon such information as he might obtain in this way, or from the natives; but should that shore prove destitute of traces, to carry out, if possible, our original plan for the completion of discovery and search upon Victoria Land, comprising the blank space between the extremes visited by Captain Collinson and Mr. Wynniatt.

I soon found that my party had to labour across a rough pack; nor was it until the third day that we completed the journey across the strait, and encamped near to the entrance of Port Parry, in King William's Island. Although the weather was clear, and that by our reckoning we passed directly over the assigned position of the two southern of the Clarence Islands, yet we saw nothing of them.

A day was devoted to securing a depot in a huge mass of grounded ice, and in repairing and drying equipments, or, to speak more correctly, in getting rid of the ice which encumbered our sleeping bags and gear; this we effected by beating them well and exposing them to the direct rays of the sun. Magnetic and other observations gave me ample employment, the only *immediate* result of which was my being almost snow-blind for the two following days.

On May 2nd we set off again briskly; our load being diminished to thirty days' provisions, and the sledge sail set, we soon reached the land, and travelled along it for Cape Sabine; it was very thick weather, and we were unable to see any distance in consequence of the mist and snowdrift. The following day was no better, and as the shore was extremely low, we dared not venture upon leaving it to cross the bays and indentations, lest we should lose our way; for be it remembered that in such proximity to the Magnetic Pole the compass is wholly useless.

We soon discovered that we had strayed inland; but, guided by the wind, continued our course. Upon May 4th we descended into Wellington Strait, and the weather being tolerably clear, we crossed over to the south-west extreme of Matty Island, in the hope of meeting with natives, no traces of them having been met with since leaving Cape Victoria. Off this south-west point we found a deserted village of nearly twenty snow huts, besides several others, within a few miles upon either side of it; in all of them I found shavings or chips of different kinds of woods from the lost expedition; they appeared to have been abandoned for only a fortnight or three weeks. Abundance of blubber was gathered up to increase our stock of fuel, and, had we encamped here, the dogs would have feasted sumptuously off the scraps and bones of seals strewed about.

The runners (or sides) of some old sledges left here were very ingeniously formed out of pointed rolls of sealskin, about 3½ feet long, and flattened so as to be 2 or 3 inches wide and 5 inches high; the sealskins appeared to have been well soaked and then rolled up, flattened into the required form and allowed to freeze. The underneath part was coated with a mixture of moss and ice laid smoothly on by hand before being allowed to freeze, the moss, I suppose, answering the purpose of hair in mortar, to make the compound adhere more firmly.

From this spot the shore-line of Matty Island turned sharply to the N.N.E.; there were some considerable islands to the east, but thinking the most southerly of this group—named "Owut-tā" by the Esquimaux—the most likely place to find the natives, I pushed on in that direction until we encamped. Thick fog enveloped us for the next two days;

we could not find the island, but found a very small islet near it, off which was another snow village very recently abandoned, the sledge tracks plainly showing that the inhabitants had gone to the E.N.E., which is straight for Nĕitchīllĕe. It was now evident that these places of winter resort were deserted, and that here at least we should not find any natives; I was the more sorry at having missed them, as, from the quantity of wood-chips about the huts, they probably had visited the stranded ship alluded to by the last Esquimaux we had met, and the route to which lies up an inlet visible from here, and then overland three or four days' journey to the westward, until the opposite coast of King William's Land is reached.

The largest huts measured 12 feet in diameter, by 6 or 7 feet high; most of them were constructed in pairs, having a passage 20 or 25 feet long, which served as the common entrance; at the place where this passage divided into two branches, there was a small hut, which served as a sort of antechamber for the reception of such articles as were intended to remain frozen.

Sledge under Sail.

CHAPTER XIV.

Meet Esquimaux — News of Franklin's people — Frighten a solitary party — Reach the Great Fish River — On Montreal Island — Total absence of all relics — Dog-driving — Examine Ogle Peninsula — Discover a skeleton — Vagueness of Esquimaux information — Cape Herschel — Cairn.

7th May.—To avoid snow-blindness, we commenced night-marching. Crossing over from Matty Island towards the shore of King William's Island, we continued our march southward until midnight, when we had the good fortune to arrive at an inhabited snow village. We found here ten or twelve huts and thirty or forty natives of King William's Island; I do not think any of them had ever seen white people alive before, but they evidently regarded us as friends. We halted at a little distance, and pitched our tent, the better to secure small articles from being stolen whilst we bartered with them.

I purchased from them six pieces of silver plate, bearing the crests or initials of Franklin, Crozier, Fairholme, and McDonald; they also sold us bows and arrows of English woods, uniform and other buttons, and offered us a heavy sledge made of two short stout pieces of curved wood, which no mere boat could have furnished them with, but this of course we could not take away; the silver spoons and forks were readily sold for four needles each.

They were most obliging and peaceably disposed, but could not resist the temptation to steal, and were importunate to barter everything they possessed. There was not a trace of fear, every countenance was lighted up with joy; even the children were not shy, nor backward either, in crowding about us, and poking in everywhere. One man got hold of our saw, and tried to retain it, holding it behind his back, and presenting his knife in exchange; we might have had some trouble in getting it from him, had not one of my men mistaken his object in presenting the knife towards me, and run out of the tent with a gun in his hand; the saw was instantly returned, and these poor people seemed to think they never could do enough to convince us of their friendliness; they repeatedly tapped me gently on the breast, repeating the words "Kammik toomee" (We are friends).

Having obtained all the relics they possessed, I purchased some seal's flesh, blubber, frozen venison, dried and frozen salmon, and sold some of my puppies. They told us it was five days' journey to the wreck—one day up the inlet still in sight, and four days overland; this would bring them to the western coast of King William's Island; they added that but little now remained accessible of the wreck, their countrymen having carried almost everything away. In answer to an enquiry, they said she was without masts; the question gave rise to some laughter amongst them, and they spoke to each other about *fire*, from which Petersen thought they had burnt the masts through close to the deck in order to get them down.

There had been *many books*, they said, but all have long ago been destroyed by the weather; the ship was forced on shore in the fall of the year by the ice. She had not been visited during this past winter, and an old woman and a boy were shown to us who were the last to visit the wreck; they said they had been at it during the preceding winter (*i. e.* 1857–8).

Petersen questioned the woman closely, and she seemed anxious to give all the information in her power. She said many of the white men dropped by the way as they went to the Great River; that some were buried and some were not; they did not themselves witness this, but discovered their bodies during the winter following.

We could not arrive at any approximation to the numbers of the white men nor of the years elapsed since they were lost.

This was all the information we could obtain, and it was with great difficulty so much could be gleaned, the dialect being strange to Petersen, and the natives far more inclined to ask questions than to answer them. They assured us we should find natives upon the south shore of King William's Island only three days' journey from here, and also at Montreal Island; moreover they said we might find some at the wreck. For these reasons I did not prolong my stay with them beyond a couple of hours. They seemed to have but little intercourse with other communities, not having heard of our visit to the Boothians two months before: one man even asked Petersen if he had seen his brother, who lived in Boothia, not having heard of him since last summer.

It was quite a relief to get away from these good-humoured, noisy thieves, and rather difficult too, as some of them accompanied us for miles. They had abundance of food, were well clothed, and are a finer race than those who inhabit North Greenland, or Pond's Inlet: the men had their hair cropped short, with the exception of one long, straggling lock hanging down on each side of the face; like the Boothians, the women had lines tattooed upon their cheeks and chins.

We now proceeded round a bay which I named Latrobe, in honour of the late Governor of Victoria, and of his brother, the head of the Moravian Church in London, both esteemed friends of Franklin.

Finding the "Mathison Island" of Rae to be a flat-topped hill, we crossed over low land to the west of it, and upon the morning of the 10th May reached a single snow hut off Point Booth. I was quite astonished at the number of poles and various articles of wood lying about it, also at the huge pile of walrus' and reindeer's flesh, seal's blubber, and skins of various sorts. We had abundance of leisure to examine these exterior articles before the inmates would venture out; they were evidently much alarmed by our sudden appearance.

A remarkably fine old dog was tied at the entrance—the line being made fast within the long passage—and although he wagged his tail, and received us as old acquaintances, we did not like to attempt an entrance. At length an old man and an old woman appeared; they trembled with fear, and could not, or would not, say anything except "Kammik toomee:" we tried every means of allaying their fears, but their wits seemed paralysed, and we could get no information. We asked where they got the wood? They purchased it from their countrymen. Did they know the Great River? Yes, but it was a long way off. Were there natives there now? Yes. They even denied all knowledge of white people having died upon their shores. A fine young man came out of the hut, but we could learn nothing of him; they said they had nothing to barter, except what we saw, although we tempted them by displaying our store of knives and needles.

The wind was strong and fair, and the morning intensely cold, and as I could not hope to overcome the fears of these poor people without encamping, and staying perhaps a day with them, I determined to push on, and presented the woman with a needle as a parting gift.

The principal articles which caught my attention here were eight or ten fir poles, varying in length from 5 to 10 feet, and up to 2½ inches in diameter (these were converted into spear handles and tent poles), a kayak paddle constructed out of the blades of two ash oars, and two large snow shovels 4 feet long, made of thin plank, painted white or pale yellow; these might have been the bottom boards of a boat. There were many smaller articles of wood.

Half a mile further on we found seven or eight deserted snow huts. Bad weather had now fairly set in, accompanied by a most unseasonable degree of cold. On the morning of the 12th May we crossed Point Ogle, and encamped upon the ice in the Great Fish River the same evening; the cold, and the darkness of our more southern latitude, having obliged us to return to day-travelling. All the 13th we were imprisoned in our tent by a most furious gale, nor was it until late on the morning of the 14th that we could proceed; that evening we encamped 2 miles from some small islands which lie off the north end of Montreal Island.

On the morning of the 15th we made only a short march of 6 miles, as one of the men suffered severely from snow-blindness, and I was anxious to recommence night-travelling; encamped in a little bay upon the N.E. side of Montreal Island. The same evening we again set out, although it was blowing very strongly, and "snowing for a wager," as the men expressed it, but it was only necessary for us to keep close along the shore of the island: we discovered, however, a narrow and crooked channel which led us through to the west side of the island, and, one of the men (Robert Hampton) appearing seriously ill, we encamped about midnight.

Whilst encamped this day, explorations were made about the N.E. quarter of the island; islets and rocks were seen to abound in all directions; eventually it proved to be a separate island upon which we had encamped. The only traces or relics of Europeans found were the following articles, discovered by Petersen, beside a native mark (one large stone set upright on the top of another), at the east side of the main—or Montreal—island:—A piece of a preserved meat tin, two pieces of iron hoop, some scraps of copper, and an iron hook-bolt. These probably are part of the plunder obtained from the boat, and were left here until a more favourable opportunity should offer, or perhaps necessity should compel the depositor to return for them.

All the 16th we were unable to move, not only because Hampton was still very ill, but the weather was extremely bad, and snow thickly falling with temperature at zero; certainly strange weather for the middle of May! We have not had a single clear day since the 1st of the month.

On the 17th the weather, though dull, was clear, so Mr. Petersen, Thompson, and I set off with the dog-sledge to complete the examination of Montreal Island, leaving the other three men with the tent: we also still hoped to find natives, although we had not seen any recent traces of them since passing Point Booth. Petersen drove the dog-sledge close along shore round the island to the south, and as far up the east side as to meet our previously explored portion of it, whilst Thompson and I walked along on the land, the one close down to the beach, and the other higher up, examining the more conspicuous parts: in this order we traversed the remaining portion of the island.

Although the snow served to conceal from us any traces which might exist in hollows or sheltered situations, yet it rendered all objects intended to serve as marks much more conspicuous; and we may remember that the retreating crews saw Montreal Island in its winter garb, precisely as we ourselves saw it. The island was almost covered with small native marks, usually of one stone standing upright upon another, sometimes consisting of three stones, but very rarely of a greater number.

No trace of a cairn could be found.

In examining, with pickaxe and shovel, a collection of stones which appeared to be arranged artificially, we found a quantity of seal's blubber buried beneath; this old Esquimaux *câche* was near the S.E. point of the island. The interior of the island and the principal islets adjacent were also examined without success, nor was there the slightest evidence of natives having been here during the winter: it is not to be wondered at that we returned in the evening to our tent somewhat dispirited. The total absence of natives was a bitter disappointment; circles of stones, indicating the sites of their tenting places in summer, were common enough.

Montreal Island is of primary rock, chiefly grey gneiss, traversed with whitish vertical bands in a north and south direction (by them I often directed my route when crossing the island). It is of considerable elevation, and extremely rugged. The low beaches and grassy hollows were covered with a foot or two of hard snow, whilst all the level, elevated, or exposed parts were swept perfectly bare; had a cairn, or even a grave, existed (raised as it must be, the earth being frozen hard as rock), we must at once have seen it. If any were ever constructed, they must have been levelled by the natives; every doubtful appearance was examined with the pickaxe.

A remark made by my men struck me as being shrewd; they judged from the washed appearance of the rock upon the east side of Montreal Island that it must often be exposed to a considerable sea, such as would effectually remove everything not placed far above its reach; when looking over the smooth and frozen expanse one is apt to forget this.

Since our first landing upon King William's Island we have not met with any heavy ice; all along its eastern and southern shore, together with this estuary of the Great Fish River, is one vast unbroken sheet formed in the early part of last winter, where *no ice previously existed;* this I fancy, from the accounts of Back and Anderson, is unusual, and may have caused the Esquimaux to vary their seal-hunting localities. Mr. Petersen suggested that they might have retired into the various inlets after the seals; and therefore I determined to cross over into Barrow's Inlet as soon as we had examined the Point Ogle Peninsula.

Upon Montreal Island I shot a hare and a brace of willow-grouse. Up to this date we had shot during our journey only one bear and a couple of ptarmigan. The first recent traces of reindeer were met with here.

On the 18th May crossed over to the mainland near Point Duncan, but, Hampton again complaining, I was obliged to encamp. When away from my party, and exploring along the shore towards Elliot Bay, I saw a herd of eight reindeer and succeeded in shooting one of them. In the evening Petersen shot another. Some willow-grouse also were seen. Here we found much more vegetation than upon King William's Island, or any other arctic land I have yet seen.

On the evening of the 19th May we commenced our return journey, but for the three following weeks our route led us over new ground. Hampton being unable to drag, I made over my puppy team to him, and was thus left free to explore and fully examine every doubtful object along our route. I shall not easily forget the trial my patience underwent during the six weeks I drove that dog-sledge. The leader of my team, named "Omar Pasha," was very willing, but very lame; little "Rose" was coquettish, and fonder of being caressed than whipped, from some cause or other she ceased growing when only a few months old, she was therefore far too small for heavy work; "Darky" and "Missy" were mere pups; and last of all came the two wretched starvelings, reared in the winter, "Foxey" and "Dolly." Each dog had its own harness, formed of strips of canvas, and was attached to the sledge by a single trace 12 feet long. None of them had ever been yoked before, and the amount of cunning and perversity they displayed to avoid both the whip and the work was quite astonishing. They bit through their traces, and hid away under the sledge, or leaped over one another's backs, so as to get into the middle of the team out of the way of my whip, until the traces became plaited up, and the dogs were almost knotted together; the consequence was I had to halt every few minutes, pull off my mitts, and, at the risk of frozen fingers, disentangle the lines. I persevered, however, and, without breaking any of their bones, succeeded in getting a surprising amount of work out of them. Their strength and endurance are astonishing. When an Esquimaux dog feels the whip, he usually bites his neighbour; the bite is passed along to the next, and a general fight and howling match ensues; then the driver lays about him with the whip-handle until order is restored. Hobson drove his own dog-sledge likewise, and as long as we were together, we helped each other out of difficulties; and they were frequently occurring, for, apart from those I have above mentioned, directly a dog-sledge is stopped by a hummock, or sticks fast in deep snow, the dogs, instead of exerting themselves, lie down, looking perfectly delighted at the circumstance, and the driver has to extricate the sledge with a hearty, one, two, three haul! and apply no trifling persuasion to set his canine team in motion again.

Having searched the east shore of this land for 7 or 8 miles farther north, we crossed over into Barrow's Inlet, and spent a day in its examination, but not a trace of natives was met with.

Regaining the shore of Dease and Simpson's Strait, some miles to the west of Point Richardson, we crossed over to King William's Island upon the morning of the 24th, striking in upon it a short distance west of the Peffer River. The south coast was closely examined as we marched along towards Cape Herschel. Upon a conspicuous point, to the westward of Point Gladman, a cairn nearly five feet high was seen, which, although it did not appear to be a recent construction, was taken down, stone by stone, carefully examined, and the earth beneath was broken up with the pickaxe, but nothing was discovered.

The ground about it was much exposed to the winds, and consequently devoid of snow, so that no trace could have escaped us. Simpson does not mention having landed here or anywhere upon the island, except at Cape Herschel; yet it seemed to me strange that natives should construct such a mark here, since a huge boulder, which would equally serve their purpose, stood upon the same elevation, and within a couple of hundred yards. We had previously examined a similar but smaller cairn, a few miles to the eastward.

We were now upon the shore along which the retreating crews must have marched. My sledges, of course, travelled upon the sea-ice close along the shore; and although the depth of snow which covered the beach deprived us of almost every hope, yet we kept a very sharp look-out for traces, nor were we unsuccessful. Shortly after midnight of the 25th May, when slowly walking along a gravel ridge near the beach, which the winds kept partially bare of snow, I came upon a human skeleton, partly exposed, with here and there a few fragments of clothing appearing through the snow. The skeleton—now perfectly bleached—was lying upon its face, the limbs and smaller bones either dissevered or gnawed away by small animals.

A most careful examination of the spot was, of course,

made, the snow removed, and every scrap of clothing gathered up. A pocket-book afforded grounds for hope that some information might be subsequently obtained respecting the unfortunate owner and the calamitous march of the lost crews, but at the time it was frozen hard. The substance of that which we gleaned upon the spot may thus be summed up :—

This victim I supposed to have been a young man, slightly built, and perhaps above the common height; the dress appeared to be that of a steward or officer's servant, the loose bow-knot in which his neck-handkerchief was tied not being used by seamen or officers. In every particular the dress confirmed our conjectures as to his rank or office in the late expedition—the blue jacket with slashed sleeves and braided edging, and the pilot-cloth great-coat with plain covered buttons. We found, also, a small clothes-brush near, and a horn pocket-comb, in which a few light-brown hairs still remained. This poor man seems to have selected the bare ridge top, as affording the least tiresome walking, and to have fallen upon his face in the position in which we found him. It is probable that, hungry and exhausted, he suffered himself to fall asleep when in this position, and that his last moments were undisturbed by suffering; at least I felt strongly impressed with this idea, and the spectacle before me brought most forcibly to my recollection the extreme danger of being overcome by sleep under intense cold.

It was a melancholy truth that the old woman spoke when she said, "they fell down and died as they walked along."

Of this skeleton only a portion of the skull appeared above the snow, and it so strongly resembled a bleached rounded stone that the man I called from the sledge, mistaking it for one, rested his shovel upon it, but started back with horror when the hollow sound revealed to him its true nature.

Were it not for their shroud of snow, it is more than probable that our anxious search would have brought to light many another skeleton, and have still further confirmed the old woman's brief story—unsurpassed in graphic simplicity.

I do not think the Esquimaux had discovered this skeleton, or they would have carried off the brush and comb: superstition prevents them from disturbing their own dead, but would not keep them from appropriating the property of the white man if in any way useful to them. Dr. Rae obtained a piece of flannel, marked, "F. D. V., 1845," from the Esquimaux of 'Boothia or Repulse Bay: it had doubtless been a part of poor Des Vœux's garments.

At the time of our interview with the natives of King William's Island, Petersen was inclined to think that the retreat of the crews took place in the fall of the year, some of the men in boats, and others walking along the shore; and as only five bodies are said to have been found upon Montreal Island with the boat, this fact favoured his opinion, because so small a number could not have dragged her there over the ice, although they could very easily have taken her there by water. Subsequently this opinion proved to be erroneous. I mention it because it shows how vague our information was—indeed all Esquimaux accounts involving dates and numbers are necessarily so—and how entirely we were dependent upon our own exertions for bringing to light the mystery of their fate.

The information obtained by Dr. Rae was mainly derived second-hand from the Fish River Esquimaux, and should not be confounded with that received by us from the King William's Island Esquimaux. These people told us they did not find the bodies of the white men (that is, they did not know any had died upon the march) until the following winter. This is probably true, as it is only in winter and early spring they can travel overland to the west shore, or that they make a practice of wandering along the shore in search of seals and bears.

The remains of those who died in the Fish River may very probably have been discovered in the summer shortly after their decease: in fact, the Esquimaux report brought home by Dr. Rae does state that the bodies were found before the thaw.

Along the south coast of King William's Land, as upon the mainland, I was sadly disppointed in my expectation of meeting natives. We found only six or eight deserted snow huts, showing that they had recently been here, and consequently there was the less chance of meeting with them on our further progress, as the season had now arrived when they seek the rivers, and the favourite haunts and passes of the reindeer in their northern migration.

Hobson was however upon the western coast, and I hoped to find a note left for me at Cape Herschel containing some piece of good news. After minutely examining the intervening coast-line, it was with strong and reasonable hope I ascended the slope which is crowned by Simpson's conspicuous cairn. This summit of Cape Herschel is perhaps 150 feet high, and about a quarter of a mile within the low stony point which projects from it, and on which there was considerable ice pressure and a few hummocks heaped up, the first we had seen for three weeks. Close round this point, or by cutting across it as we did, the retreating parties *must* have passed; and the opportunity afforded by the cairn of depositing in a known position—and that, too, where their own discoveries terminated, including the *discovery of the North-West Passage*—some record of their own proceedings, or, it might be, a portion of their scientific journals, would scarcely have been disregarded.

Simpson makes no mention of having left a record in this cairn, nor would Franklin's people have taken any trouble

Cape Herschel, and Remains of Simpson's Cairn.

to find it if he had left one; but what now remained of this once "ponderous cairn" was only four feet high; the south side had been pulled down and the central stones removed, as if by persons seeking for something deposited beneath. After removing the snow with which it was filled, and a few loose stones, the men laid bare a large slab of limestone: with difficulty this was removed, then a second, and also a third slab, when they came to the ground. For some time we persevered with a pickaxe in breaking up the frozen earth, but nothing whatever was found, nor any trace of European visitors in its vicinity. There were many old *câches* and low stone walls, such as natives would use to lurk behind for the purpose of shooting reindeer; and we noticed some recent tracks of those animals which had crossed direct hither from the mainland.

CHAPTER XV.

The cairn found empty — Discover Hobson's letter — Discovery of Crozier's record — The deserted boat — Articles discovered about the boat — The skeletons and relics — The boat belonged to the 'Erebus' — Conjectures.

As the Esquimaux of this land, as well as those of Boothia and Pond's Inlet, have long since given up the practice of building stone dwellings — passing their winters in snow huts and summers in tents — no other traces of them than those described remain; so that when or in what numbers they may have been here, one cannot form any opinion, the same *caches* and hiding-places serving for generations.

I cannot divest myself of the belief that *some record was left here* by the retreating crews, and perhaps some most valuable documents which their slow progress and fast failing strength would have assured them could not be carried much further. If any such were left, they have been discovered by the natives, and carried off, or thrown away as worthless. Doubtless the natives, when they ascertained that famine and fatigue had caused many of the white men "to fall down and die" upon their fearful march, and heard, as they might have done, of its fatal termination upon the mainland, lost no time in following up their traces, examining every spot where they halted, every mark they put up, or stone displaced.

It is easy to tell whether a cairn has been put up or touched within a moderate period of years; if very old, the outer stones have a weathered appearance, lichens will have grown upon the sheltered portions and moss in the crevices;

but if recently disturbed, these appearances are altered. If a cairn has been recently built, it will be evident, because the stones picked up would be bleached on top by the exposure of centuries, whilst underneath they would be coloured by the soil in which they were imbedded. When at Melville Island, in 1853, I visited several places explored by Parry in 1820, and was perfectly astonished at the freshness which his traces presented; at one place the rut of his cart-wheels was distinctly impressed in spungy moss; the stones with which his cairn was built retained the colouring of the earth on the one side, the other being bleached with the frosts of ages; even their impressions remained so distinct that we could have replaced several of them in their own moulds in the earth from which Parry had removed them thirty-three years before! To the observant eye of the native hunter these marks are at once apparent; and, therefore, unless Simpson's cairn (built in 1839) had been disturbed by Crozier, I do not think the Esquimaux would have been at the trouble of pulling it down to plunder the *cache;* but, having commenced to do so, would not have left any of it standing, *unless they found what they sought.*

I noticed with great care the appearance of the stones, and came to the conclusion that the cairn itself had been erected many years ago, but was reduced to the state in which we found it by people having broken down one side of it, the displaced stones, from being turned over, looking far more fresh than those in that portion of the cairn which had been left standing. It was with a feeling of deep regret and much disappointment that I left this spot without finding some certain record of those martyrs to their country's fame.

A few miles beyond Cape Herschel the land becomes very low; many islets and shingle-ridges lie far off the coast; and as we advanced, we met with hummocks of unusually heavy ice, showing plainly that we were now travelling upon a far more exposed part of the coast-line. We were approaching a spot where a revelation of intense interest was awaiting me.

About 12 miles from Cape Herschel I found a small cairn built by Hobson's party, and containing a note for me. He had reached this, his extreme point, six days previously, without having seen anything of the wreck, or of natives, but he had found a record[1]—THE RECORD so ardently sought for of the Franklin Expedition—at Point Victory, on the N.W. coast of King William's Land.

That record is indeed a sad and touching relic of our lost friends, and, to simplify its contents, I will point out separately the double story it so briefly tells. In the first place, the record paper was one of the printed forms usually supplied to discovery ships for the purpose of being enclosed in bottles and thrown overboard at sea, in order to ascertain the set of the currents, blanks being left for the date and position; any person finding one of these records is requested to forward it to the Secretary of the Admiralty, with a note of time and place; and this request is printed upon it in six different languages. Upon it was written as follows :—

"28th of May, 1847. H. M. ships 'Erebus' and 'Terror' wintered in the ice in lat. 70° 05' N., long. 98° 23' W. Having wintered in 1846–7 at Beechey Island, in lat. 74° 43' 28" N., long. 91° 39' 15" W., after having ascended Wellington Channel to lat. 77°, and returned by the west side of Cornwallis Island.

"Sir John Franklin commanding the expedition.

"All well.

"Party consisting of 2 officers and 6 men left the ships on Monday, 24th May, 1847.

"GM. GORE, Lieut.
"CHAS. F. DES VŒUX, Mate."

There is an error in the above document, namely, that the

---

[1] The stains upon the record—as represented in the facsimile—were caused by the rusting of the tin cylinder in which it was contained (see p. 257): the original record, together with all the relics brought home in the 'Fox,' have been deposited in the Museum of the United Service Institution, Whitehall Yard.

'Erebus' and 'Terror' wintered at Beechey Island in 1846-7, —the correct dates should have been 1845-6 ; a glance at the date at the top and bottom of the record proves this, but in all other respects the tale is told in as few words as possible of their wonderful success up to that date, May, 1847.

We now know that, after the last intelligence of Sir John Franklin was received (bearing date 26th July, 1845) from the whalers in Melville Bay, his Expedition passed on to Lancaster Sound, and entered Wellington Channel, of which the southern entrance had been discovered by Sir Edward Parry in 1819. The 'Erebus' and 'Terror' sailed up that strait for one hundred and fifty miles, and reached in the autumn of 1845 the same latitude as was attained seven years subsequently by H.M.S. 'Assistance ' and ' Pioneer.' Whether Franklin intended to pursue this northern course, and was only stopped by ice in that latitude of 77° north, or purposely relinquished a route which seemed to lead away from the known seas off the coast of America, must be a matter of conjecture ; but the document assures us of one thing, that Sir John Franklin's Expedition, having accomplished this examination, returned southward from latitude 77° north, which is at the head of Wellington Channel, and re-entered Barrow's Strait by a new channel between Bathurst and Cornwallis Islands.

Seldom has such an amount of success been accorded to an arctic navigator in a single season, and when the 'Erebus' and 'Terror' were secured at Beechey Island for the coming winter of 1845-6, the results of their first year's labour must have been most cheering. These results were the exploration of Wellington and Queen's Channel, and the addition to our charts of the extensive lands on either hand. In 1846 they proceeded to the south-west, and eventually reached within twelve miles of the north extreme of King William's Land, when their progress was arrested by the approaching winter of

1846-7. That winter appears to have passed without any serious loss of life; and when in the spring Lieutenant Gore leaves with a party for some especial purpose, and very probably to connect the unknown coast-line of King William's Land between Point Victory and Cape Herschel, those on board the 'Erebus' and 'Terror' were "all well," and the gallant Franklin still commanded.

But, alas! round the margin of the paper upon which in 1847 those words of hope and promise were written, the following words had subsequently been faintly traced :—

"April 25, 1848.—H. M. ships 'Terror' and 'Erebus' were deserted on the 22nd April, 5 leagues N.N.W. of this, having been beset since 12th September, 1846. The officers and crews, consisting of 105 souls, under the command of Captain F. R. M. Crozier, landed here in lat. 69° 37' 42" N., long. 98° 41' W. Sir John Franklin died on the 11th June, 1847; and the total loss by deaths in the expedition has been to this date 9 officers and 15 men.

(Signed)	(Signed)
" F. R. M. CROZIER,	" JAMES FITZJAMES,
" Captain and Senior Officer.	" Captain H. M. S. 'Erebus.'
"and start (on) to-morrow, 26th, for Back's Fish River."	

With the exception of the signatures, and the note stating when and where they were going, which was added by Captain Crozier, the whole record was written by Captain Fitzjames.

There is some additional marginal information relative to the transfer of the document to its present position : I insert it here by itself, having omitted it in its proper place in order to simplify the more interesting part of the record.

"This paper was found by Lt. Irving under the cairn supposed to have been built by Sir James Ross in 1831, 4 miles to the northward, where it had been deposited by the late Commander Gore in June, 1847. Sir James Ross' pillar has not, however, been found, and the paper has been transferred to this position, which is that in which Sir James Ross' pillar was erected."

This little word *late* shows us that poor Graham Gore was one of those who had passed away within the twelvemonth.

In the short space of twelve months how mournful had become the history of Franklin's expedition; how changed from the cheerful "All well" of Graham Gore! The spring of 1847 found them within 90 miles of the known sea off the coast of America; and to men who had already in two seasons sailed over 500 miles of previously unexplored waters, how confident must they then have felt that that forthcoming navigable season of 1847 would see their ships pass over so short an intervening space! It was ruled otherwise. Within a month after Lieutenant Gore placed the record on Point Victory, the much-loved leader of the expedition, Sir John Franklin, was dead; and the following spring found Captain Crozier, upon whom the command had devolved, at King William's Land, endeavouring to save his starving men, 105 souls in all, from a terrible death by retreating to the Hudson Bay territories up the Back or Great Fish River.

So sad a tale was never told in fewer words. There is something deeply touching in their extreme simplicity, and they show in the strongest manner that both the leaders of this retreating party were actuated by the loftiest sense of duty, and met with calmness and decision the fearful alternative of a last bold struggle for life, rather than perish without effort on board their ships; for we well know that the 'Erebus' and 'Terror' were only provisioned up to July, 1848.

Lieutenant Hobson's note also told me that he had experienced extremely bad weather—constant gales and fogs—and thought he might have passed the wreck without seeing her; he hoped to be more successful upon his return journey.

Encouraged by this important news, we exerted our utmost vigilance in order that no trace should escape us.

Our provisions were running very short, therefore the three remaining puppies were of necessity shot, and their sledge used for fuel. We were also enabled to lengthen our journeys, as we had very smooth ice to travel over, the off-lying islets keeping the rough pack from pressing in upon the shore.

Upon the 29th of May we reached the western extreme of King William's Island, in lat. 69° 08′ N., and long 100° 08′ W. I named it after Captain Crozier of the 'Terror,' the gallant leader of that "Forlorn Hope" of which we had just now obtained tidings. The coast we marched along was extremely low—a mere series of ridges of limestone shingle, almost destitute of fossils. The only tracks of animals seen were those of a bear and a few foxes—the only living creatures a few willow-grouse. Traces even of the wandering Esquimaux became much less frequent after leaving Cape Herschel. Here were found only a few circles of stones, the sites of tenting-places, but so moss-grown as to be of great age. The prospect to sea was not less forbidding—a rugged surface of crushed-up pack, including much heavy ice. In these shallow and perpetually ice-packed channels, seals are but seldom found; and it is highly probable that all animal life in them is as scarce as upon the land.

From Cape Crozier the coast-line was found to turn sharply away to the eastward; and early in the morning of the 30th May we encamped alongside a large boat—another painful relic which Hobson had found and examined a few days before, as his note left here informed me; but he had failed to discover record, journal, pocket-book, or memorandum of any description.

A vast quantity of tattered clothing was lying in her, and this we first examined. Not a single article bore the name of its former owner. The boat was cleared out and carefully swept that nothing might escape us. The snow was then removed from about her, but nothing whatever was found.

This boat measured 28 feet long, and 7 feet 3 inches wide; she was built with a view to lightness and light draught of water, and evidently equipped with the utmost care for the ascent of the Great Fish River; she had neither oars nor rudder, paddles supplying their place; and as a large remnant of light canvas, commonly known as No. 8, was found, and also a small block for reeving a sheet through, I suppose she had been provided with a sail. A sloping canvas roof or rain-awning had also formed part of her equipment. She was fitted with a weather-cloth 9 inches high, battened down all round the gunwale, and supported by 24 iron stanchions, so placed as to serve likewise for rowing thowells. There was a deep-sea sounding line, fifty fathoms long, near her, as well as an ice-grapnel; this line must have been intended for river work as a track line. She had been originally "carvel" built; but for the purpose of reducing weight, very thin fir planks had been substituted for her seven upper strakes, and put on "clincher" fashion.

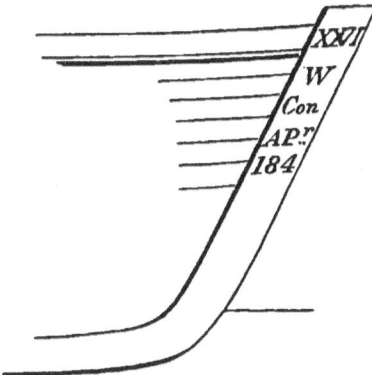

The only markings about the boat were those cut in upon her stem; besides giving her length, they indicated that she was built by contract, numbered 61, and received into Woolwich Dockyard in April, 184—; the fourth figure to the right hand was lost, as the stem had been reduced as much as possible in order to lessen her weight; from this cause part of the Roman numerals indicating her length were also lost.

The weight of the boat alone was about 700 or 800 lbs. only, but she was mounted upon a sledge of unusual weight and strength. It was constructed of two oak planks 23 feet 4 inches in length, 8 inches in width, and with an average thickness of $2\frac{1}{2}$ inches. These planks formed the sides or runners of the sledge; they were connected by five cross-bars of oak, each 4 feet long, and 4 inches by $3\frac{1}{2}$ inches thick, and bolted down to the runners; the underneath parts of the latter were shod with iron. Upon the cross-bars five saddles or supporting chocks for the boat were lashed, and the drag-ropes by which the crew moved this massive sledge, and the weights upon it, consisted of $2\frac{3}{4}$-inch whale-line.

I have calculated the weight of this sledge to be 650 lbs.; it could not have been less, and may have been considerably more. The total weight of boat and sledge may be taken at 1400 lbs., which amounts to a heavy load for seven strong healthy men.

The ground the sledge rested upon was the usual limestone shingle, perfectly flat and probably overflowed at times every summer, as the stones were imbedded in ice.

The boat was partially out of her cradle upon the sledge, and lying in such a position as to lead me to suppose it the effect of a violent north-west gale. She was barely, if at all, above the reach of occasional tides.

One hundred yards from her, upon the land side, lay the stump of a fir-tree 12 feet long, and 16 inches in diameter at 3 feet above the roots. Although the ice had used it roughly during its drift to this shore, and rubbed off every vestige of bark, yet the wood was perfectly sound. It may have been and probably has been lying there for twenty or thirty years, and during such a period would suffer less decay in this region of frost than in one-sixth of the time at home. Within two yards of it I noticed a few scanty tufts of grass.

But all these were after observations; there was in the boat that which transfixed us with awe, viz., portions of two human skeletons! One was that of a slight young person; the other of a large, strongly-made, middle-aged man. The former was found in the bow of the boat, but in too much disturbed a state to enable Hobson to judge whether the sufferer had died there; large and powerful animals, probably wolves, had destroyed much of this skeleton, which may have been that of an officer. Near it we found the fragment of a pair of worked slippers, of which I give the pattern, as they may possibly be identified. The lines were white, with a black margin; the spaces white, red, and yellow. They had originally been 11 inches long, lined with calf-skin with the hair left on, and the edges bound with red silk ribbon. Besides these slippers there were a pair of small strong shooting half-boots.

The other skeleton was in a somewhat more perfect state; it lay across the boat, under the after-thwart, and was enveloped with cloths and furs. This would seem to have been the survivor of the two men whose remains were lying in the boat. Close beside it were found five watches; and there were two double-barrelled guns—one barrel in each loaded and cocked—standing muzzle upwards against the boat's side. It may be imagined with what deep interest these sad relics were scrutinised, and how anxiously every fragment of clothing was turned over in search of pockets and pocket-books, journals, or even names. Five or six small books were found, all of them scriptural or devotional works, except the 'Vicar of Wakefield.' One little book, 'Christian Melodies,' bore an inscription upon the title-page from the donor to G. G. (Graham Gore?). Another small book, 'A Manual of Private Devotion, by C. J. Blomfield, D.D.,' bore on its title-page, "G. Back,[1] to Graham Gore. May, 1845." A small Bible contained numerous marginal notes, and whole passages underlined. Besides these books, the covers of a New Testament and Church of England Prayerbook were found.

Amongst an amazing quantity of clothing there were seven or eight pairs of boots of various kinds—cloth winter boots, sea boots, heavy ankle boots, and strong shoes. I noted that there were silk handkerchiefs—black, white, and figured—towels, soap, sponge, tooth-brush, and hair-combs; macintosh gun-cover, marked outside with paint A 12, and lined with black cloth. Besides these articles we found twine, nails, saws, files, bristles, wax-ends, sail-makers' palms, powder, bullets, shot, cartridges, wads, leather cartridge-case, knives—clasp and dinner ones, needle and thread cases, slow-match, several bayonet scabbards cut down into knife-sheaths, two rolls of sheet-lead, and, in short, a quantity of articles of one description and another truly astonishing in variety, and such as, for the most part, modern sledge-travellers in these regions would consider a mere accumulation of dead weight, of little use, and very likely to break down the strength of the sledge-crews.

The only provisions we could find were tea and chocolate; of the former very little remained, but there were nearly 40 pounds of the latter. These articles alone could

---

[1] The present Admiral Sir George Back, poor Graham Gore's former Captain in the Arctic Expedition of 1836-7, when they both served on board of H.M.S. 'Terror.'

never support life in such a climate, and we found neither biscuit nor meat of any kind. A portion of tobacco, and an empty pemmican-tin capable of containing 22 pounds weight, were discovered. The tin was marked with an E; it had probably belonged to the 'Erebus.' None of the fuel originally brought from the ships remained in or about the boat, but there was no lack of it, for a drift-tree was lying on the beach close at hand, and had the party been in need of fuel, they would have used the paddles and bottom-boards of the boat.

In the after-part of the boat we found eleven large spoons, eleven forks, and four tea-spoons, all of silver. Of these twenty-six pieces of plate, eight bore Sir John Franklin's crest, the remainder had the crests or initials of nine different officers, with the exception of a single fork which was not marked; of these nine officers, five belonged to the 'Erebus'—Gore, Le Vesconte, Fairholme, Couch, and Goodsir. Three others belonged to the 'Terror'—Crozier (a teaspoon only), Hornby, and Thomas. I do not know to whom the three articles with an owl engraved on them belonged, nor who was the owner of the unmarked fork, but of the owners of those we can identify, the majority belonged to the 'Erebus.' One of the watches bore the crest of Mr. Couch, of the 'Erebus,' and as the pemmican tin also came from that ship, I am inclined to think the boat did also. One of the pocket chronometers found in the boat was marked, "Parkinson and Frodsham 980," the other, "Arnold 2020;" these had been supplied one to each ship.

Sir John Franklin's plate perhaps was issued to the men for their use, as the only means of saving it; and it seems probable that the officers generally did the same, as not a single iron spoon, such as sailors always use, has been found. Of the many men, probably twenty or thirty, who were attached to this boat, it seems most strange that the remains of only two individuals were found, nor were there any graves upon the neigbouring flat land; indeed, bearing in mind the season at which these poor fellows left their ships, it should be remembered that the soil was then frozen hard as rock, and the labour of *quarrying* a grave very great indeed.

I was astonished to find that the sledge was directed to the N.E., exactly for the next point of land for which we ourselves were travelling!

The position of this abandoned boat is about 50 miles—as a sledge would travel—from Point Victory, and therefore 65 miles from the position of the ships; also it is 70 miles from the skeleton of the steward, and 150 miles from Montreal Island: it is moreover in the depth of a wide bay, where, by crossing over 10 or 12 miles of very low land, a great saving of distance would be effected, the route by the coast-line being about 40 miles.

A little reflection led me to satisfy my own mind at least that this boat was *returning to the ships.* In no other way can I account for two men having been left in her, than by supposing the party were unable to drag the boat further, and that these two men, not being able to keep pace with their shipmates, were therefore left by them supplied with such provisions as could be spared, to last them until the return of the others from the ship with a fresh stock.

Whether it was the intention of this boat party to await the result of another season in the ships, or to follow the track of the main body to the Great Fish River, is now a matter of conjecture. It seems more than probable that they fully intended to revisit the boat, not only on account of the two men left in charge of it, but also to obtain the chocolate, the five watches, and many other small articles which would otherwise scarcely have been left in her.

The same reasons which may be assigned for the return of this detachment from the main body (which, it will be remembered, had started under the command of Captain Crozier for the Great Fish River) will also serve to account for the party not having come back to their boat. In both instances they appear to have greatly overrated their strength, and the distance they could travel in a given time.

Taking this view of the case, we can understand why their provisions would not have lasted them for anything like the distance they required to travel; and why they would be obliged to send back to the ships for more, first taking from the detached party all provisions they could possibly spare. Whether all or any of the remainder of this detached party ever reached their ships is uncertain; all we know is, that they did not revisit the boat, otherwise more skeletons would probably have been found in its neighbourhood; the Esquimaux report is, that there was no one alive in the ship when she drifted on shore, and that they found but one human body on board of her.

After leaving the boat we followed an irregular coast-line to the N. and N.W., up to a very prominent cape, which is probably the extreme of land seen from Point Victory by Sir James Ross, and named by him Point Franklin, which name, as a cape, it still retains.

I need hardly say that throughout the whole of my journey along the shores of King William's Land, we all kept a most vigilant look-out for any appearance of the stranded ship spoken of by the natives; but our search for her was utterly fruitless.

CHAPTER XVI.

Errors in Franklin's records — Relics found at the cairn — Reflections on the retreat — Returning homeward — Geological remarks — Difficulties of summer sledging — Arrive on board the 'Fox' — Navigable N.W. passage — Death from scurvy — Anxiety for Captain Young — Young returns safely.

On the morning of 2nd June we reached Point Victory. Here Hobson's note left for me in the cairn informed me that he had not found the slightest trace either of a wreck anywhere upon the coast, or of natives to the north of Cape Crozier.

Although somewhat short of provisions, I determined to remain a day here in order to examine an opening at the bottom of Back Bay, called so after Sir George Back, by his friend Sir James Ross, and which had not been explored. This proved to be an inlet nearly 13 miles deep, with an average width of 1½ or 2 miles; I drove round it upon the dog sledge, but found no trace of human beings; it was filled with heavy old ice, and was therefore unfavourable for the resort of seals, and consequently of natives also.

The direction of the inlet is to the E.S.E.; we found the land on either side rose as we advanced up it, and attained a considerable elevation, except immediately across its head, where alone it was very low; I have conferred upon it the name of Collinson, after one who will ever be distinguished in connexion with the Franklin search, and who kindly relieved Lady Franklin of much trouble by taking upon himself the financial business of this expedition.

An extensive bay, westward of Cape Herschel, I have named after Captain Washington, the hydrographer, a stedfast supporter of this final search. But, all the intermediate coast-line—along which the retreating crews performed their fearful death-march—is sacred to their names alone.

Hobson's note informed me of his having found a second record, deposited also by Lieutenant Gore in May, 1847, upon the south side of Back Bay, but it afforded no additional information. It was a duplicate of the Point Victory record, and shows that Gore and Des Vœux merely left them under cairns, without adding further particulars at the time of depositing: their attention was probably directed to a more important matter, the completion of their discovery of the North-West Passage. This record had not been opened by the retreating crews in 1848; when found by Hobson, it was soldered up, as when taken from the ship on the 24th May, 1847.

It is remarkable that both these papers state the ships to have wintered in 1846–7 at Beechey Island! So obvious a mistake would hardly have been made had any importance been attached to these documents. They were soldered up in thin tin cylinders, having been filled up on board prior to the departure of the travellers; consequently, the day upon which they were *deposited* was not filled in; but already the papers were much damaged by rust—a very few more years would have rendered them wholly illegible. When the record left at Point Victory was opened to add thereto the supplemental information which gives it its chief value, Captain Fitzjames (as may be concluded by the colour of the ink) filled in the date—28th—of May, when the record was originally deposited. The cylinder containing this record had not been soldered up again; I suppose they had not the means of doing so; it was found on the ground amongst a few loose stones which had evidently fallen along with it from the top of the cairn. Hobson removed every stone of this cairn down to the ground and rebuilt it.

Brief as these records are, we must needs be contented with them; they are perfect models of official brevity. No log-book could be more provokingly concise. Yet, that *any record at all* should be deposited after the abandonment of the ships, does not seem to have been at first intended; and we should feel the more thankful to Captains Crozier and Fitzjames, to whom we are indebted for the invaluable supplement, and our gratitude ought to be all the more sincere when we remember that the ink had to be *thawed*, and that writing in a tent during an April day in the arctic regions is by no means an easy task.

Before moving forward from that known position, however, they seem to have reflected upon the importance of leaving there information as to their route. They must have felt that their countrymen were seeking, and would seek for them until some clue was obtained; and that such definite points as Simpson's cairn at Cape Herschel, and James Ross's cairn at Point Victory (between which lay the only unexplored portion of the North-West Passage) would be examined, as instinctively as McClure, and Kellett, made for well-known sandstone rock-beacon at Melville Island, to seek, and to deposit information. This is the only explanation I can offer of their having sent to Sir James Ross's pillar in May, 1847, and of their taking such pains in April, 1848, to seek out the exact position where it stood, there to erect a cairn five or six feet high, and place their record in it.

Besides placing a copy of the record taken away by Hobson from the cairn, we both put records of our own in it; and I also buried one under a large stone ten feet true north from it, stating the explorations and discoveries we had made.

A great quantity and variety of things lay strewed about the cairn, such as even in their three days' march from the ships the retreating crews found it impossible to carry further. Amongst these were four heavy sets of boat's cooking stoves, pickaxes, shovels, iron hoops, old canvas, a large single block, about four feet of a copper lightning conductor, long pieces of hollow brass curtain rods, a small case of selected medicines containing about twenty-four phials, the contents in a wonderful state of preservation; a dip circle by Robinson, with two needles, bar magnets, and light horizontal needle all complete, the whole weighing only nine pounds; and even a small sextant engraved with the name of "Frederic Hornby" lying beside the cairn without its case. The coloured eye-shades of the sextant had been taken out, otherwise it was perfect; the movable screws and such parts as come in contact with the observer's hand were neatly covered with thin leather to prevent frost-bite in severe weather.

The clothing left by the retreating crews of the 'Erebus' and 'Terror' formed a huge heap four feet high; every article was searched, but the pockets were empty, and not one of all these articles was marked,—indeed sailors' warm clothing seldom is. Two canteens, the property of marines, were found, one marked "88 C°. Wm. Hedges," and the other "89 C°. Wm. Heather." A small pannikin made out of a two-pound preserved-meat tin had scratched on it "W. Mark."

These abandoned superfluities afford the saddest and most convincing proof that here—on this spot—our doomed and scurvy-stricken countrymen calmly prepared themselves to struggle manfully for life.

When continuing my homeward march, and, as nearly as I could judge, $2\frac{1}{2}$ or $2\frac{3}{4}$ miles to the north of Point Victory, I saw a few stones placed in line, as if across the head of a tenting place to afford some shelter; here it was I think that Lieutenant Gore deposited the record in May, 1847, which was found in 1848 by Lieutenant Irving, and finally deposited at Point Victory. Some scraps of tin vessels were lying about, but whether they had been left by Sir James Ross's party in May, 1830, or by the Franklin Expedition in 1847 or 1848, is uncertain.[1]

Here ended my own search for further traces of our lost countrymen. Hobson found two other cairns, and many relics, between this position and Cape Felix. From each place where any trace was discovered the most interesting of the relics were taken away, so that the selection we have made is very considerable.

Of these northern cairns I will give a description when I have received Hobson's account of his journey; but here it is as well to state that in his opinion, as well as my own, no part of the coast between Cape Felix and Cape Crozier has been visited by Esquimaux since the fatal march of the lost crews in April, 1848; no cairn disturbed; none of the numerous articles strewed about them, nor the scanty driftwood we noticed at long intervals—although invaluable to the natives—had been touched. From this very significant fact it is quite certain that they had not been discovered by the Esquimaux, whose knowledge of the "white men falling down and dying as they walked along" must be limited to the shore-line southward and eastward of Cape Crozier, and where, of course, no traces were permitted to remain for us to find. It is not probable that such fearful mortality could have overtaken them so early in their march as within 80

---

[1] It is remarkable that, when Sir James Ross discovered Point Victory in 1830, he named two points of land, then in sight, Cape Franklin, and Cape Jane Franklin respectively. Eighteen years afterwards Franklin's ships were abandoned almost within sight of those headlands. Point Victory, where the survivors landed, is almost identical with Cape Jane Franklin.

miles by sledge-route from the abandoned ships—such being the distance of the latter from Cape Crozier; nor is it probable that we could have passed the wreck had she existed there, as there are no off-lying islands to the northward of Cape Crozier, to prevent a ship drifting in upon the beach; whilst to the southward they are very numerous, so much so that a drifting ship could hardly run the gauntlet between them so as to reach the shore.

The coast from Point Victory northward is considerably higher than that upon which we have been so many days; the sea also is not so shallow, and the ice comes close in; to seaward all was heavy close pack, consisting of all descriptions of ice, but for the most part old and heavy.

From Walls' Bay I crossed overland to the eastern shore, and reached my depot near the entrance of Port Parry on the 5th June, after an absence of thirty-four days. Hence I purposed travelling along shore to Cape Sabine, in order to avoid the rough ice which we encountered when crossing direct from Cape Victoria in April, and also hoping to obtain a few more observations for the magnetic inclination.

The weather became foggy as we approached Prince George's Bay, therefore we were obliged to go well into it before attempting to cross. We gained the land—upon the opposite side, as I supposed—and which would lead us direct to Cape Sabine; but when the weather cleared up, we saw a long low island to seaward of us, which puzzled me much. Eventually I found we had discovered a strait leading from Prince George's Bay into Wellington Strait, about 8 miles south of Cape Sabine.

This discovery cost us a day's delay, and was therefore unwelcome, as we were then in daily expectation and dread of the thaw, which renders all travelling so very difficult; and we were still 230 long miles from our ship. In this strait we found a deserted snow village of seventeen huts;

one of them was unusually large, its internal diameter being 14 feet. Strewed about on the ice or in every snow hut, were shavings and chips of fresh wood; in one of them I found a child's toy—a miniature sledge—made of wood; and the men soon collected enough seal's blubber to supply us with fuel for our homeward march. No traces of natives were found upon either shore at this place, nor had I met with any since leaving the western coast of the island to the southward of Cape Crozier.

Having passed through nearly to the eastern end of the strait, we cut off some distance by crossing overland, so as to reach the sea-coast 3 or 4 miles southward of Cape Sabine. A few willow grouse, two foxes, and a young reindeer were seen. There was some vegetation upon the land, and animals appeared to resort to this locality in tolerable abundance; the contrast between it and the low, barren shores we had so recently come from was striking indeed!

Nothing can exceed the gloom and desolation of the western coast of King William's Island; Hobson and myself had some considerable experience of it; his sojourn there exceeded a month. Its climate seems different from that of the eastern coast; it is more exposed to north-west winds, and the air was almost constantly loaded with chilling fogs. Everywhere upon the shores of the island I noticed boulders of dark gneiss; upon the west coast they were generally small, and of a dark gray colour. About the north part of the island Hobson found a good deal of sandstone, the probable result of ice-drift from Melville Island or Banks Land.

The west coast gives one the idea of its having risen within a recent geological period from the sea—not suddenly, but at regular intervals; the numerous terraces or beach-marks form long horizontal lines, rising very gradually, and in due proportion as their distance increases from the sea; near the shore they are of course most distinct; some fossils were picked up, chiefly impressions of shells.

King William's Island is for the most part extremely barren, and its surface dotted over with innumerable ponds and lakes. It is not by any means the "land abounding with reindeer and musk oxen" which we expected to find: the natives told us there were none of the latter and very few of the former upon it.

On the 8th June the first ducks and brent geese were seen flying northward. Passing over the extreme point of Cape Victoria, Boothia Land, near which we saw the deserted snow huts of our March acquaintances, and shortly afterwards crossing the mouth of the deep bay to the north of it, in which, sheltered by the island, a ship would find security from ice pressure, and very tolerable winter quarters, we again reached the straight low limestone coast of Boothia Felix.

I was unable to make any delay at the Magnetic Pole, nor could I find a trace of Ross's cairn;[1] but at each of our encampments along the coast the magnetic inclination was carefully observed. Throughout my whole journey I availed myself of every opportunity of obtaining these most interesting observations, often remaining up, after we had encamped for rest, six or seven hours in order to do so; but the instruments supplied for this purpose were not well adapted for use in this climate or in the open air, consequently they occasioned me a vast deal of labour and loss of time, so as to diminish to almost one-third the results I should otherwise have obtained.

Much snow has disappeared off the land; and the ridges

[1] This cairn, as well as the one built on Point Victory in 1830, had been destroyed by the natives; fortunately they had not visited Point Victory whilst the Franklin cairn and record remained there, otherwise neither cairn nor record would have remained for us to discover.

or ancient beaches, being the parts most free from snow, showed out strongly in long, dark, horizontal lines, rising above each other until lost to view in the interior. Here and there a few fossil shells and corals were picked up; and four or five willow grouse were shot.

13th June.—We passed from limestone to granite in lat. 71° 10′ N. Here the land attains to considerable elevation. In the hollows of the dark granite rocks we found abundance of water, and also in a few places upon the sea-ice; it was quite evident that in another day or two the snow would altogether yield to the warmth of summer; birds were now frequently seen.

We discovered a narrow channel to the eastward of the one between the Tasmania Group, through which we had passed with so much difficulty in April; our new channel was covered with smooth ice, and was also much shorter.

At one of our depots lately visited, a note left by Hobson informed me of his being six days in advance of me, and also of his own serious illness; for many days past he had been unable to walk, and was consequently conveyed upon the sledge; his men were hastening home with all their strength and speed, in order to get him under the Doctor's care. We also were doing our best to push on, lest the bursting out of melting snow from the various ravines should render the ice impassable.

On the 15th the snow upon the ice everywhere yielded to the effects of increased temperature; I was indeed most thankful at its having remained firm so long. To make any progress at all after this date was of course a very great labour, requiring the utmost efforts of both the men and the dogs; nor was the freezing mixture through which we trudged by any means agreeable: we were often more than knee-deep in it.

We succeeded in reaching False Strait on the morning of

the 18th June, and pitched our tent just as heavy rain began to descend; it lasted throughout the greater part of the day. After travelling a few miles upon Macgregor Laird Lake, further progress was found to be quite impossible, and we were obliged to haul our sledges up off the flooded ice, and commence a march of 16 or 17 miles overland for the ship. The poor dogs were so tired and sore-footed, that we could not induce them to follow us; they remained about the sledges. After a very fatiguing scramble across the hills and through the snow valleys we were refreshed with a sight of our poor dear lonely little 'Fox,' and arrived on board in time for a late breakfast on 19th June, after an absence of seventy-eight days.

I may here, at the conclusion of our journey, and as the result of our experience, express my opinion that, had the barrier of ice which lay across the western outlet of Bellot Strait permitted us last season to reach the open water beyond, the chances would have been greatly in favour of our reaching Cape Herschel on the S. side of King William's Island, by passing (as I intended to do) along its *eastern* side.

The wide channel between Prince of Wales' Land and Victoria Land admits a continuous stream of very heavy ocean-formed polar ice from the N.W., which presses upon the north-western shore of King William's Island; thus opposing a formidable barrier to the descent of Victoria Strait with ships, and involving to the navigator the very heavy risk of drifting through in the pack.

No one seeing Victoria Strait as we saw it could entertain a doubt of this being the only way to get a ship through.

From Bellot Strait to Cape Victoria we found a mixture of old and new ice, showing the exact proportion of pack and of clear water at the setting in of winter. Once to the southward of the Tasmania Group, I think our chief difficulty would have been overcome; and south of Cape Victoria I doubt whether any further obstruction would have been experienced, as but little if any ice remained. The natives told us the ice went away, and left a clear sea every year. As our discoveries show Victoria Strait to be but little more than 20 miles wide, the ice pressed southward through so narrow a space could hardly have prevented our crossing southward of it, to Victoria Land, and Cambridge Bay, the wintering place reached by Collinson, from the *west*, in 1852.

In a season so favourable for navigation as to open Peel Sound (as, for instance, in 1846, when Franklin sailed down it), I think but comparatively little difficulty would be experienced until Victoria Strait was reached. Had Sir John Franklin known that a channel existed on the eastern side of King William's *Land*—so named by Sir John Ross, and laid down by him as part of the mainland—he would not have risked the besetment of his ships in the very heavy ice to the westward of it; but would have taken the eastern, although more circuitous passage, and would in all probability have carried his ships safely through to Behring Strait, in 1846.

But Franklin had no alternative; he was furnished with charts which indicated no opening to the eastward of King William's *Land*;[1] consequently he had but one course open to him, and that the one he adopted.

My own preference for the route by the east side of the island has been formed with a knowledge of Rae's observations on that locality, and of the experience of Collinson to the westward. I am of opinion that the barrier of ice off Bellot Strait, some 3 or 4 miles wide, was the only obstacle to our carrying the 'Fox,' according to my original intention, southward between Boothia and King William's Island

[1] It was not until 1854 that its insularity was determined, by Dr. Rae.

towards the Great Fish River, and from thence to a wintering position on Victoria Land. Perhaps some future voyager, profiting by the experience of Franklin, and the observations which my journey round King William's Island has enabled me to make, may succeed in carrying his ship through from sea to sea; at least he will be enabled to direct all his efforts *in the true and only direction.* Nevertheless, to Franklin must be assigned the virtual completion of the North-West Passage,[1] as well as the priority of its discovery. This fact will be readily understood when it is recollected that a navigable passage is known to exist along the continent of North America, from Boothia to Behring Strait. Franklin himself, and his companion Richardson, discovered and surveyed by far the greater portion of that vast extent, which overlaps in longitude the discoveries of Parry in a more northern latitude; and for the last thirty years or more, the discovery of a North-West Passage has been reduced to the discovery of a link uniting the two. Therefore, to reach those well-known waters along the continental shore was the guiding object of all Franklin's efforts; and that heroic leader, having conducted his ships *almost* within reach of the goal, sent forth his parties to explore : to me a striking parallel here suggests itself.

But neither Franklin nor any one of his heroic band was destined to bring home the news of their achievement ; nor perhaps would it ever have been fully brought to light, had not the 'Fox' been sent on her noble mission, and returned in safety.

Intelligence of the discovery of a North-West Passage in 1850 by Sir Robert McClure, who entered the Arctic Sea by Behring Strait, reached England in 1853; but it is only now that we have become aware of Franklin's prior discovery, which was probably made in the spring of 1847.

[1] See Preface, page xiii.

Saturday, 2nd July.—Upon my arrival at the ship on the morning of the 19th June, my first enquiries were about Hobson; I found him in a much worse state than I had expected. He reached the ship on the 14th, unable to walk or even to stand, without assistance; but already he was beginning to amend, and was in excellent spirits. Christian had shot several ducks, which, with preserved potato, milk, strong ale, and lemon-juice, completed a very respectable dietary for a scurvy-stricken patient. All the rest were tolerably well; slight traces only of scurvy in two or three of the men. The ship was as clean and trim as I could have expected, and all had well and cheerfully performed their duties during my absence; hardly any game had been shot, except one bear.

The Doctor now acquainted me with the death of Thomas Blackwell, ship's steward, which occurred only five days previously, and was occasioned by scurvy. This man had scurvy when I left the ship in April, and no means were left untried by the Doctor to promote his recovery and rally his desponding energies; but his mind, unsustained by hope, lost all energy, and at last he had to be forcibly taken upon deck for fresh air. For months past the ship's spirits had been of necessity removed from under his control.

When too late, his shipmates made it known that he had a dislike to preserved meats, and had lived the whole winter upon salt pork! He also disliked preserved potato, and would not eat it unless watched, nor would he put on clean clothes, which others in charity prepared for him. Yet his death was somewhat unexpected; he went on deck as usual to walk in the middle of the day, and, when found there, was quite dead. His remains were buried beside those of our late shipmate Mr. Brand.

The news of our success to the southward in tracing the

footsteps of the lost expedition, greatly revived the spirits of my small crew; we wished only for the safe and speedy return of Young and his party.

Captain Young commenced his spring explorations on the 7th April, with a sledge party of four men, and a second sledge drawn by six dogs under the management of our Greenlander, Samuel; almost incessant gales greatly retarded his progress: and finding that a channel existed between Prince of Wales' Land and Victoria Land whereby his field for discovery and search would be lengthened, he sent back one sledge, the tent, and four men to the ship, in order to economise provisions, and for forty days journeyed with one man (George Hobday) and the dogs, encamping in such snow lodges as they were able to build.

For many days together no sun appeared; they journeyed when the storms abated, pushing on—without regard to day or night on these occasions—as long as their strength permitted. Once, when quite worn out with fatigue, they slept an unbroken sleep of many hours, their snow-hut so buried in the drift as to be unusually warm and snug, and the storm without supplying an appropriate lullaby; and so a day slipped by unnoticed! It would have been a marvel had they retained their reckoning during those forty dreary, diurnal periods, those days without nights.

Young, being a skilful navigator, tested and corrected his calendar, by comparing his observed lunar distance with that given in the Nautical Almanack.

Hobday is a fine young man-of-war's man, and also a man of few words; his faith in his leader was unbounded, and of the unquestioning sort: all he cared to understand, were his *orders*.

When Young contemplated the possibility of still further extending his journey, by substituting a lame dog or two for pemmican, the only response his taciturn companion vouchsafed to this announcement was—"If you can eat dog, why, so can I!"

But this great exposure and fatigue, together with extremely bad weather, and a most difficult coast-line to trace, greatly injured Young's health; he was compelled to return to the ship on 7th June for medical aid, but purposing at all hazards to renew his explorations almost immediately. Dr. Walker met this determination by a strong protest in writing against his leaving the ship again, his health being quite unequal to it; but after three days Young felt himself somewhat better, and, with a zeal which knew no bounds, set off to complete his branch of the search, taking with him both his sledge parties.

From the Doctor's account I felt most anxious for his return, lest his health, or that of his companions, should receive permanent injury; in fact this was now my only cause of anxiety. The season was rather forward here, and advancing with unusual rapidity, rain and wind dissolving the snow and ice; there was much water in Bellot Strait, extending from Half-way Island eastward to the table land, and thence in a narrow lane to Long Island.

After a day or two I could perceive a vast improvement in Hobson; and my own four men, with the exception of Hampton who required a long rest, were in sound health; so also was my companion Petersen. On 24th June Christian shot two small reindeer, which gave us 170 lbs. of meat; a few days before that he shot a seal, which afforded two sumptuous meals for all on board.

The time had now elapsed during which Young expected to remain absent, and supposing the difficulty of the transit from the western sea to have still further increased, I set off early on the 25th June with my four men, intending to visit Pemmican Rock; but failing to come across him there, I resolved to carry on provisions as far as Four River Point, in the hope of meeting with him, and of facilitating his return. To our surprise the water had all drained off the frozen surface of the Long Lake, and it therefore afforded excellent travelling. We found the poor dogs lying quietly beside our sledges; they had attacked the pemmican, and devoured a small quantity which was not secured in tin, also some blubber, some leather straps, and a gull that I had shot for a specimen; but they had not apparently relished the biscuit. Poor dogs! they have a hard life of it in these regions. Even Petersen, who is generally kind and humane, seems to fancy they must have little or no feeling: one of his theories is, that you may knock an Esquimaux dog about the head with any article, however heavy, with perfect impunity to the brute. One of us upbraided him the other day because he broke his whip-handle over the head of a dog. "*That was nothing at all*," he assured us: some friend of his in Greenland found he could beat his dogs over the head with a heavy hammer—it stunned them certainly— but by laying them with their mouths open to the wind, they soon revived, got up, and ran about "*all right.*"

We lost no time in giving them a good feed, the first for seven days, yet they did not seem unusually hungry, and soon coiled themselves up to sleep again. Whilst the men and dogs were employed next day in conveying a sledge to the east end of the lake, I walked to Cape Bird to look out for the absent party, but they had not yet returned to Pemmican Rock.

When vainly endeavouring, with felonious intentions, to climb up a steep cliff to the breeding-places of some silvery gulls, I saw and shot a brent goose, seated upon an accessible ledge, and made a prize of four eggs; that this bird should have selected so unusual a breeding-place is a proof that in cunning she was more than a match for the foxes, for her nest was quite beyond their reach. Many seals were basking on the ice, and the watercourse by which our sledges ascended a week before to the Long Lake was now a strong and rapid stream. A few reindeer were seen.

On the 27th I sent three of the men back to the ship, and with Thompson and the dogs went on to Pemmican Rock, where, to our great joy, we happily met Young and his party, who had but just returned there, after a long and successful journey, the particulars of which I will give hereafter.

Young was greatly reduced in flesh and strength, so much weakened indeed that for the last few days he had travelled on the dog sledge; Harvey—also far from well—could just manage to keep pace with the sledge; his malady was scurvy. Their journies had been very depressing; most dismal weather, low dreary limestone shores devoid of game, and no trace of the lost expedition. The news of our success in the southern journies greatly cheered them. On the following day we were all once more on board, and indulging in an enormous consumption of eatables, such as only those can do who have been much reduced by long-continued fatigue and exposure to cold. Venison, ducks, beer, and lemon-juice, daily; preserved apples and cranberries three times a week; and pickled whaleskin—a famous antiscorbutic—*ad libitum* for all who liked it. The weather, which for the last week had been wet, windy, and miserable, now set in fair. The carpenter's hammer, and the men's voices at their work, were new and animating sounds.

CHAPTER XVII.

Signs of release — Seal-stalking — Dearth of animal life — Birthdays — Break out of winter quarters — Game lists — Steam out of Port — Escape from Regent's Inlet — In Baffin's Bay — Bears — Captain Allen Young's journey — Hobson's journey — Disco ; sad disappointment — Part from our Esquimaux friends — Adieu to Greenland — Arrive home.

DURING the long absence of Hobson, Young, and myself, the Doctor has had but a dreary time of it on board; no wonder he felt "very lonely and often thought of home."

Once a white wolf came very near to the ship, but the rifles would not go off. Another time a bear with her two cubs actually came alongside the ship and went away unobserved; but another bear was less fortunate, it was shot, and the steaks were eagerly devoured. Gradually the birds arrived from the south; an occasional hare, or perhaps a deer-track, would enliven his solitary ramble over the hills; at length the thawing commenced, the welcome sound of running water was heard, and the wild plants put forth their tiny flowers.

Later still, a few insects appeared, and convinced him that *the Summer* had at length arrived.

To-day (*2nd July*) I took a long and delightful walk, but shot only two ducks; Petersen went in another direction, and got nothing; Christian, after toiling all day in his kayak, returned with only two divers and a duck. Lately he has obtained for us several king and long-tailed ducks (no eider ducks have been seen), two red-throated divers, and two brent geese, and caught an ermine in its summer coat.

T

Yesterday one of the men brought on board a trout weighing 2 lbs. ; he saw a glaucous gull and a fox disputing for it on the margin of a small lake; the former seems to have killed and brought it to land.

We have seen that Bellot Strait continued unfrozen throughout the entire winter. In this respect it bears an exact resemblance to the various water-spaces which have, from time to time, been reported, and were regarded as proofs of an open polar sea—the polynia of some writers. In every instance where more extended observation has been made, not only have the hypotheses which attributed this open water to modifications of temperature, or subcurrents of warm water, &c., been proved to have no foundation in fact, but it has been ascertained that the existence of these water-spaces is solely due to the strength of the currents or tides.

The Bellot Strait water now washes the south side of the Fox Islands, and extends to the south point of Long Island. The month of June has been somewhat warmer than usual, its mean temperature being $+ 35\frac{1}{2}°$.

9th.—The ship has been thoroughly cleaned and restowed, remaining provisions examined, tanks filled with fresh water, 12 tons of stone ballast taken in, and everything brought on board that was landed last autumn. Hobson is the only one upon the sick list; but he is able to walk about and does duty. Very few birds, and only one small seal, have been obtained during the week; an occasional great northern diver is seen, and a rare land bird has been shot. We cannot discover the nests of eider ducks or geese, and the breeding cliffs of the gulls being inaccessible, we have not got any eggs. I am a close prisoner at the corner of my table, poring over my observation and angle book, and have at length laid down upon paper the west coast of King William's Land to my satisfaction. Tidal observations are commenced; and the aneroid and mercurial barometers are again being compared in order to verify the former.

16th. Saturday night.—We are now almost ready for sea. There is a much larger space of water in Bellot Strait, reaching within 300 or 400 yards of us. Long cracks or lanes of water have been seen in Prince Regent's Inlet. The decay of the ice continues, though not with equal rapidity, yet with very satisfactory despatch. Westerly winds and clear weather prevail. Christian has seen two reindeer this week, and has shot a very few birds, and seven seals. As these creatures lie basking upon the ice, he crawls up to them behind a small calico screen, fitted upon a miniature sledge about a foot long, on which there is a rest for the muzzle of his rifle, and a slit in the calico through which he fires.

Christian Seal-stalking.

The seals afford an average weight of thirty pounds of excellent fresh meat, which we relish greatly, and consider much better suited to our present condition, than such poor venison as reindeer would furnish at this season. A single hare has been shot; the white fur has nearly all disappeared, and left exposed the summer coat of dull lead colour. Several small birds not common to the northward are found here. Insects abound; the Doctor is perpetually in chase, unless busily occupied in grubbing up plants. Young is surveying the harbour. Hobson fully occupied with preparing the ship for sea. I have been giving some attention to the engines and boiler, and hope, with the help of the two stokers, to be able to make use of our steam power.

With regard to Christian's stratagem for approaching a seal upon the ice, I have heard that the Greenlanders caught the idea from a bear who was seen holding up a piece of ice in his paws, and thus shielded from its view, steal up to a seal! I do not insist on the truth of the story. Esquimaux require no such prompting; their tradition is that by concealing their boats and kayaks behind pieces of ice, and drifting in before the wind, clothed in white furs, they succeeded in surprising the last of the Scandinavian settlements in South Greenland; they surrounded it, set fire to it, and slaughtered the wretched inhabitants as they rushed out, one powerful old man alone escaping with his young son to the mountains of the interior. History tells us that the lost colonies of Greenland, which were first settled in the eleventh century, became extinct in the fourteenth.

The men have received my hearty thanks for their great exertions during the travelling period. I told them I considered every part of our search to have been fully and efficiently performed. Our labours have determined the exact position of the extreme northern promontory of the continent of America; I have affixed to it the name of Murchison, after the distinguished President of the Royal Geographical Society—the strenuous advocate for this "further search"—and the able champion of Lady Franklin when she needed all the support which private friendship and public spirit could bestow.

23rd.—The ice in Prince Regent's Inlet is broken up into pack, but the prevalence of easterly winds keeps it close in upon this shore. The ice about us is very much decayed, holes through it in many places. No reindeer seen this week, and only two seals procured; one of them shot by Christian, the other was killed by a bear, which ran off before Samuel could come within shot of him. A fox, a gull, a couple of ducks, and one or two lemmings, complete our game list for the week, yet our two Esquimaux are indefatigable in the pursuit. We eat all the birds and seals we can shoot, as well as mustard and cress as fast as we can grow it, but the quantity is very small. We sometimes refresh ourselves with a salad of sorrel-leaves, or roots of the little plant with lilac flower of snapdragon shape, named *Pedicularis hirsuta.*

The seine has been hauled in the narrow lake at the head of the harbour, but as it was not well managed, only a dozen small trout were taken, though more were seen. We have tried for rock-cod, but without success. The relics of the lost expedition have been aired, exhibited to the crew, labelled, and packed away. The Doctor has been dredging lately. A record detailing our proceedings has been placed in a cairn upon the west point of Depot Bay.

1st August.—Birthdays have been numerous lately; the men have compared notes, and have discovered that *two*, or even *three*, of them were born on the same day! Hobson's good nature is appealed to for aid in these celebrations, for pipes, or tobacco, a glass of grog, or a holiday and a gun, to try and shoot something for the pot.

A few evenings ago our steward was looking remarkably

like an owl—next morning his appearance was ghastly; he was brought up for judicial investigation. His eldest daughter, he said, had on that day attained her ninth year; to do honour to the event, he had saved up a little grog, *quite contrary to his usual custom*, and that its effect, together with the excitement of his feelings, overpowered him, &c. In short, he supplied most ingenious excuses, and in return I gave much excellent advice. In truth, I felt somewhat indebted to the unconscious little maiden for even this shadow of an excuse; but not wishing either the paternal feelings, or the good effects of my counsel to be put to a severe test, I do hope no more birthdays will occur in that family during the remainder of our sojourn in the 'Fox.'

A long continuance of unusually calm, bright, and warm weather has been favourable to our painting and cleaning the ship, scraping masts, and so forth. The result is that she looks unusually smart and gay, and our impatience to exhibit her, and *ourselves*, at home is much increased. With the exception of a few gulls, and a duck, our hunters have shot nothing lately, although constantly out, either darting about in their kayaks, or ranging over the hills; in fact, there is nothing which they *can* shoot; the ducks are tolerably numerous, but extremely wild; the valleys are respectably clothed with vegetation, yet only one animal—a hare—has been seen. I was so fortunate as to shoot a snowy owl, the flesh of which was white and tender, but, to my palate, tasteless, although Petersen considers that "owl is the best beef in the country."

On Thursday night we found the harbour-ice to be quietly drifting out, of course taking us with it. The night was calm, the current in Bellot Strait very strong, we were almost helpless under the circumstances, and therefore felt the danger of our position. To warp the ship along the ice-edge, out of the way of the shore and rocks as it turned round and drifted along the cliffs to the westward, gave us some hours' occupation. At length it stuck fast between Fox Island and the main.

At turn of tide on Friday morning the ice began to drift eastward, and by this time being much broken up, and a breeze coming to our aid, we managed to extricate ourselves, and reach a secure anchorage in Port Kennedy.

On Saturday night some ice that was left came drifting out of the inner harbour, and obliged us to slip our cable; but after a few hours we regained our berth in safety, and have since been undisturbed. There is no immediate prospect of escape, but we expect a prodigious smashing up of the ice whenever a strong wind comes to set it in motion. To-day the steam was got up, and with the help of our two stokers I worked the engines for a short time. It is very cheering to know that we still have steam power at our command, although, by the deaths of poor Mr. Brand and Robert Scott, we were deprived of our engineer and engine-driver.

The mean temperature for July has been 40·14°, which is above the average for this region; the July temperatures have usually varied from 36° to 42°.

All are now in good health, but Hobson is still a little lame. The issue of lemon-juice has been reduced to the ordinary allowance of half an ounce daily (as we have but little that is really good), lest another winter should become inevitable, which, I can devoutly say, may God forbid!

Monday night, 8th.—Very anxiously awaiting an opportunity to escape. We have constantly watched the ice from the neighbouring hills, including the lofty summit of Mount Walker—named after the Doctor, who was the first to ascend it (1123 feet)—from which Fury Point can be distinguished, but nothing very cheering has been seen. We had a N.E. gale, accompanied by rain and a considerable fall of the barometer, a few days ago; and as it blew freshly from the westward this morning, I went to a hill-top, and saw that much ice had been broken up in Brentford Bay, and that there were streaks of water along the land between Possession Point and Hazard Inlet; this water, however, was not accessible to us.

The ice about Pemmican Rock was much in the same position as we found it last year, but Bellot Strait was perfectly clear. All the ice in this harbour, in Depot Bay, and Hazard Inlet, is gone, by far the greater part having decayed, not drifted away.

Later in the day, and from loftier hill-tops, a good deal of water was seen off Cape Garry, and a water-sky beyond. It now blows very strongly from the S.W., the most desirable quarter; and as the anxious desire to escape has become oppressive, it is not to be wondered at that now our hopes have become extravagant. We may even make a start to-morrow! On the other hand, a careful examination of our provision store shows that, should we be obliged to spend another winter here, we must curtail our allowance of meat—fresh and salt—to three-quarters of a pound, and have to use but very indifferent lemon-juice. The spirits, I rejoice to say, will very shortly be entirely expended.

On the morning of the 3rd instant, when the rain ceased and a N.E. gale sprang up, two claps of thunder were distinctly heard; this occurs but very rarely in these latitudes. There is ample occupation for the men, but not much for the officers; as for myself, I write a great deal, and work occasionally at our chart of discoveries; the only refreshment I indulge in is an occasinal dive into packets of old letters. All yesterday the harbour was full of ice, driven in by southerly and westerly winds, and so closely packed that one might have walked over it to the shore; to-day it has nearly all drifted out again. The subjoined table will show what game we have been able to obtain, by constant and arduous labour from the resources of these regions during two years' sojourn : also the game lists of most of the Arctic Expeditions. The pursuit of game was perhaps more systematically and perseveringly followed at Port Leopold, and at Dealy Island, than at any other stations.

The very small game list for Winter Harbour is accounted for by the inexperience of all on board the ships; and compared with that for Dealy Island—only forty miles from it, and not in any way more favoured—furnishes a striking contrast between the *first* winter and the *last*, which our Government ships have ever passed in the arctic regions.

At Port Kennedy several ermines were caught; a few seals were seen in the waterspace in Bellot Strait as early as February; only two dovekies were seen—one in summer plumage, and the other in winter plumage. A few ptarmigan and willow grouse remained all the winter; many came from the south in early spring, but all of them went northward before April. During the four months occupied in sailing from Davis' Strait to Bellot Strait, several hundreds of looms and dovekies, and five or six bears, were shot.

We had hoped to find musk oxen at Port Kennedy, but were not so fortunate as even to see one of those most interesting animals. Nothing in these dreary solitudes brings home to one so forcibly the wonderful power of adaptation which nature so frequently displays, as the first sight of a herd of these tremendously shaggy little arctic buffaloes, contentedly scraping away the snow, and browsing such scanty vegetation as the soil affords. Their lips are so flattened, and incisors so sharp, that they shave the frozen ground more closely than sheep or goats could do.

Nowhere have we found them more numerous than at Melville Island, where 114 were shot during the twelve

LIST OF ANIMALS KILLED AT THE VARIOUS LOCALITIES WHERE ARCTIC EXPEDITIONS HAVE WINTERED, DURING A PERIOD OF ABOUT ELEVEN MONTHS AT EACH STATION.

Date.	Place.	Lat. N.	Long. W.	Musk Oxen.	Reindeer.	Hares.	Bears.	Wolves.	Foxes.	Lemmings.	Seals.	Ptarmigan.	Geese and Ducks.	Gulls and Divers.	Looms.	Dovekies.	Fish.	Remarks.
	Average weight of each when cleaned and cut up, in lbs.			166	60	7	..	..	..	..	..	1	2¼	..	1	10 oz.	4	*Note.*—The flesh of bears, foxes, wolves, and seals, is not noticed here; it was given to the dogs.
1819–20	Winter Harbour	74¾°	111°	3	24	68	..	..	30	numerous	..	144	112	..	1866	2200	..	3766 lbs. of fresh meat issued to the crews.
1848–9	Port Leopold	73¾	90	..	..	..	1	..	22	1	1	9	40	50	..	..	..	3350 lbs. ,, ,, ,,
1850–1	Griffith Island	74¾	95	..	..	8	9	..	22	very few	1	88	61	90	..	..	..	2746 lbs. ,, ,, ,,
,,	Princess Royal Islands	73	118	5	..	27	4	..	40	..	..	249	50	..	..	..	..	
1851–3	Bay of Mercy	74	118	2	70	142	..	3	..	numerous	3	323	180	..	..	..	..	10,167 lbs., including 100 lbs. of small lake-trout, during a period of nineteen months.
1851–2	Walker Bay	71¼	117¾	..	5	127	4	..	22	numerous	3	118	280	50	..	..	1153	The fish were caught in lakes, in midsummer.
1852–3	Dealy Island	75	109	114	95	161	4	3	52	numerous	2	711	357	very few	..	..	..	13,202 lbs. consumed on board: 6,637 lbs. by detached parties; 2,406 lbs. unfit for use; small game, 513 lbs.; total, 27,483 lbs.
,,	Cambridge Bay	69	105¾	..	1	13	2	..	..	numerous	..	122	680	35	..	..	3230	The fish were caught in a large lake and a river.
1853–4	Beechey Island	74¾	92	..	..	3	3	..	..	..	4	20	20	..	..	1900	..	The game procured by travelling parties is not included here.
1857–8	Baffin's Bay	Drifting in mid-channel		..	..	..	2	..	1	..	73	..	..	..	..	..	..	For eight months only.
1858–9	Port Kennedy	72	94	..	8	9	2	..	19	several	18	82	100	20	..	38	..	

months passed there by the ships commanded by Captain Kellett and myself. On its western shores our exploring parties would sometimes see forty, fifty, or even sixty oxen in a single day's march.

The largest bulls approach to 800 lbs. in weight. The uniform colour is a dark brownish black; one cow was seen of a pure white colour, but she was accompanied by a black calf. They clamber up the steepest rocky ascents like goats, and when running, their long black hair heaves up and down, and, streaming in the breeze, gives them a peculiarly savage appearance; it is so long that they occasionally tread on it, and you find hairs almost two feet in length, stamped into the snow. There is an undergrowth of very thick wool, so soft and silky that the warmest gloves have been made of it. The musk ox is not absolutely deficient of a tail, but it never exceeds one inch and a half in length.

They do not seem to cross from one island to another, as the reindeer do, but usually roam about in small herds. Unaccustomed to man, they seldom deigned to notice us until we came tolerably near, then they would generally close together in an attitude of defence. Whilst facing you, their massive horns so effectually shield every vital part that it is useless to fire, therefore a single sportsman must wait until their patience is exhausted, and they alter their position. But it is desirable to get behind a patch of glassy ice, a rock, or some rough ground, where they cannot charge straight at you, which we have known them do, before, as well as after being fired at.

I once came rather suddenly upon a solitary old bull; he instantly faced me, rubbed the tips of his horns against his forelegs for a few seconds, and then rushed on at full speed. At the moment I was standing quite still, waiting for him to expose his shoulder, and examining my priming; I had, however, taken the precaution to approach him along the edge of a ravine, so by retreating a few paces down the steep slope I was able to shoot him when he halted on the brink above me. Another time three bulls allowed me to walk close up to them. I shot one, but the other two only stared stupidly, as if they *could not* understand it. I was obliged to shoot a second, as he seemed inclined to be troublesome, having begun to rub his horns against his forelegs—a sure sign that mischief is brewing; even then we had to pelt the remaining one with clods, hitting him repeatedly, but holding our guns ready cocked, for the musk ox is as impetuous as he is fearless—before he would move away.

Three or four sportsmen may station themselves about a herd, close in to seventy or eighty yards, and then by picking off the restless ones first, so bewilder the remainder as to secure them all. I have been one of three to shoot down a herd of ten oxen in this manner, in three or four minutes. No wonder then that we looked out anxiously for musk oxen at Port Kennedy; one such *battue* as this would have supplied us with fresh beef every day for three months! Their flesh is decidedly beef, but the fat is as decidedly mutton fat; in autumn the flesh of the males is often so strongly tainted with musk that only the dogs can eat it.

Musk oxen are unknown in Greenland; and the only instance that has ever come to my knowledge of their existence on the western shores of Baffin's Bay, or eastward of Wellington Channel and Prince Regent's Inlet, is the solitary one of a skull found near Cape Horsburgh (lat. $75°$ N.) in 1865, when the whaler 'Queen' wintered in its vicinity. Dr. Kane's expedition found some of their skulls on the shore of Smith's Sound, where the mean annual temperature is $34°$ *below* the freezing point! How much farther north they may exist, is not known.

Wednesday, 10th.—The S.W. wind proved a good friend to us; by the morning of the 9th it had moved the ice off shore, and cleared away a passage for us out of Brentford Bay. We started under steam at eleven o'clock yesterday morning, and, passing round Long Island, made sail along the land towards Cape Garry, there being a channel about 2 or 3 miles wide between the pack and the shore.

The wind now failed us, and I experienced some little difficulty in the management of the engines and boiler; the latter primed so violently as to send the hot water and steam over our top-gallant yard, to the dismay of Young, who was up there piloting the ship through the ice, and who was of course very speedily compelled to descend from his eyrie: and the tail valve of the condenser by some means had got out of its seat, and admitted air to the condenser; but eventually we got the engines to work well, and steamed across Cresswell Bay during the night. The pack rested against Fury Point, and an east wind springing up, we made fast to a large grounded mass of ice in Adelaide Bay, about ¼ mile off shore and in 3 fathoms' water, at eleven o'clock this morning. Having managed the engines for twenty-four consecutive hours, I was not sorry to get into bed. We were hardly out of Brentford Bay when fulmar petrels and white whales were seen—the first we have noticed for eleven and a half months; dovekies are likewise abundant, and a seal has already been shot. Cresswell Bay is perfectly clear of ice, but this pale limestone land is the perfection of sterility, even with the rugged hills of Brentford Bay in lively recollection.

Upon the east side of Port Kennedy the bones of whales were found in two places a mile apart from each other; the lowest of them was 180 feet above the sea, the second was more than 300 feet high. The latter I examined, and found a jawbone, two ribs, a joint of the vertebræ, and fragments of other bones, all more or less buried in the soil, and much heavier than the bones of a recent animal; they lay within 40 or 50 yards of each other, and upon a little flat patch of rather rich earth. a rocky hill above, and steep slope below; they are also nearly a mile inland.

When did the skeletons of these whales drift to their present positions? When did the forest trees grow in Baring's and Prince Patrick's Land, many of which are still fit for firewood? And when were the lofty table-lands of North Devon and North Somerset scored by these immense ravines, broad and deep, with sides almost perpendicular, and rocky beds sometimes a hundred yards wide, where no rivers now exist, nor even streamlets, except during the few weeks of summer's thaw? Will geology ever solve these enigmas?

Of the traces which we have left behind us, the most considerable are the graves of our two shipmates within the western point of our little harbour; they were tastefully sodded round, and planted over with the usual arctic flowers. There is our record in a conspicuous cairn at the west point of Depot or Transition Bay: we left also three cases of pemmican near the east end of Macgregor Laird Lake, and our travelling boat near its west end, at the head of False Strait, but she is damaged, a bear having put his paw through her thin planking.

Monday, 15th.—Strong east winds, with much rain, have imprisoned us here for the last four days, and driven the whole pack close in, completely filling up Cresswell Bay. We remain fast to the grounded ice, which shields us from pressure, otherwise we should have been irretrievably driven on shore. A couple more seals and a white whale have been shot; the latter measured $13\frac{1}{2}$ feet long, and proved to be a female of ordinary dimensions, and of an uniform cream colour; the eyes are extremely small, and orifices of the ears scarcely large enough to admit a crow-quill. We dined off steaks of the flesh, and prefer it to seal, which it very much resembles, but is not quite so tender; the skin is greatly prized by the Greenlanders as an antiscorbutic; it is a sort of gristly gelatinous substance, nearly half an inch thick, and possessing very little taste; fried and eaten with fish-sauce, it reminded me of cod-sound, though not so good.

The blubber fills two twenty-gallon casks; it produces oil of a quality superior to seal oil; not an ounce of the flesh or skin of this huge animal has been thrown away, the men having a wholesome dread of scurvy, and unbounded confidence in "blood-meat," such as this! The Doctor has picked up a few fossils very similar to those formerly brought home from Port Leopold.

To our great joy the east wind died away this morning, and immediately a west wind sprang up, which very quickly freshened to a smart gale. At four o'clock this afternoon we were able to make sail, the ice having moved about three miles off shore; passed within a mile of Fury Beach two hours afterwards, and saw the framing of the house, the boats and casks very distinctly.

17*th*.—After passing Fury Beach, it fell calm, so we steamed up as far as Batty Bay. On Tuesday afternoon we were off Port Leopold, and running fast, when thick fog came on; we became involved in loose ice, and seriously damaged our rudder. The boats and stores at Port Leopold appeared to remain as we left them last year. The flag-staff on the summit of North-east Cape (over Whale Point) is still standing, but not erect.

Fog and ice obstructed our progress during the night; but this morning when I came on deck at eight o'clock, the day was bright, clear, and charming; no ice visible, except about Leopold Island, which was now some miles behind us. Towards evening the wind became contrary.

Sunday evening, 21st.—Position, 72° 43' N., 72° 6' W. At sea—out of sight of land!

On the 19th we were somewhat delayed by loose ice off Cape Hay, but by noon yesterday were close off Cape Burney, and whilst almost becalmed there, a mother bear swam off to us with two interesting cubs about the size of very large dogs—foolish creatures! a volley of rifles decided their fate in a very few seconds. Not finding any whaling vessels off Pond's Inlet, the land-ice which shelters the whales having all disappeared, we concluded that the whalers had left in consequence, so, without seeking for them further south, we at once changed our course for Disco.

To-day only a few icebergs have been seen. There is a good deal of swell, so we tumble about. Roast *veal* has appeared amongst the delicacies of our table since the battue of yesterday, and Christian has asked for a portion of the old bear to carry home to his mother. Bear's flesh is a real delicacy in Greenland.

This is probably the last time that we shall fall in with bears, or have any occasion to allude to them. We see, we talk, and we dream more of bears than of any other animals, and are wont to write about them also, more perhaps than is necessary; nevertheless, I cannot let slip this opportunity of saying a few last words about our old acquaintance, the polar bear.

When we find him roaming over fields of drifting ice more than a hundred miles from land, we are filled with wonder; when there is no ice, we find him swimming off to our ships two, three, or more leagues, and we are scarcely less astonished. Arctic blue-books contain the official diaries of more than a hundred sledge-journeys, and in these the ubiquitous bear is constantly mentioned.

It is only when wounded or pressed by extreme hunger that the polar bear becomes fierce; as a rule he endeavours to avoid both men and dogs; therefore our plan was to lie down and remain quite still, the bear would then cautiously approach, sheltering himself from view as long as possible. Polar bears, hares, and foxes sometimes stand erect to reconnoitre, and I once shot a bear in this attitude; had I hesitated for a second or two, he would have completed his survey of us, and would probably have cautiously and safely retreated as he had advanced, by keeping behind hummocks of ice. In all our adventures with bears not previously acquainted with man, we found them to be inquisitive, timid except when hungry, and somewhat stupid, although in the capture of their prey they display a degree of instinct almost akin to reason; their endurance of cold, hunger, and fatigue, and their acute sense of smell, are quite extraordinary. They are perpetually roaming over the ice across the direction of the wind, scenting out the breathing holes of the seals. More than one officer records seeing a bear scrape away the snow, and enlarge the breathing hole of a seal with his claws, or break the ice by jumping up into the air and alighting with his whole weight on his fore-paws; and, when sufficiently enlarged, he would lie down beside the hole, and patiently watch for the doomed seal to pop up—almost between the paws of his wily enemy. These seal holes enlarged by bears have frequently been noticed.

Captain G. H. Richards mentions seeing "a bear with blood stains on his fur indulging in all the gambols of a kitten, and when approached, he moved off head over heels in a very unusual manner for so grave an animal:" but one of these holes through the ice with much blood and the claws of a seal, explained the whole affair. Footprints on the snow of a bear and a wolf have shown where the former had tracked the latter to his lair, had made a successful spring, and, after a sharp struggle, had supped off wolf. Captain Sherard Osborn mentions seeing a bear with her two cubs at some distance (perhaps a couple of miles) inland; the mother diligently turning over loose rocks which strewed the plain, and the cubs watching the opportunity to rush in and seize the unlucky lemmings which were thus dislodged, and tossing them up in the air in their wantonness; after repeating this operation until they must have made a tolerable meal, the dam seated herself on her haunches in a convenient posture for her purpose, and the young ones suckled in a standing position. But the lemmings were speedily avenged, for Osborn shot the whole of this interesting family.

An officer, on ascending a tall cliff to obtain an extensive view over the frozen sea, found a contemplative old bear sitting there; fortunately he was completely absorbed in watching for seals to appear on the ice, and the officer—being unarmed—tells us "that he came down much faster than he went up." Another officer, evidently on his first sledging journey, looks out of his tent and sees a young bear about ten yards off quietly devouring some pemmican which had been left upon the sledge; his first shot "takes effect over the left eye, taking the eye and a piece of the skull with it;" the bear falls, but is only stunned for the moment, jumps up, and runs off "at full trot;" a second shot breaks his hind leg, but he only trots faster than before; a third bullet "passes through his neck, and sends him off at full gallop!" At length, exhausted from loss of blood, this most unlucky young bear lies down, and a fourth bullet despatches him by passing through his heart. Only a novice would have aimed at the head, which is a very massive structure, or at the *whole* bear; the vital region is just behind the fore-shoulder.

It has happened that one of these animals, more inquisitive or more hungry than usual, actually looked into a tent, and threw the party into such confusion that they pulled the tent down on themselves! but bruin had snuffed the pemmican on the sledge, and turned deliberately to inspect it, when he was, of course, shot.

The sleepers in one of the 'Fox's' tents were aroused by a bear's paw breaking through their calico shelter!

The motive which usually led our searching parties to slaughter bears was to obtain their blubber for fuel, and their flesh for the dogs. In this way we have made them very useful to us; but they have often damaged our *câches* of provisions, destroyed any packages not strong enough to resist both their claws and their weight, rolled the casks about, and have invariably broken down the oars or poles erected as marks.

Captain Collinson records that "a bear broke open his depot, helped himself to pork and sugar, and"—worst of all —" extracted the bung from a barico of spirits and capsized it." It has occasionally happened that a man and a bear have unexpectedly found themselves close together, when, after an anxious gaze, they have mutually avoided each other, with as little loss of dignity and as much show of deliberation as possible!

I believe the only part of the arctic regions where bears have not been found is on the northern shores of Melville and Prince Patrick's Islands.

In the summer of 1850, one was shot within twenty-five miles of Beechey Island, at which it will be remembered that Franklin's ships spent the winter of 1845-6; under an old scar a large belted bullet was found; it had been fired from a two-grooved rifle, such as was formerly used in the naval service, and had been supplied to Franklin's expedition. In no other way can we account for the presence of this leaden messenger!

Throughout our winter at Port Leopold, in 1848-9, there were some very steep banks of hard snow against the face of a cliff, and I well remember seeing my excellent friend and messmate, the Paymaster of the 'Enterprise,' accidentally make a most rapid descent of at least one hundred and fifty feet on one of these; none of us had either the inclination or the courage to follow his example: our surprise may be imagined at seeing a bear at the top of one of these slopes, deliberately place himself on his haunches, and slide down to the bottom, steadying himself with his fore-paws as he went along, and thus maintaining the same posture throughout the entire descent!

25th.—Position, 70° 40′ N., 55° 17′ W. Becalmed off Hare Island, and getting the steam ready. We are only 108 miles from Godhavn, and the anxiety to clutch our letters has become intolerable. No pack-ice has been met with in our passage across Baffin's Bay, but many icebergs. This morning the lofty snow-clad lands of Noursoak, and Disco were beautifully distinct; and at the same time the wind died away, leaving us, at least, the opportunity to contemplate at our *leisure* their gloomy grandeur.

26th.—Steamed for ten hours last night. Fair winds and calms have alternated since then, but this evening we are within twenty miles, and hope soon to get into port.

I have been reading over Young's report of his spring journey. It comprises seventy-eight days of sledge travelling, and certainly under most discouraging circumstances. Leaving the ship on 7th April, he crossed Sir J. Franklin Strait to Prince of Wales' Land, and thence traced its shore to the south and west. On reaching its southern termination— Cape Swinburne, so named in honour of Rear-Admiral Swinburne, a much esteemed friend of Sir J. Franklin, and one of the earliest supporters of this final expedition—he describes the land as extremely low, and deeply covered with snow, the heavy grounded hummocks which fringed its monotonous coast alone indicating the line of demarcation

Moonlight – August 25 1859.

betwixt land and sea. To the north-east of this terminal cape the sea was covered with level floe formed in the fall of last year, whilst all to the northwestward of the same cape was pack consisting of heavy ice-masses, formed perhaps years ago in far distant and wider seas.

Young attempted to cross the channel[1] which he discovered between Prince of Wales' Island and Victoria Land, but, from the rugged nature of the ice, found it quite impracticable with the means and time remaining at his disposal. Young expresses his firm conviction that this channel is so constantly choked up with unusually heavy ice as to be quite unnavigable; it is, in fact, a *continuous ice-stream* from the N.W.. His opinion coincides with my own, and with those of Captains Ommanney and Osborn, when these officers explored the north-western shores of Prince of Wales' Land in 1851; and also with the opinion formed by Captain R. Collinson, C.B., when that officer discovered Gateshead Island, which lies near its southern shore, and at the N.E. extreme of Victoria Land.

Fearing that his provisions might run short, he sent back one sledge with four men, and continued his march with only one man and the dogs for forty days! They were obliged to build a snow-hut each night to sleep in, as the tent was sent back with the men; but latterly, when the weather became more mild, they preferred sleeping on the sledge, as the construction of a snow-hut usually occupied them for two hours. Young completed the exploration of this coast beyond the point marked upon the charts as Osborn's farthest, up nearly to lat. 73° N., but no cairn was found. Young, however, recognised the remarkably shaped conical hills noticed by Osborn when at his farthest in 1851 he struck off-shore to the westward.

The coast-line throughout was extremely low; and in the

---

[1] M'Clintock Channel; see Preface, p. xiv.

thick disagreeable weather which he almost constantly experienced, it was often a matter of great difficulty to prevent straying inland from it. He commenced his return on 11th May, and reached the ship on 7th June, in wretched health and depressed in spirits.

Directly his health was partially re-established, and in spite of the Doctor's remonstrances, as I have before said, he again set out on the 10th with his party of men and the dogs to complete the exploration of both shores of Sir John Franklin Strait, between the position of the 'Fox' and the points reached by Sir James Ross in 1849, and of Lieutenant Browne in 1851. This he accomplished without finding any trace of the lost expedition, and the parties were again on board by 28th June. The ice travelled over in this last journey was almost all formed last autumn.

The extent of coast-line explored by Captain Young amounts to 380 miles, whilst that discovered by Hobson and myself amounts to nearly 420 miles, making a total of 800 geographical miles of new coast-line which we have laid down.

Knowledge is power—a truth which these sledge journies amply demonstrate. If the reader now turns to Parry's second voyage, page 190, he will find there a most vivid description of a journey attempted to be made by Captain Lyons, R.N.

After due preparation, Lyons and a small party of men, equipped with sledge, tent, blankets, and three days' provisions, started on the 15th March, 1822, the thermometer standing at zero. Almost immediately a strong adverse gale sprang up, obliging them to pitch their tent when about six miles from the ship. The temperature fell to $-15°$, so cold that they considered it impossible to live in the tent; fortunately it was pitched on very deep snow, into which they dug a large hole or burrow, and there passed the night, the external temperature being $-25°$. So cramped and wretched were they next morning, that it was deemed less hazardous to attempt to reach the ship through the storm and densely drifting snow, than to risk another night in their snow-cavern.

Providentially they found their ship, but not until after wandering about for three hours and a half in the snow-storm, and when it was evident that four of the party could not have survived another hour! All of them were severely frost-bitten.

At this very time some Esquimaux also came to the ship for relief; but their need was very different—the seal-hunt had failed, they had nothing to eat, and their stock of blubber also being exhausted, not a lamp remained alight in their snow village!

With a proper equipment, or even a very slender one, and a snow-hut, Lyons and his companions, instead of being in imminent peril, might have been positively jolly; but this sort of knowledge is of slow growth. In his first voyage Sir Edward Parry did not venture to travel before the 1st of June, therefore this attempt of Lyons in the second voyage was a very bold step in advance.

We of the present time have, of course, benefitted largely by the dear-bought experience of our predecessors.

In the Franklin search more than 40,000 miles have been sledged, including 8000 miles of coast-line minutely examined, by parties varying from five to eleven persons, remaining absent from their ships for periods ranging up to one hundred and five days, and dragging along with them provisions for five, six, or seven weeks. Sledge parties travelled in every month excepting only the dark ones of December and January, in temperatures not unfrequently 40° below zero (of Fahrenheit), and occasionally even 10° or 15° colder still. It was found that men employed on long sledge journeys lost on the average about twelve pounds weight; and where they would drag a moderately laden sledge thirteen miles a day, an equal number of dogs would drag half the same load for twenty-seven miles.

The work of a single expedition of two ships (Kellett's and my own) with ninety officers and men, at a wintering station, amounted to 1282 statute miles, sledged in autumn, and 7352 miles in spring, by eleven parties; in this manner 1800 miles of coast-line were explored.

These great results are astonishing; and yet the system of sledge exploration is capable of still further development; already it has brought even the North Pole of the earth within our reach!

What laurels, what world-wide renown will be his, who first accomplishes this crowning feat of geographical discovery!

In his hour of triumph let him remember the ladder by which he has climbed; the successive steps of which were worked out by Lyons in 1822, and by a hundred others in the Franklin search.

Hobson's report is a minute record of all that occurred during his journey of seventy-four days, and includes a list of all the relics brought on board, or seen by him. He suffered very severely in health: when only ten days out from the ship, traces of scurvy appeared; when a month absent, he walked lame; towards the latter end of the journey, he was compelled to allow himself to be dragged upon the sledge, not being able to walk more than a few yards at a time; and on arriving at the ship on the 14th June, poor Hobson was unable to stand. How strongly this bears upon the last sad march of the lost crews! And yet Hobson's food throughout the whole journey was pemmican of the very best quality, the most nutritious description of food that we know of, and varied occasionally by such game as they were able to shoot. In spite of this fresh-meat diet, scurvy advanced with rapid strides. And here let me observe that amongst all the relics of the ill-fated expedition no preserved meat or vegetable tins were found, either about the cairns or along the line of retreat; the inference is as plain as it is painful!

His diary states that, after leaving me at Cape Victoria, "no difficulty was experienced in crossing James Ross Strait. The ice appeared to be of but one year's growth; and although it was in many places much crushed up, we easily found smooth leads through the lines of hummocks; many very heavy masses of ice, evidently of foreign formation, have been here arrested in their drift; so large are they, that in the gloomy weather we experienced, they were often taken for islands."

Again, at Cape Felix, he observes—"The pressure of the ice is severe, but the ice itself is not remarkably heavy in character; the shoalness of the coast keeps the line of pressure at a considerable distance from the beach: to the northward of the island the ice, as far as I could see, was very rough, and crushed up into large masses." Here we notice the gradual change in the character of the ice as Hobson left the Boothian shore and advanced towards Victoria Strait. The "very heavy masses of ice, evidently of foreign formation," had drifted in from the vast Polar Sea westward of Prince Patrick's Island, through M'Clure Strait; Victoria Strait contained a large proportion of this character; and Hobson's description of the ice he passed over clearly illustrates how Franklin, leaving comparatively clear water behind him, had to press his ships into the pack when he attempted to force through Victoria Strait.

Some description of this polar pack is necessary in order to convey any idea of it. Parry first met with it in 1819, near the western extreme of Melville Island, where it terminated his progress. He speaks of the floe-pieces as "haycock floes," from the rounded hummocks or mounds which studded their surfaces.

Although I have occasionally sledged over these floes, I never measured the actual height of the irregularities on their surfaces; they were, however, more than sufficient to intercept my view of the horizon.

The late lamented Commander Mecham mentions one very old floe which he sledged over, the mounds of blue ice upon it varying from five to twenty feet in height, and the ridges between them, over which he was obliged to pass, were from four to nine feet high! Another accurate observer describes some pieces of these floes which he found lying upon the shore of Banks' Land, where they had been forced up by enormous ice-pressure; they were from twenty-two to twenty-four feet thick, and one of them had a mound or knoll upon it ten feet high!

Hobson left King William's Island on the last day of May, having spent thirty-one days on its desolate shores. During that period, one bear and five willow-grouse were shot; one wolf and a few foxes were seen. One poor fox was either so desperately hungry or so charmed with the rare sight of animated beings, that he played about the party until the dogs snapped him up, although in harness and dragging the sledge at the time. A few gulls were seen, but not until after the first week in June.

It was at a short distance westward of Cape Felix that Hobson first came upon the traces of the Franklin Expedition; he found a large cairn, and close beside it three small tents, with blankets, old clothes, and other vestiges of a shooting, or a magnetic station; but although the cairn was dug under, and a trench dug all round it at a distance of ten feet, no record was discovered. A sheet of white paper folded up was found in the cairn, but even under the microscope no trace of writing appears.

Two broken bottles (corked) lay amongst the loose stones which had fallen off the cairn, and these may perhaps have contained records. The most interesting of the relics, including a small English ensign, and the iron heads of two boarding pikes, were brought away.

The tents lay prostrate, and without tent-poles; it seems highly probable that the pikes had been used for that purpose, and were subsequently burnt for fuel.

Two miles farther to the south-west a small cairn was found, but neither record nor relics; and about three miles northward of Point Victory a third cairn was examined, but only a broken pickaxe and empty tin canister found.

I have already explained how Hobson found the records and the boat; he exercised his discretionary power with sound judgment, and completed his search so well that, in coming over the same ground after him, I could not discover any trace that had escaped him.

I quite agree with him that there may be many small articles beneath the snow; but that cairns, graves, or any conspicuous objects could exist upon so low and uniform a shore, without our having seen them, is *almost* impossible.

The natives told Petersen that the ships were destroyed in the autumn of the same year in which they were abandoned; but not understanding their Esquimaux names of places upon King William's Island, we could not ascertain whereabouts the one was crushed and sunk, and the other driven on shore. But as the natives had not visited the north-west shore since the landing there of the lost crews, it seems tolerably certain that it was off the south-west shore of King William's Island that the abandoned ships were destroyed.

Sunday evening, 28th.—Calm, warm, lovely weather; and we are thoroughly enjoying it in the quiet security of Lievely harbour, or Godhavn. Although Friday night was dark, we managed to find out the harbour's mouth, and slowly steamed into it. The inhabitants were awoke by Petersen demanding our letters, but great indeed was our disappointment at finding only a very few letters and two or three papers, and these for the officers only! It appears that on the arrival of the whalers in early spring, the ice prevented their usual communication with the settlement, therefore the letters on board of them were unavoidably carried northward. Some few, however, which came out in the 'Truelove,'[1] were landed at the neighbouring settlement of Noursoak, and from thence were sent back to Godhavn.

It is rather a nervous thing opening the first letters after a lapse of *more than two years!* We received them in our beds at three o'clock in the morning, and, when we met at breakfast, were able, thank God! to congratulate each other upon the receipt of cheering home news. Lady Franklin

---

[1] The history of the old 'Truelove,' of Hull, is a very remarkable one. In 1764, before the question of American Independence was raised, she was built at Philadelphia, of the famous live-oak. This wood was plentiful and cheap in those days, and was used without stint in her construction, so much so that, although originally a packet, and possessing rather superior sailing qualities, yet her massive beams and unusual strength rendered her so peculiarly adapted for battling with the arctic ice, that she was converted into a Greenland whaler. For more than forty years she plied those dangerous seas, escaping by innumerable hair-breadths the destruction which overwhelmed numberless other vessels, and eventually she was only driven from the trade by the introduction of steam.

Yet still (1869) she plies the northern seas, under some icy spell, it would seem, conveying to us cargoes of Norwegian ice; and steered by a compass which dates back to 1818.

Her stout timbers are quite sound, and as the original planking is doubled over with African oak, it is not impossible that she may continue for another century to defy the storms of ocean, and set at nought the adage which her name suggests.

and Miss Cracroft wrote to me from Bournemouth in March last. They have travelled more in the time than we have, having visited almost all the countries bordering the Mediterranean and Black Seas, posted through the Crimea, and steamed up the Danube ! I am gratified to find that I have been elected a member of the Royal Yacht Squadron during my absence.

Yesterday morning I called upon the Inspector, Mr. Olrik, who has been home to Denmark since I saw him last spring. In the autumn he took Mrs. Olrik and his family to Copenhagen, and has but just returned alone. He received me with his usual kindness, and promised me such supplies as we require, notwithstanding that my demands are unsustained by any authority—even my expected letters of credit have not arrived; neither is there any hint thrown out as to where I am to take the 'Fox.' Mr. Olrik gave me a large bundle of the 'Illustrated London News,' which was exceedingly acceptable, and told us that Austria was at war with France and Sardinia. By the latest news a battle had been fought and won by the latter Powers. Most fortunately a 'Navy List' had come out to Hobson, otherwise I think we should have been utterly brokenhearted ! We study its pages daily, and delight in noticing the advancement of our many friends.

1st Sept., Thursday night.—At sea, on *the passage*, and already enjoying, by anticipation, the pleasures of home ! Five busy days were spent in Godhavn, supplying our present wants, in as far as they could be supplied, including 100 gallons of light beer. The natives were very useful, the men bringing off water, stone ballast, and sand, and a troop of lively Esquimaux girls scrubbing the paintwork and the decks.

Each evening the men went on shore, taking with them

a very limited quantity of rum-punch for the ladies, and danced for several hours in a large store; whilst the officers and myself spent the time with Mr. Olrik or the other Danish gentlemen—Messrs. Andersen, Bulbrue, and Tyner. Nothing could exceed their kindness to us, whilst their good humour and their anecdotes, sometimes expressed in quaint English, greatly amused us. We shall always retain very agreeable recollections of Godhavn; twice has it been to us an arctic home.

Mr. Petersen's nieces, the belles of the place, came on board (Miss Sophia with scented cambric handkerchief and gloves—in other respects adhering to the Esquimaux costume, of which the accompanying illustration gives a very faithful representation); they were delighted with the organ, although it is rather out of repair, and they sang together very sweetly. Our Esquimaux shipmates, Christian and Samuel, were discharged, and by their own request, their wages given in charge to Mr. Olrik, and Mr. Bulbrue; they seemed to understand the importance of husbanding their wealth. Christian said he thought it would not be all spent under three years. First of all he intended buying a rifle for his brother, and then some wood to build a house for himself.

I was gratified very much when I heard them say that the men had treated them very well—"all the same as brothers;" and they really seemed sorry to leave the ship; they would come on board and look gravely about at everything as if regretting the coming separation. Even our poor dogs seemed to think the ship their natural abode; although landed at the settlement, they soon ran round the harbour to the point nearest to the ship, and there, upon the rocks, spent the whole period of our stay; as we sailed slowly out of the harbour, they ran along the rocks abreast of the ship

Belles of Disco.

to the outermost extreme, howling most piteously; even when far out at sea we could still hear their plaintive chorus! We rejoiced that we had made the best provision in our power for their future treatment, having given them away to those who were the most likely to be kind to them.

At this place the Esquimaux do not feed their dogs during the summer months; they exist upon such scraps of offal or old skins as they can pick up about the huts, and such dead fish as are thrown up on the rocks. They may be often seen prowling along the shore and contending with the ravens for the refuse of the sea.

On Tuesday night we set off some fireworks on shore to amuse the natives for I intended sailing next day, but the wind prevented my doing so. The last day was spent in the interchange of presents between our Danish friends and ourselves; indeed, the sincere hearty good feeling which existed between every individual in the 'Fox' and the inhabitants of the settlement was as gratifying as apparent. Almost the only fresh supplies obtained here were rock cod, and salmon-trout from Disco fiord. During our stay the weather was delightful; indeed, it was the first really fine weather they had experienced at Godhavn during the present season, the summer having been cold and wet.

10th Sept., Saturday night.—To-day we passed to the eastward of Cape Farewell, but about 100 miles to the south of it. The last iceberg was seen to-day; and now we are running along swiftly before a pleasant N.W. breeze. Hitherto we have had every variety of wind and weather, from a calm to a gale, but generally the wind has been favourable. The change of temperature is already very perceptible.

Saturday night, 17th Sept.—A week of favourable gales

has brought us from Cape Farewell to within 400 miles of the Land's End, or about 1100 miles of distance. But such rough weather is not pleasant in so small a vessel, however much "like a duck" she may rise over the waves; and our two years' sojourn in the still waters of the frozen North has made us very susceptible of the change.

CONCLUSION.

We sailed all the way home from Greenland, yet the 'Fox' made the passage in only nineteen days, arriving in the English Channel on 20th September; on the evening of the 21st I reached London (having landed at Portsmouth), and made known to the Admiralty the result of my voyage.

On the 23rd September the 'Fox' was taken into dock at Blackwall; and, through the kindness and promptitude of the Lords of the Admiralty, I was enabled on the 27th, when the crew were assembled for the last time, to present the Arctic Medal to such of my companions as had not already received it for previous arctic service, and also to inform Lieutenant Hobson that his promotion to the rank of Commander would speedily take place.

I will not intrude upon the reader, who has followed me through the pages of this simple narrative, any description of my feelings on finding the enthusiasm with which we were all received on landing upon our native shores. The blessing of Providence had attended our efforts, and more than a full measure of approval from our friends and countrymen has been our reward. For myself the testimonial given me by the officers and crew of the 'Fox' has touched me perhaps more than all. The purchase of a gold chronometer, for presentation to me, was the first use the men made of their earnings; and as long as I live it will remind me of that perfect harmony, that mutual esteem and goodwill, which made our ship's company a happy little community, and contributed materially to the success of the expedition.

The names I have given to my discoveries are, with the exception of those by which I have endeavoured to honour the members of the lost expedition, the names of active supporters of the recent search, and friends of Franklin and his companions, though such names are far from exhausting the number of those who have the highest claims to distinction on both grounds.

It will be observed that I have refrained from repeating names which have already been commemorated by preceding commanders, and which therefore are already in our charts. Besides the individuals already mentioned in the narrative, Sir Thomas D. Acland, one of the most zealous promoters of the search, both in and out of the House of Commons; Monsieur De la Roquette, Vice-President of the Geographical Society of Paris, and author of an interesting biography of Franklin; Rear-Admiral Fitzroy; and Major-General Pasley, R.E., stand high amongst those whom it has been my privilege to honour.

Although much talent has been brought to bear upon the deciphering of the letters and papers found in a pocket-book near Cape Herschel (page 236, *ante*), yet, from their being so very much defaced by time, only a few detached sentences have been made out, and these do not in the slightest degree refer to the proceedings of the lost expedition.

One paper is dated "April 21st, 1847." Amongst them was a seaman's parchment certificate; by the aid of chemical re-agents, Mr. F. G. Netherclifft, of 32 Brewer Street, Golden Square, has been able to decipher the name of Hy. Peglar, together with several particulars respecting him—stature, 5 ft. 7¼ in.; hair, light-brown, &c. A reference to official documents at the Admiralty shows that Henry Peglar joined H.M.S. 'Terror' on 11th March, 1845, as Captain of the

Fore-top, his age then being 37 years. The same authority also corroborates a sort of narrative of Hy. Peglar, contained in one of these papers, apparently drawn up by himself, and showing that he entered H.M. Navy in Nov. 1825, and continued to serve in it almost without interruption; it is without date, and ends with the words "now in the 'Terror.'"

Three of these manuscripts have each word written backwards, frequently ending in a capital letter, and as the spelling is very incorrect, they were most puzzling; they are devoid of any special interest. Upon the parchment certificate are still legible the names of the six ships—'Magnificent,' 'Rattlesnake,' 'Talavera,' 'Gannet,' 'Ocean,' and 'Wanderer'—in which Peglar served previous to joining the 'Terror;' it does not appear to have ever been filled up for this latter ship, and probably the office work of filling up the seamen's certificates was left to be performed upon the long passage home. This circumstance, coupled with the fact that poor Peglar (who seems to have been a poet in a very humble way) found amusement in writing a sort of parody on a sea-song in April, 1847, after an absence of two years from England, lets in a gleam of light upon their habits, and affords some grounds for the belief that, up to that date at least, they were both cheerful and confident: it is an unlooked-for confirmation of Graham Gore's "All well!" in May, 1847.

A year later, and the possessor of the pocket-book—whom I presume to be Peglar—prepares himself for the long (and, as it proved, the fatal) march; discarding his seaman's attire,[1] he dressed himself in his best suit of *shore-going* clothes, the clothes reserved to be worn on the day of landing once more in England; he took with him the pocket-book already mentioned, with its trivial contents of songs and stories,[2] perhaps

[1] See p. 236. [2] See List of Relics in Appendix No. I., p. 320.

to be read for the amusement of his companions upon fitting occasions during their journey to the Hudson Bay Territories; he also took with him a comb and a brush. In all this there is no trace of despondency, nor of departure from ordinary customs—hence it is impossible to resist the inference that their discipline continued perfect, and that they conducted themselves throughout that fearful march like brave men to whom despair was unknown.

I gladly embrace the present opportunity of filling up an omission in this journal, which the frequent enquiries of friends has shown me exists. I am asked to explain why so few of the bones of our lost countrymen have been found. The answer is simply, because—like those who travelled in search of them—they were compelled to drag their boats and laden sledges upon the sea ice, which affords a level roadway, and which the land does not.[1] And, it is hardly needful to observe that the bodies of those who were overtaken by death upon the ice, found their final rest at the bottom of the sea, upon the summer thaw of 1848. Doubtless also, the snow which thinly covered the coastline concealed many traces, and perhaps even skeletons, of our lost countrymen, as has already been surmised (pp. 237, 301).

The supposition that some may have protracted their existence, amongst the Esquimaux or upon the resources of the country, is altogether untenable.

Upon the whole of King William's Island, and also within the mouth of the Back River, only eight or nine families were met with; and had they succoured our famishing

[1] Oftentimes the land is impracticable even for light sledges, whilst upon the sea we can march straight from point to point: this may receive illustration from my own experience: out of nearly six thousand miles which I have sledged in the "Franklin Search," not quite three hundred miles have been upon the land, and even this is a very large proportion of land-travel, compared with that of other searchers.

countrymen, they most certainly would have told us of it. During my two spring-journeys, comprising one hundred and four days' marching along these and the West Boothian shores, although constantly on the look-out for game, and accompanied by Petersen, one of the most ardent and successful of arctic sportsmen, we succeeded in shooting only two rein-deer, one bear, two foxes, a hare, and twenty birds.

The retreating crews could not have carried with them more than forty days' provisions at a very short allowance; that any considerable number of them reached Montreal Island, a distance of about 250 miles by sledge-route, is marvellous; yet here they were separated by 600 or 800 miles from any land sufficiently abounding in animal life to sustain them, and the Back River, by which they hoped to obtain access to this more favoured region, was still frozen to a depth of five or six feet.

Under these appalling circumstances, I cannot but conclude that all superfluous weights, such as logbooks[1] and journals, were thrown away very early upon the march, the officers themselves setting the example; Sir Robert M'Clure did not attempt to save his logbooks, he left them behind him on board the 'Investigator' when that ship was abandoned in Mercy Bay.

It has been the generally received opinion that one hundred and thirty-eight individuals sailed on board the 'Erebus' and 'Terror,' that number being the sum of their united complements. I am enabled to state, on the authority of the Admiralty, that only one hundred and thirty-four persons left England; and of these, one subsequently returned in H.M.S. 'Rattler,' and four in the transport 'Barretto Junior'—so that only one hundred and twenty-nine, the exact number mentioned in the record, actually entered the ice.

[1] See p. 242.

The relics we have brought home have been deposited by the Admiralty in the Museum of the United Service Institution, and now form a national memento—the most simple and most touching—of those heroic men who perished in the path of duty, but not until they had achieved the grand object of their voyage—the *Discovery of the North-West Passage.*

London, 24*th Nov.* 1859.

APPENDIX.

No. I.

List of Relics of the Franklin Expedition brought to England in the 'Fox,' and deposited in the Museum of the United Service Institution.

Relics brought from the boat found in lat. 69° 8' 43" N., long. 99° 24' 42" W., upon the West Coast of King William's Island, May 30, 1859:—

Two double-barrelled guns, one barrel in each is loaded. Found standing up against the sides in the after part of the boat.

A small Prayer-Book; cover of a small book of 'Family Prayers;' 'Christian Melodies,' an inscription within the cover to "G. G." (Graham Gore?); 'Vicar of Wakefield;' a small Bible, interlined in many places, and with numerous references written in the margin; a New Testament in the French language.

Two table knives with white handles—one is marked "W. R." (wardroom); a gimlet; an awl; two iron stanchions, 9 inches long, for supporting a weather cloth, which was round the boat.

26 pieces of silver plate—11 spoons, 11 forks, and 4 teaspoons; 3 pieces of thin elmboard (tingles) for repairing the boat, and measuring 11 inches by 6 inches, and 3-10ths inch thick.

Piece of canvas:—Bristles for shoemaker's use, bullets, short clay pipe, roll of waxed twine, a wooden button, small piece of a port fire, two charges of shot tied up in the finger of a kid glove, fragment of a seaman's blue serge frock. Covers of a small Testament and Prayer-Book, part of a grass cigar-case, fragment of a silk handkerchief, thread-case, piece of scented soap, three shot charges in kid glove fingers, a belted bullet, a piece of silk pocket-handkerchief. Two pairs of goggles, made of stout leather, and wire gauze instead of glass; a sail-maker's palm, two small brass pocket compasses, a snooding line rolled up on a piece of leather, a needle and thread case, a bayonet scabbard altered into a sheath for a knife, tin water bottle for the pocket, two shot pouches (full of shot).

Three spring hooks of sword belts, a gold lace band, a piece of thin gold twist or cord, a pair of leather goggles with crape instead of glass; a small green crape veil.

Two small packets of blank cartridge in green paper, part of a cherry-stick pipe stem, piece of a port-fire, a few copper nails, a leather boot-lace, a seaman's clasp-knife, two small glass stoppered bottles (full), three glasses of spectacles, part of a broken pair of silver spectacles, German silver pencil-case, a pair of silver (?) forceps, such as a naturalist might use for holding or seizing small insects, &c.; a small pair of scissors rolled up in blank paper, and to which adheres a printed Government paper, such as an officer's warrant or appointment; a spring hook of a sword belt, a brass charger for holding two charges of shot.

A small bead purse, piece of red sealing-wax, stopper of a pocket flask, German silver top and ring, brass matchbox, one of the glasses of a telescope, a small tin cylinder, probably made to hold lucifer matches; a linen bag of percussion caps of three sizes, a very large and old-fashioned kind, stamped "Smith's patent;" a cap with a flange similar to the present musket caps used by Government, but smaller; and ordinary sporting caps of the smallest size.

Five watches.

A pair of blue glass spectacles or goggles with steel frame, and wire gauze encircling the glasses, in a tin case.

A pemmican tin, painted lead colour, and marked " E." (Erebus) in black. From its size it must have contained 20 lbs. or 22 lbs.

Two yellow glass beads, a glass seal with symbol of Freemasonry.

A 4-inch block, strapped, with copper hook and thimble, probably for the boat's sheet.

Relics seen in lat. 69° 9′ N., long. 99° 24′ W., not brought away, 30th of May, 1859 :—

A large boat, measuring 28 ft. in extreme length, 7 ft. 3 in. in breadth, 2 ft. 4 in. in depth. The markings on her stem were —"XXI, W. Con. N61., APr. 184." It appears that the fore part of the stem has been cut away, probably to reduce weight, and part of the letters and figures removed. An oak sledge under the boat, 23 ft. 4 in. long, and 2 ft. wide; 6 paddles, about 60 fathoms of deep-sea lead line, ammunition, 4 cakes of navy chocolate, shoemaker's box with implements complete, small quantities of tobacco, a small pair of very stout shooting boots, a pair of very heavy iron-shod knee boots, carpet boots, sea boots and shoes—in all seven or eight pairs; two rolls of sheet lead, elm tingles for repairing the boat, nails of various sizes for boat, and sledge irons, three small axes, a broken saw, leather cover of a sextant case, a chain-cable punch, silk handkerchiefs (black, white, and coloured), towels, sponge, tooth-brush, hair comb, a macintosh, gun cover (marked in paint "A 12"), twine, files, knives; a small worsted-work slipper, lined with calfskin, bound with red riband; a great quantity of clothing, and a wolfskin robe; part of a boat's sail of No. 8 canvas, whale-line rope with yellow mark, and white-line with red mark; 24 iron stanchions, 9½ inches high, for supporting a weather cloth round the boat; a stanchion for supporting a ridge pole at a height of 3 ft. 9 in. above the gunwale.

Relics found about Ross's Cairn, on Point Victory, May and June, 1859, brought away :—

A 6-inch dip circle by Robinson, marked I 22. A case of medicines, consisting of 25 small bottles, canister of pills, ointment, plaster, oiled silk, &c. A 2-foot rule, two joints of the cleaning rod of a gun, and two small copper spindles, probably for dog-vanes of boats. The circular brass plate broken out of a wooden gun-case, and engraved "C. H. Osmer, R.N." The field glass and German silver top of a 2-foot telescope, a coffee canister, a piece of a brass curtain rod. The record tin, and the record dated 25th of April, 1848. A 6-inch double frame sextant, on which the owner's name is engraved, "Frederick Hornby, R.N."

Found in a small cairn on the south side of Back Bay, brought away:—

A tin record case and record.

Seen about Ross's Cairn, Point Victory, not brought away :—

Four sets of boat's cooking apparatus complete, iron hoops, 4 feet of a copper lightning conductor, hollow brass curtain rod three-quarters of an inch in diameter, 3 pickaxes, 1 shovel, old canvas, a pile of warm clothing and blankets 4 feet high; 2 tin canteens stamped "89 Co., Wm. Hedges," "88 Co., Wm. Heather," and a third one not marked. A small pannikin, made on board out of a 2-lb. preserved meat tin, and marked "W. Mark;" a small deal box for gun wadding, the heavy iron work of a large boat, part of a canvas tent, part of an oar sawed longitudinally and a blanket nailed to its flat side, three boat-hook staves, strips of copper, a 9-inch single block strapped, a piece of rope, and spunyarn. Among the clothing was found a stocking marked "W. Green," and a fragment of one marked "W. S."

Relics obtained at the Northern Cairn, near Cape Felix, May, 1859 :—

Fragments of a boat's ensign, metal lid of a powder case, two eye-pieces of sextant tubes, brass button; worsted glove, colours red, white, and blue; bung-stave of a marine's water keg or bottle; brass ornaments of a marine's shako; brass screw for screwing down lid, also a copper hinge of the lid of powder-case; a few patent wire cartridges containing large shot; part of a pair of steel spectacles, glass being replaced by wood, having a narrow slit in it; two small rib bones, probably out of salt pork; six or eight packets of needles; small flannel cartridge containing an ounce of damaged powder; a small, roughly made copper apparatus for cooking; some brimstone matches. Piece of white paper folded up found in the North Cairn, two pike-heads, narrow strip of white paper, found under one of the tent places: their tent places were within a few yards of the cairn.

Beside a small cairn, about three miles north of Point Victory, was :—

A pickaxe, with broken handle: brought away an empty tea or coffee canister.

Articles noticed about the North Cairn, not brought away :—

Fragments of two broken bottles, several pieces of broken basins or cups, blue and white delf-ware, hoops of marine's water keg, small iron hoops, fragments of white-line, spunyarn, canvas, and twine; three small canvas tents, under which lay a bearskin and fragments of blankets; two blanket frocks, several old mittens, stockings, gloves, pilot cloth and box cloth jackets and trousers, large shot, piece of tobacco and broken pipe, metal part of powder-case, top of tin canister marked "cheese," preserved-potato tin, feathers of ptarmigan, and salt-meat bones.

Seen near Cape Maria Louisa :—

Part of a drift tree, white spruce fir, 18 feet long, 10 inches in diameter; it appeared to have but recently (*i. e.* since thrown on the coast) been sawed longitudinally down the centre, and one-half of it removed.

Relics obtained from the Boothian Esquimaux, near the Magnetic Pole, in March and April, 1859 :—

Seven knives made by the natives out of materials obtained from the lost expedition, one knife without a handle, one spear-head and staff (the latter has broken off), two files; a large spoon or scoop, the handle of pine or bone, the bowl of musk-ox horn; six silver spoons and forks, the property of Sir John Franklin, Lieutenants H. D, Le Vesconte, and Fairholme, A. M'Donald, Assistant Surgeon, and Lieutenant E. Couch (supposed from the initial letter C and crest, a lion's head); a small portion of a gold watch-chain, a broken piece of ornamental work apparently silver gilt, a few small naval and other metal buttons, a silver medal obtained by Mr. M'Donald as a prize for superior attainments at a medical examination in Edinburgh, April,

1838; some bows and arrows, in which wood, iron, or copper has been used in the construction—but of no other interest.

Remarks upon these Articles.

The spear-staff measures 6 feet 3 inches in length, and appears to have been part of a light boat's gunwale; it measured (before being partially rounded to adapt it to its present use) about $1\frac{1}{2}$ by $1\frac{3}{4}$ inch, is made of English oak, and upon the side has been painted white over green. The spear-head is of steel, riveted to two pieces of hoop, with bone between, and lashed on to the staff. The rivets are of copper nails. The native who sold it said he himself got it from the boat in the Fish River. Another spear of the same kind was seen. The knives are made either of iron or steel, riveted to two strips of hoop, between which the handle of wood is inserted, and rivets passed through, securing them together. The rivets are almost all made out of copper nails, such as would be found in a copper-fastened boat, but those which have been examined do not bear the Government mark. It is probable that most of the boats of the 'Erebus' and 'Terror' were built by contract, and therefore would not have the broad arrow stamped upon their iron and copper work. One small knife appears to have been a surgical instrument. A large knife obtained in April bears some marking, such as a sword or a cutlass might have. The man who sold it said he bought it from another, who picked it up on the land where the ship was driven ashore by the ice, and where the white people had thrown it away; it was then about as long as his arm. This was the first information we received of one of the ships having drifted on shore. One knife and one file are stamped with the broad arrow. The handles are variously composed of oak, ash, pine, mahogany, elm, and bone. The spoons and forks were readily sold for a few needles each, also the buttons, which they wore as ornaments on their dresses. Bows and arrows were readily exchanged for knives. Previously to the stranding on the neighbouring shore of the lost Expedition these people must have been almost destitute of wood or iron. Some of them even had only bone knives and bone spear-points. Some of their sledges were seen, consisting of two rolls of sealskin, flattened and frozen, to serve as runners, and connected together by cross bars of bones. Many more knives, bows, and buttons, similar to those brought away, might have been obtained, but no personal or important relics.

Seen in a Snow Hut in lat. $70\frac{1}{2}°$ N., 20th of April, 1859, not brought away :—

Two wooden shovels, one of them made of mahogany board, some spear-handles and a bow of English wood, a deal case which might have served for a telescope or barometer. Its external dimensions were :— length, 3 ft. 1 in.; depth, $3\frac{1}{2}$ in.; width, 9 in.; two brass hinges remained attached to it.

Relics obtained from the Esquimaux near Cape Norton, upon the East Coast of King William's Island, in May, 1859 :—

Two tablespoons ; upon one is scratched " W. W.," on the other " W. G. ; " these bear the Franklin crest ; two table forks, one bearing the Franklin crest, the other is also crested, probably Captain Crozier's ; silversmith's name is " I. West ;" two teaspoons, one engraved " A. M. D." (A. M'Donald), the other bears the Fairholme crest and motto ; handle of a dessert knife, into which had been inserted a razor (since broken off) by Millikin, Strand ; buttons, wood, and iron, were here in abundance, but as enough of these had already been obtained, no more were purchased.

Taken out of some deserted snow-huts near here :—

Some scraps of different kinds of wood, such as could not be obtained from a boat—teak or African oak.

Found lying about the skeleton, 9 miles eastward of Cape Herschel, 26th May, 1859 :—

The tie of black silk neckerchief; fragments of a double-breasted blue cloth waistcoat, with covered silk buttons, and edged with braid ; a scrap of a coloured cotton shirt, silk-covered buttons of blue cloth great-coat, a small clothes-brush, a horn pocket-comb, a leathern pocket-book, which fell to pieces when thawed and dried ; it contained 9 or 10 letters, a few leaves apparently blank ; a sixpence, date 1831 ; and a half-sovereign, dated 1844.

A subsequent most careful examination proved these letters, or rather papers folded as letters, to be :—

(No. 1.)   Simply an address—"Mr. John Cowper, No. 47, John Street, Commercial Road, London."

(No. 2.)   An account of Hy. Peglar's sea services.

(No. 3.)   An address—" O. J. Rezzoe, a Squier, R.N., Sandile Harbor. John T. Couart, ... eth   "—

(No. 4.)   The words of a sea-song, with the date " April 21, 1847."

(No. 5.)   " Lines writ . . . . on a party wot happened at Trinidad," &c., each word being spelt backwards.

(No. 6.)   An account of some festive trip, each word spelt backwards, —" Sir, in one of my jerneys to the old City of Cumanar," &c.

(No. 7.)   Lines beginning " Oh Death where is thy sting ; " and spelt backwards.

(No. 8.)   The parchment certificate of Henry Peglar. Also, two or three wholly illegible papers and a scrap of ' Lloyd's Weekly Newspaper.'

There are two handwritings here; the MSS. numbered 1, 2, and 4, are by the same person ; Nos. 3, 5, 6, and 7, are by some one else.

Articles seen among the natives at Cape Norton, not purchased :—

Bows made of wood, knives, uniform and plain buttons, a sledge made of two long pieces of hard wood.

From beside an Esquimaux stone-mark, on the east side of Montreal Island :—

Part of a preserved-meat tin, painted red; part of the rim of some strong copper case or vessel; pieces of iron hoop, two pieces of flat iron, an iron hook-bolt, a piece of sheet copper.

Articles seen about a snow-hut near Point Booth, not purchased :—

Eight or ten fir poles, varying from 5 feet to 10 feet in length, the stoutest being 2½ inches in diameter. Two wooden snow shovels about 3½ feet long, and made of pieces of plank painted white or pale yellow; it occurred to me that the pieces of plank might have been the bottom-boards of a boat. There was abundance of wood fashioned into smaller articles.

Contents of Boat's Medicine Chest, found on Point Victory:—

One bottle labelled as zinzib. R. pulv., full; ditto, spirit. rect., empty; ditto, mur. hydrarg., seven-eighths full; ditto, ol. caryophyll., one-fifth full; ditto, ipec. P. co., full; ditto, ol. menth. pip., empty; ditto, liq. ammon. fort., three-quarters full; ditto, ol. olivæ, full; ditto, tinct. opii camph., three-quarters full; ditto, vin. sem. colch., full; ditto, quarter full; ditto, calomel, full (broken); ditto, hydrarg. nit. oxyd., full; ditto, pulv. gregor., full (broken); ditto, magnes. carb., full; ditto, camphor, full; two bottles tinct. tolut., each quarter full; one bottle ipec. R. pulv., full; ditto, jalap. R. pulv., full; ditto, scammon. pulv., full; ditto, quinine bisulph., empty; ditto (not labelled), tinct. opii, three-quarters full; one box (apparently) purgative pills, full; ditto, ointment, shrunk; ditto, emp. adhesiv., full; one probang, one pen wrapped up in lint, one lead pencil, one pewter syringe, two small tubes (test) wrapped up in lint, one farthing, bandages, oil silk, lint, thread.

No. II.

REPORTS OF SCIENTIFIC OBSERVATIONS OBTAINED DURING THE VOYAGE OF THE 'FOX;' OR REFERENCES TO SUCH OF THESE REPORTS AS ARE PUBLISHED ELSEWHERE.

ZOOLOGY.—Notes on the zoology of the voyage, by the Surgeon, David Walker, M.D.; also Notes on some of the diatomous forms collected, by the Rev. Eugene O'Meara. Published in the 'Royal Dublin Society's Journal' for 1860.

BOTANY.—The botanical specimens collected and brought home by Dr. Walker consisted of about 170 species of plants. They were placed in the hands of Dr. J. D. Hooker, F.R.S., and the account drawn up by him will be found in the 'Journal of Proceedings of the Linnean Society,' *Botany*, vol. v.

GEOLOGY.—The geological collection made during the voyage of the 'Fox,' together with the collections brought home by me in three previous arctic Expeditions, were submitted to the Rev. Professor Samuel Haughton, F.R.S., President of the Geological Society of Dublin. From all these specimens, Dr. Haughton constructed a highly interesting geological map of the Arctic Archipelago to accompany his description, which will be found in Appendix IV. of the former editions of this work. The specimens are in the Museum of the Royal Dublin Society, and, together with those collected in Greenland by Sir Charles L. Giesecke, form a more extensive collection of arctic rocks and fossils than is to be found in any other museum in Europe. It includes ammonites from lat. $76\frac{1}{2}°$ N.; specimens of pine trees found in great abundance in lat. $74°$ N., also in $76°$ N., both recent and fossil; coal plants; fossils from the carboniferous and silurian rocks of similar high latitudes; and miocene fossils from lat. $70°$ N.

These latter fossils have been described by Professor Oswald Heer, of Zürich, in his 'Flora Fossilis Arctica,' published in 1868. An abstract taken from this work by R. H. Scott, M.A. (which includes all miocene specimens brought home by Captain E. A. Inglefield, R.N.; Lieutenant P. Columb, R.N.; Herr C. S. M. Olrik; and by myself) will be found in the 'Journal of the Royal Dublin Society' for 1867, No. xxxvi.

A collection more recently brought home by F. Whymper, Esq., F.R.G.S., is noticed in the 'Proceedings of the Royal Society' for 1869, No. 110.

The total number of these most interesting miocene plants, discovered in Greenland, now amounts to 137 species.

METEOROLOGY.—It is not proposed to do more here than invite the attention of the scientific enquirer to a very able and complete discussion on the meteorological observations made on board the 'Fox,' as published in the 13th volume of the 'Smithsonian Contributions to Knowledge,' April 1861.

A few brief remarks, such as may not be uninteresting to the general reader, are all that we can find room for here.

At Port Kennedy the highest temperature observed during the year was $55°$ Fahr., the lowest $-49.8°$ Fahr., consequently the extreme range was $105°$. The average maximum temperature occurred between noon and 1 P.M., and the minimum between 2 and 3 A.M.

The mean annual temperature is $+2°$ Fahr. By calculation, the warmest day is 20th July, the coldest day is 19th January; and the days of mean annual temperature are 23rd April and 22nd October.

The mean monthly diurnal fluctuations of temperature in autumn and winter do not exceed 3°; whereas in spring and summer—the sun then being generally above the horizon—it amounts to 9°.

Even during mid-winter, when the sun is absent, the diurnal variation does not altogether disappear.

The effect of the moon during winter, in producing a clear sky and fall of temperature, has long been known. From the observations of the 'Fox,' it appears that the temperature is lower at full moon than at new moon by about 7°.

The effect of a calm is also to lower the temperature.

At Port Kennedy the most windy months were October and November; the calmest months were March and April.

In Baffin's Bay, February, March, and April, were the most windy months, and June and July the calmest.

On 30th Sept., 1858, a tube, containing a Thermometer, was sunk 2 ft. 2 inches into the ground; the earth for the first six inches was not frozen, but all below that depth had evidently never thawed. In a few days this spot was covered to a depth of 5 ft. with snow, and remained so until the middle of June, 1859. During this period the buried Thermometer indicated the following temperatures:—

Dates.	Buried Thermometer.	Mean Temperature of the Air during the seven days preceding each observation.
1858.	°	°
13th November	+16	−10·7
11th December	+12·9	−29·8
1859.		
8th January	+7	−36·8
12th February	+3	−34·1
10th March	+0·5	−17
7th April	+1·1	−3·5
7th May	+2·8	+5·9
4th June	+5	+26·5

It may, therefore, be assumed that the earth at that depth reached its minimum temperature—zero—on 16th March.

I subjoin an abstract of the 'Fox' temperatures; also one of mean annual temperatures at various stations where arctic expeditions have wintered, having obtained them from published accounts, or from the officers employed. They are given more in detail with the 'Fox' observations in the 'Smithsonian Contributions;' many valuable additions could be furnished from the registers kept in Greenland, also from Moravian stations in Labrador, and from the various Hudson's Bay Company's trading posts.

TABLE OF MEAN MONTHLY TEMPERATURES OF THE AIR IN THE SHADE, ALSO THE RANGE OF THE THERMOMETER; REGISTERED ON BOARD THE 'FOX.'

Date.	Lat., N.	Long., W.	Mean Temperature, Fahr.	Range.
1857.	°	°	°	°
August	74	59	+34·6	28
September	75	65	19·5	38
October	75	68	5·7	45
November	74	69	− 4·7	63
December	74	67	21·6	41
1858.				
January	73	64	25	38
February	71	61	15·5	50
March	69	59	3·4	59
April	66	58	+ 8	64
May	69	54	29·9	35
June	75	60	36	22
July	74	76	36·6	18
August	73	88	34·5	20

IN PORT KENNEDY—Latitude 72° N., Longitude 94° W.

September	..	..	25·1	30
October	..	..	7·1	49
November	..	..	−11·9	48
December	..	..	33·7	31
1859.				
January	..	..	34·4	34
February	..	..	36·9	36
March	..	..	17·4	51
April	..	..	2	58
May	..	..	+15·9	35
June	..	..	35·7	32
July	..	..	40	25
August	..	..	36·7	17

TABLE OF MEAN ANNUAL TEMPERATURES REGISTERED BY MODERN ARCTIC EXPEDITIONS AT THEIR WINTERING STATIONS.

Temp., Fahr.	Locality.	Lat., N.	Long., W.	Date.
°		°	°	
+ 9·63	Winter Island	66¼	83¼	1821–2
5·96	Repulse Bay..	66·32	87	1846–7
3·0	Cambridge Bay	69	105¼	1852–3
5·51	Igloolik..	69¼	81¾	1822–3
6·0	Felix Harbour	70	92	1829–30
2·5	Sheriff's Harbour ..	70	91¾	1830–31
5·0	Camden Bay..	70·8	145½	1853–4
7·3	Point Barrow	71·36	156	1852–3–4
8·1	Walker Bay..	71·36	117⅔	1851–2
2·0	Port Kennedy	72·1	94¼	1858–9
1·0	Prince of Wales' Strait	72·47	117½	1850–51
4·0	Port Bowen	73·14	89	1824–5
1·1	Port Leopold	73·51	90	1848–9
1·5	Mercy Bay	74·6	118¼	1851–2–3
0·5	Griffith Island	74·34	95⅓	1850–51
− 2·5	Cape Cockburn	74·41	101⅓	1853–4
+ 3·0	Beechey Island	74·43	92	1852–3–4
0·4	Winter Harbour.. ..	74·47	111	1819–20
0·9	Dealy Island	74·56	108¾	1852–3
− 1·8	Wellington Channel ..	75·31	92⅓	1853–4
+ 4·3	Wolstenholme Sound	76½	69	1849–50
− 0·6	Northumberland Sound	76·52	97	1852–3
− 2·2	Rensselaer Harbour ..	78·37	70⅔	1853–4–5

MAGNETISM.—Under this head are included observations for inclination, declination, intensity, and hourly deviation of declination. The hourly observations made at Port Kennedy were continued throughout a period of five months; they have been discussed by Major-General Sir Edward Sabine, R.A., President of the Royal Society, and are published in the 'Philosophical Transactions' for 1863, vol. 153. The entire series of magnetical observations have been laid before the Royal Society; those for inclination possess more than ordinary interest, as many of them were taken in the vicinity of the Magnetic Pole; they were made with one of Gambey's 9½-inch dip circles. The only other magnetic observations which we possess from this interesting locality were made by the late Sir James C. Ross, in 1830–31, when that talented officer discovered the Magnetic Pole.

AURORAS.—Observations on the Aurora, its influence on an electroscope, periods of maximum and minimum atmospheric electricity, &c., by Surgeon David Walker, M.D., are contained in Appendix No. VI. of former editions of this work.

POLARISCOPE.—Observations made with a polariscope during the voyage by Surgeon D. Walker, M.D., will be found in the 'Proceedings of the Royal Society' for 1859-60, vol. x. p. 558.

TIDES.—The tidal observations made at Port Kennedy have been placed in the hands of the Rev. Professor Samuel Haughton, F.R.S., who is engaged in the discussion of several sets of similar observations made in various parts of the arctic regions where our searching expeditions have wintered. In Appendix No. V. of the former editions of the 'Fox Voyage' will be found Dr. Haughton's notes "on the Tidal Streams of the Arctic Archipelago;" and in the 'Philosophical Transactions of the Royal Society' for 1861-2, his discussion of the tidal observations made at Port Leopold in 1848-9.

ICE.—Observations on ice, by Surgeon D. Walker, M.D., were published in the 'Royal Dublin Society's Journal' for 1860, vol. ii. p. 376.

ICE MOVEMENTS.—*On the Effect of Wind in producing Ice Movement.*—In the 1st and 5th chapters I have noticed, in the former, the Spitzbergen current, in the latter, the probable result of wind, as effecting the drift of the 'Fox.'

The Spitzbergen or Polar current sets round Cape Farewell, follows the trend of the shore to the northwest, bearing heavy ice as far, usually, as 65° N., and still continues northward until deflected off shore to the westward, apparently by banks which lie in 67° N. Here uniting with such current as sets out of Baffin's Bay, it curves southwestward, runs swiftly past Cape Walsingham, and as the "Labrador current" continues its course along that coast towards Newfoundland.

It is obvious that, to estimate the volume of water setting out of Baffin's Bay, our observations should be limited to the north of 67°.

The winter drift of the 'Terror,' in 1836-7, from Frozen Strait through Hudson Strait into the Atlantic, appears to me to be due to wind alone, since a polar current is there an impossibility, and that any considerable current—during winter—issues from Hudson's Bay, is highly improbable. From all that I have been able to observe during our winter drift down the middle of Baffin's Bay to Davis' Strait, the ice movement was almost entirely due to wind, and not to an arctic or polar current.

As this is not the generally received opinion, I give a carefully pre pared table of our monthly winds and drifts. The direction of duration of the wind has been worked out like a day's work, the number of hours upon each point of the compass being regarded as miles. The direction of the force has been similarly obtained, but regarding the accumulated hourly force (according to the Beaufort notation), upon each point, as so many miles. The directions of duration and of force thus obtained nearly agree; and, compared with our true drift, show at once whether other causes were at work in effecting the movement of the ice.

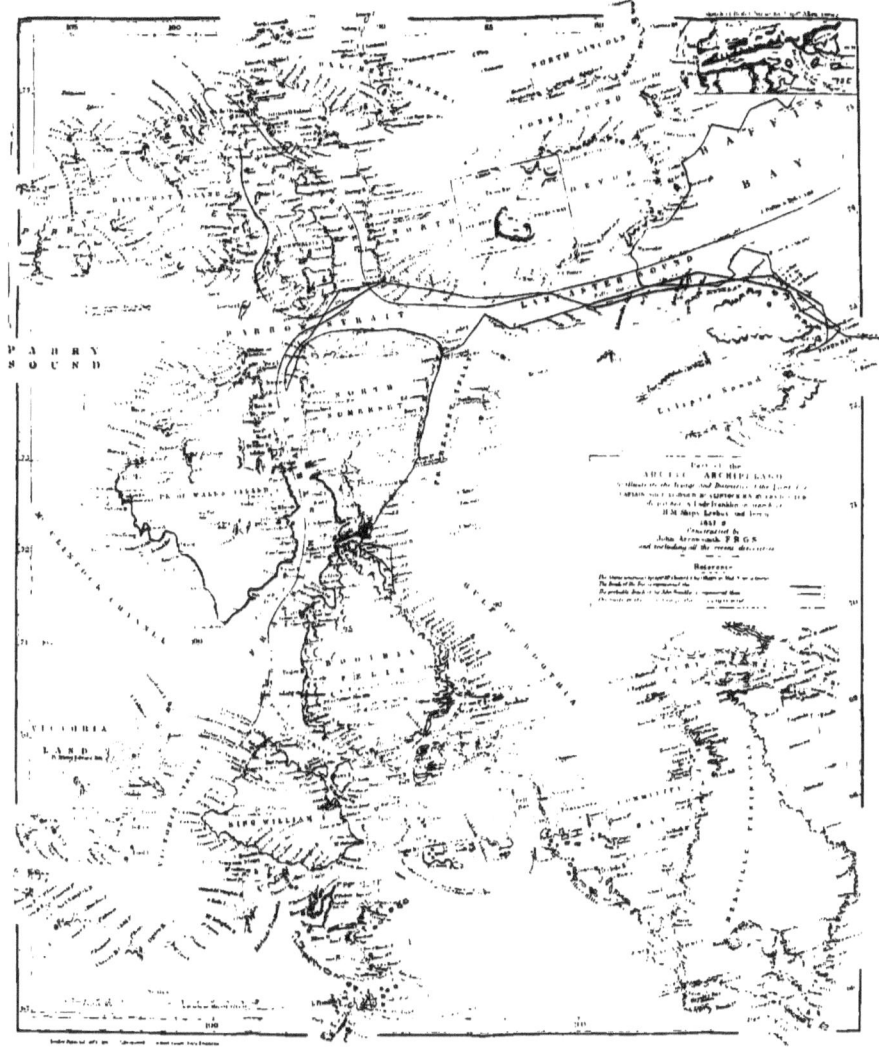

No. II. APPENDIX. 327

To ascertain whether our mileage was proportional to the strength of the prevailing wind, I used a simple formula dependent thereon, which answered the purpose sufficiently well.

Formula. $\left\{ \begin{array}{c} \text{No. of hours in excess} \\ \text{of prevailing wind} \end{array} \right\} \times \text{its mean force} \times \frac{1}{10} = \text{drift of free packed ice.}$

For example: March, 1858. $\frac{246 \times 4\cdot 05}{10} = 99\cdot 6$ miles.

An ordinary fresh breeze (force 5), when blowing in the direction of open water, would usually drift the pack twelve miles in twenty-four hours.

A TABLE OF THE WINDS AND ICE-DRIFTS EXPERIENCED BY THE ARCTIC SEARCHING YACHT 'FOX.'

Date.	Mean Force of all Winds.	Direction of Prevailing Wind.		Wind in Prevailing Quarter.		True Drift.	Drift from Empirical Formulæ.	REMARKS.
		Of Duration.	Of Force.	Hours in Excess.	Mean Force.			
1857. Sept.	3·18	° N. 17 W.	° N. 8 E.	N. to W. 126 hrs.	2·83	° ′ S. 40 W. 37	° ′ S. 12 E. 35	In Melville Bay, 25 to 40 miles off shore. Ice-drift affected by local causes.
Oct.	3·05	N. 42 W.	N. 13 W.	144 ,,	2·85	N. 75 W. 49	S. 28 E. 41	Water to the W. and N.W., and ice free to move in those directions; much ice to the southward.
Nov.	3·84	N. 73 W.	N. 75 W.	224 ,,	3·83	S. 9 W. 32	S. 74 E. 85	Similar to last month, but ice accumulating to the northward.
Dec.	2·88	N. 62 W.	N. 61 W.	244 ,,	3·18	S. 47 E. 68	S. 61 E. 77	In mid-channel; a tendency to drift westward; the cause unknown.
1858. Jan.	3·41	N. 43 W.	N. 44 W.	252 ,,	4·58	S. 45 E. 113	S. 44 E. 116	In mid-channel.
Feb.	4·45	N. 28 W.	N. 26 W.	334 ,,	5·13	S. 5 E. 166	S. 27 E. 171	Parallel to the Greenland coast, and distant from it about 120 miles.
Mar.	3·96	N. 15 W.	N. 19 W.	246 ,,	4·05	S. 16 E. 94	S. 17 E. 100	As last month.
April, 17th	4·39	N. 11 W.	N. 11 W.	214 ,,	5·34	South 168	S. 11 E. 114	Parallel to the Greenland coast, but much nearer to the west land, which

appeared to deflect the ice eastward. Our near approach to the open sea may account for our rapid increase of drift; the ice appearing by the sounding line to drift more freely than heretofore. I could not ascertain the existence of current, up to this date.

INDEX.

INDEX.

A.

ADELAIDE BAY, 285.
Admiralty, supplies to the 'Fox,' 7.
Agnew River, the, 173.
Ale, freezing of, 68.
Aluik, in East Greenland, 194.
Amusements of the seamen, 39.
Ancient beach-marks, 262, 264.
Anderson, Mr., his searching expedition, 2.
Araneet, the Esquimaux, 137.
Arcedeckne, Andrew, Esq., 7; *footnote*, 174.
—— Island, 174, 217.
Arctic highlanders, or northern Esquimaux, 67, 113-14, 194.
—— Medal conferred upon the crew of the 'Fox,' 309.
—— palates, 51.
—— regions, drifting out of, 79.
Atānekerdlūk, fossilized forest of, 19, 99.
Aurora, the, remarks on, 63; *Appendix*, 325.
Awāhlah, the Ponds Bay Esquimaux Chief, 135, 139.
Ayweelik, the land of, 138.

B.

BAALS RIVER, 11, 18.
Back, Admiral Sir George, 252, 256.
Baffin, William, the Navigator, 121.
—— Bay, 24, 288, 292.
Banks Land, 128.
Barrow, John, Esq., 145.
—— Strait, 143, 147.
—— Inlet, 233-4.
Bathurst, Cape Walter, 126.
Bear, the arctic, 80-82, 125, 142, 173, 288-92.
——, fight with the dogs, 74.
——, hunt by night, 48.
Bear's flesh, 82, 288.
—— blubber, 208.

CAIRN.

Bearded seal, shot, 158, 167.
Beechey Island, Depot, &c., 143-4, 147, 291.
Beer, receipts for making it on board, 199.
——, sugar, 181, 199.
Bellot, Lieutenant, tablet in memory of, 145.
—— Strait, 153, 162, 165, 167, 274, 280.
—— Strait, boat exploration in, 165.
Beset, in Melville Bay, 31.
——, off Cape Hay, 124.
Bird, Cape, 165-6, 168, 173, 271.
Birthdays, unusual prevalence of, &c., 277-8.
Blackwell, Thomas, Ship's Steward, the death of, 268.
Board of Trade, contributions to our voyage, 7.
Boat, the, found, 248.
Booth Point, meet an Esquimaux family at, 229.
Boothia, western coast of, 170, 203.
——, natives of, 173, 203, 218.
Botany of the voyage, *Appendix No. II.*, 322.
Brand, Mr. George, the death of, 185.
Brent geese, 158, 271, 273.
Brentford Bay, 153, 161, 285.
Buchan Island, nearly wrecked at, 105.
Burial in the pack, 59.
Bullen, Cape, 143.
Burgomasters (*Larus Glaucous*), 116, 176.
Bushnan Island, 108.
Button Point, 126.

C.

CAIRNS, 124, 235, 242-3, 257, 263, 277, 300.
Cairn, Sir John Ross's, 161.
——, Simpson's, 238, 241.

INDEX.

CANINE APPETITE.

Canine appetite, 37, 40, 45.
—— force, our, 188, 196.
Cape York, 37, 110, 112.
Cave, description of a seal's, 75.
Charts, Esquimaux, 129, 136–9.
Christian, the Esquimaux dog-driver, 20, 33, 91, 93, 270, 275, 304.
Christmas Day, in the pack, 64.
——, our second, 189.
Clavering, Captain, R.N., 192.
Clay River, 100.
Clear of the pack, 87.
Coalfields of Greenland, 21, 99.
Coastline, extent of new, explored by our parties, 296.
Cobourg Island, 120.
Cod fishing, 17.
—— oil, *foot-note*, 18.
Collinson, Captain Richard, R.N., C.B., 62, 188, 223, 256, 266, 291, 295.
Comet, the, seen, 169.
Couch, the late Lieutenant Edward, R.N., *Introduction*, xlii ; 253 ; *Appendix*, 318.
Cranes, seen, 128.
Cresswell Bay, 211, 285–6.
Crimson Cliffs, the, 110, 112, 116, 119.
Croker Bay, 122.
Crow's-nest, the, 30, 42.
Crozier, Cape, 248, 260.
——, the late Captain F. R. M., R.N., *Introduction*, xxxiv ; 226, 246–7, 253 ; *Appendix*, 320.
Cunningham, Mount, 92.

D.

DANISH HOLIDAY in Greenland, 91.
Death, the first on board, 59.
—— of the Engineer, Mr. G. Brand, 185.
—— of the Ship's Steward, Thos. Blackwell, 268.
Declinometer, the, 213.
Deer. *See* Reindeer.
De Haven, Lieutenant, U. S. Navy, 78–9.
Depot (or Transition) Bay, 153, 154, 159, 161, 277.

ESQUIMAUX.

Des Vœux, the late Lieutenant C. F., R.N., *Introduction*, xlii ; 244, 257.
De Ros Islet, 121.
Deuchars, Captain, 106–7, 127, 140.
Diana, the whaleship, 126.
Dietary scale, our, 198.
Disco Island, 19, 21, 292.
——, the belles of, 304.
—— Fiord, 20, 307.
Dogs, Esquimaux, their nightly foraging expeditions, 48, 55.
——, how fed, 37, 52.
——, lose five of them, 81.
——, the, 22, 29, 38, 45, 114, 174, 196, 271, 307.
Dog-driving, 212, 233–4.
Drift of the 'Fox,' 89 ; *Appendix No. II.*, 327.
Duck Island, 106.
Durbin Island, coal said to exist there, 98.

E.

EAGLES, seen as far north as Upernivik, 45.
Earthquake in Greenland, 92.
East Greenland, our limited knowledge of, 192.
Egede, Hans, the missionary father of Greenland, 18, 102.
Elberg, the chief trader, or Governor, of Holsteinborg, 91.
Electric current, the, observed, 64.
Emma, the whaleship, 101.
Epitaph, the, at Beechey Island, 146.
Equipment, sledging, 201, 217.
Erebus Bay, Beechey Island, 144.
Ermine, 132, 169, 175, 177, 210, 273.
Escape, the, out of the pack, 86.
Evening school, our, 46.
Evaporation, through ice, 63.
Esquimaux, in British Possessions, 13, 97.
—— of Greenland, remarks on the, 13, 15, 192–194.
—— of Cape York (arctic highlanders), 113, 114, 194.
—— of Cape Horsburgh, 122.

ESQUIMAUX.

Esquimaux of Boothia Felix, 173, 203, 218.
—— of King William's Island, 226-9.
—— of Ponds Bay, 126-41.
——, where alone no traces of them were seen, 260.
——, charts, 129, 136-9.
——, their tradition of the Scandinavians, 276.
——, their information of the Franklin Expedition, 204-6, 220, 227-9, 301.

F.

FAIRHOLME, the late Lieutenant J. W., R.N., *Introduction*, xxxix; 226, 253; *Appendix*, 318.
Falcons, 167, 169, 174.
False Strait, 168, 264, 286.
Fanshawe, Cape, 125.
Farewell, Cape, passed by the 'Fox,' 11, 307.
Felix, Cape, 222, 260, 299, 300.
Fiskernaes, arrive at, 16, 17.
Fitzjames, the late Captain James, R.N., *Introduction*, xxxvii; 246.
Fliescher, chief trader or Governor, 22, 23, 101.
Flour, a barrel of, found, 211.
Four-River Point, 165, 170.
Fossilized Forest, 19, 99.
'Fox,' the yacht, purchase and equipment of, 4.
'Fox' Islets, 170, 274.
——, the arctic, remarks on, &c., 61, 62, 70, 194, 200, 208, 300.
Fox's Hole, 159.
Franklin, Lady, resolves to make a final search, 3.
——, Lady, letter of instructions from, 9.
——, Sir John, *Introduction*, xxix; 226, 246, 253; *Appendix*, 318, 320.
——, Sir John, and his companions, monument to, London, *Introduction*, xlviii.
——, Sir John, and his companions, tablet to, at Beechey Island, 146.
——, Cape, 255.

GRAVES.

Franklin, Sir John, Strait (or Channel), 168, 209, 292.
—— Search, miles sledged over, &c., in the, 297.
Franklin's ships, Esquimaux report of their fate, 206, 220, 227, 301.
Frederickshaab, arrive at, &c., 13, 14.
Freezing of salt water, 54.
Frobishers Strait, 97.
Frost-cracks in the ice, 186.
Funeral on the ice, 59.
Funnels, ice forms in the, 191.
Fury Point (or Beach), 152, 209, 211, 212, 287.

G.

GALE HAMKES BAY, Esquimaux seen there, 193.
Game lists for several arctic localities, and remarks on, 281-2.
Garnets, 17.
Garry, Cape, 212, 280.
Gateshead Island, 170, 295.
Geology of the voyage, &c., *Appendix No. II.*, 322.
Gilbert Sound, 17.
Glacier, the great, of Greenland, 12, 25-7.
—— of Kaparŏktolik, 132.
Gladman Point, a cairn near, 235.
Godhaab, 17, 18.
Godhavn, 19, 99, 145, 302-7.
Goldner's preserved meat tins, 135.
Goodsir, the late Dr. H. D. S., R.N., *Introduction*, xli; 253.
Gore, the late Commander Graham, R.N., *Introduction*, xxxviii; 244-6, 252-3, 257, 315.
Government, declines to renew the search, 3.
——, contributes stores, &c. to the 'Fox,' 6.
Graach, Captain, Royal Danish Navy, 192, 194.
Graham Moore, Cape, 128, 137.
Grampus, or Killer, 41-2.
Graves, 185, 205, 228, 286.
——, the difficulty of making, in frozen ground, 254.

GREAT FISH RIVER.

Great Fish (or Back) River, *Preface*, viii; 2, 170, 230, 313.
Green, W., *Appendix*, 317.
Greenland, its south-west coast, trade, population, &c., 11, 13.
——, its eastern coast, 192-4.
Guy Fawkes' day, in the pack, 50.

H.

HALFWAY ISLAND, 165, 270.
Halkett, boat, 127.
Hall, Capt. C. F., his search for the Franklin Expedition, *Introduction*, xxxvi.
Hampton, Robert, 144, 230-1, 233.
Hare, the arctic, 93, 169, 178, 276.
—— Island, coal found there, 99.
Harness Jack, 45.
Harvey, William, 55, 91, 152, 272.
Hay, Cape, 124, 137, 288.
Hayes, Dr. I. I., *foot-note*, 67; *List of Illustrations*, xxiv.
Hazard Inlet, 153, 166, 280.
Heather, William, 259; *Appendix*, 317.
Hedges, William, 259; *Appendix*, 317.
Heroine, whaleship, 95.
Herschel, Cape, 235, 238.
——, Cape, Simpson's cairn on, 238, 241.
Highlanders, arctic (northern Esquimaux), 110-15.
Hobday, George, 269.
Hobson, Lieut. W. R., R.N., appointed to the 'Fox,' 5, 174, 177-8, 182, 214, 244, 268, 298, 309.
Hodgson, the late Lieutenant G. H., R.N., *Introduction*, xxxix.
Holiday in Greenland, 90.
Holsteinborg, 90, 92-4.
Home Bay, supposed to be a strait, 97.
Hornby, the late Lieut. F. J., R.N., *Introduction*, xlii; 253, 259; *Appendix*, 317.
Horsburgh, Cape, 121.
Hotham, Cape, land at, 148.
Human skeleton found near Cape Herschel, 235-6.

JOURNEYS.

Human skeletons found in the boat, 251.
Hurd, Cape, 144.
Huts. *See* Snow-huts.

I.

ICE, experiments with, to obtain fresh water, 53-4.
——, the middle, or main pack, of Baffin Bay, 23-4.
——, the, about King William's Island, 233, 243, 248, 261, 299.
——, the, in Prince Regent Inlet, 161, 277.
——, the, in Sir John Franklin Strait, 166, 168, 173, 182, 208, 265.
——, the, ocean-formed polar, 265, 299.
——, the, observation on, by Dr. Walker, *Appendix No. II.*, 326.
—— blasting, 34.
——, movements and noises, 47, 77; *Appendix No. II.*, 326-7.
——, artillery, 51.
——, nip, 76, 115.
——, navigation, uncertainty of, 97, 107.
——, quake, 72.
——, tournament, 85.
Icebergs, the grounded, 36-7.
—— drifting with us, 53, 71, 78.
—— yield fresh water, 30.
Icicles issuing from the stove-pipes, 191.
Igloolik, 129-30, 136-7, 139.
Inglefield, Captain E. A., R.N., 16, 130.
'Intrepid,' H.M.S., probable traces of, 107.
Irving, the late Lieut. John, R.N, *Introduction*, xl; 246.

J.

JANE, the whaleship, 95.
Jones, Wm., the dog-driver, 50.
—— Sound, 121.
Journeys, departure of Hobson on, 174, 178, 214.
——, return of Hobson from, 177, 182, 268.

JOURNEYS.

Journeys, M'Clintock's, 200-7, 214-65, 270-2.
——, departure of Young on, 200, 209, 269, 270.
——, return of Young from, 208, 211, 270, 272.
——, the earliest spring, 197, 200-8.
——, Hobson's reports of his, 182, 298-301.
——, Young's reports of his, 208, 269, 292-6.
——, some particulars of sledging, 297-8.

K.

KAL-LEK, the bald Esquimaux, 122.
Kane, Dr. E. K., boat-party from his expedition, 66.
——, Dr. E. K., his observations on melted sea-ice, 53.
Kaparōktolik, 127, 131, 136, 138.
Kayak, the Esquimaux canoe, or, 21, 95, 113, 137, 193, 278.
Kennedy, Mr. William, 153, 157, 170, 200.
——, Port, 170, 174, 279, 285.
Killer, the, or Grampus, 41.
King William's Island (or Land), 160, 170, 206, 214, 255, 262, 300, 312.

L.

LAKE; Macgregor Laird, 166, 200, 265, 271, 286.
Lancaster Sound, 122, 143.
Lapis ollaris, the (Potstone), 132.
Lemming, 132, 169, 176, 210, 290.
Leopold, Port, 151, 209, 287.
Levesque Harbour, in Brentford Bay, 157.
Le Vesconte, the late Lieut. H. T. D., R.N.; *Introduction*, xxxix; 253; *Appendix*, 318.
Lichtenfels, Moravian missionary station of, 16.
Lightning, vivid flash of, 174.
Limestone Island, the 'Fox' sails past, 148.

MORAVIAN MISSIONS.

List of officers of Franklin's Expedition, *Introduction*, xxviii.
Little, the late Commander Edw., *Introduction*, xxxix.
Little Auk, the, or Rotchie, 116, 123.
Long Island, 157, 170.
Loom soup, 128.
Looms and Loomeries, 120, 125, 128.
Lunar phenomena, 59.
Lyon, Captain, R.N., his attempted journey, 296.

M.

M'CLINTOCK CHANNEL, *Preface*, xiv; 295.
M'Clure, Sir Robert, *Preface*, xii; 128, 258, 267, 313.
Macgregor Laird Lake, 166, 200, 265, 271, 286.
M'Donald, the late Dr. Alex., R.N., *Introduction*, xli; 205, 226, 318, 320, 321.
Magnetic, the, observatory, 178, 181, 189.
—— observations, 223, 263; *Appendix No. II.*, 325.
—— Pole, the, 170, 173, 203, 222, 263.
Maguire, Capt. Rochfort, R.N., 8.
Makkak's Elvin, River, 100.
Mark, W., 259; *Appendix*, 317.
Matty Island, 224, 226.
Melville Bay, 24-5, 108-9.
—— Island, 176, 187, 243, 258, 281, 299.
Mercury, the, frozen, 196, 201.
Meteor, a, seen, 46.
Meteorology of the voyage, *Appendix No. II.*, 322.
Midwinter day, 64.
Montreal Island, 214, 228, 230-3, 313.
Monument, the, at Beechey Island, 145.
——, the national, to Franklin and his companions, *Introduction*, xlviii.
Moravian missions in Greenland, 18.

INDEX. 333

MOUSE.

Mouse, one found alive on board, 169.
Mouth, the, of an Esquimaux, 22.
Murchison, Sir Roderick I., *Preface by him*, 3, 276.
Musk-oxen, observations, &c. on, 60, 158, 175, 281-4.
Mustard and cress, the growth of, &c., 198, 277.

N.

NARWHALS, and narwhals' horns, 51, 130, 139.
Native auxiliaries, our, 38.
Natives of Boothia, first meeting with, &c., 203-7.
—— of King William's Island, 226-8.
—— of Cape York (arctic highlanders), 110.
—— of Ponds Inlet, 126.
Navy-board Inlet, 126, 128, 130, 132, 136.
Nets for catching seals, 187-8.
New Herrnhut, Moravian mission at, 18.
New Year's Day, 65, 189.
Noises from ice-movements, 47.
North Water, the, 115.
North-West Passage, remarks on the, 265-7.
Noursak, 100.

O.

OBSERVATIONS, scientific, Reports &c. on, *Appendix No. II.*, 321.
Ogle, Point, 230, 233.
Officers, list of, &c. of Franklin's expedition, *Introduction*, xxviii.
Olrik, Herr C. S. M., Inspector of North Greenland, 19, 98, 302.
Ommanney, Capt., R.N., first traces discovered by, &c., 1, 147, 295.
Omenak's Fiord, 101.
Oomiak, or women's boat, 15.
Oonalee, the Boothian Esquimaux, 206, 218, 220-2.
Oot-loo-lik, the stranded ship at, 220.
Open water in Bellot Strait all the winter, 190, 196-7, 274.
Organ, our, 43, 304.
Orkney Isles, the shores of, 10.

PORT KENNEDY.

Osborn, Capt. Sherrard, R.N., 197, 289, 295.
Osmer, the late C. H., Esq., R.N., *Introduction*, xli; *Appendix*, 317.
Owls, 169, 194, 278.
Ow-wang-nooot, the Ponds Bay native, 137, 139.
Ozone, experiments to detect the presence of, 46.

P.

PACK, the polar, 265, 299, 300.
——, release from the, 86.
Paraselenæ, 59.
Parry, Sir Edward, 85, 124, 126, 130, 138, 243, 299.
Passage, northern, across Baffin Bay, 24.
——, southern, 24.
——, middle, 24.
——, the, North-West, its discovery, *Preface*, xii; *Introduction*, xlviii; 267.
Peel Sound (or Strait), 151, 166, 168.
Peddie, the late Dr. J. S., R.N., *Introduction*, xli.
Peglar, Henry, his certificate, &c., deciphered, 310; *Appendix No. I.*, 320.
Pemmican, its composition, 6.
—— Rock, 167, 174, 200, 272.
Pendulum, experiments, 46.
—— Islands, 193.
Pentland Firth, the 'Fox' passes through, 10.
Petersen, Carl, appointed to the 'Fox,' *Preface*, ix; 6.
——, Carl, his skill as an ice-pilot, &c., 33.
——, Carl, his sufferings in Dr. Kane's expedition, 66.
Philpots, Dr. E. P., his interesting information, *foot-notes*, 121, 184.
Pitcher, James, gets scurvy, 197.
Ponds Bay (or Inlet), 119, 126, 131, 137, 142.
Port Kennedy, 170, 174, 279, 285.
——, observations on the temperature at, *Appendix No. II.*, 322.

PORT LEOPOLD.

Port Leopold, 151, 209, 287.
Possession Bay, 125.
—— Point, 153, 161.
Prince Patricks Land (or Island), 176, 299.
—— Regent Inlet, 160, 161.
—— of Wales' Land, 170, 208, 292.
'Princess Charlotte,' the, destroyed by the ice, 107.
Prospects for a winter in the pack, 38.
Proven, settlement of, 22.
Ptarmigan, 181, 187, 190, 200.

Q.

'QUEEN,' whaleship, winters in Baffin Bay, *foot-note*, 121 ; 284.

R.

RAE, Dr., his information of the Franklin expedition, *Preface*, viii ; 1, 2, 206, 237.
——, Dr., Esquimaux information relating to, 138, 139, 204.
Raven, the arctic, 39, 93, 181, 307.
Records, the Franklin, 214, 244, 257.
—— of our own Expedition, 145, 148, 152, 258, 277.
——, cases, 257.
Redpole, the smallest of arctic birds, 81.
Red snow, 116.
Reindeer, 28, 92, 124, 158, 167, 175, 177, 186, 233.
Relics, the, obtained of Franklin's expedition, 205, 219, 226, 231, 248, 259, 314 ; *Appendix No. I.*
——, personal, of fifteen individuals obtained, 253, 259 ; *Appendix No. I.*
Rensselaer Harbour, 66.
Repulse Bay, 138, 141, 204.
'Resolute,' H.M.S., her ice-drift, &c., 81.
Revolving storms, 53, 65, 72.
Richards, Captain G. H., R.N., 289.
Riley, Cape, we arrive at, 143.
Rink, Dr. Henry, Inspector of South Greenland, 13, 14.

SOUP.

Ross, Sir James C., 151; *foot-notes*, 153, 260; 173, 205, 246, 255, 296.
——, Sir John, 153, 173, 266.
Rotchies (*Alca alle*), 116, 123.
Royal Society, the, contributions of to the 'Fox,' 7.
Royal Yacht Clubs, the 'Fox' received into, 7.

S.

SABINE, Cape, 261.
——, Captain, now Major-General Sir Edward, 192 ; *Appendix No. II.*, 325.
Sailor's expressions, 48.
Samuel, our Esquimaux dog-driver, 99, 212, 269, 277, 304.
School, opened on board, 46.
Scoresby's Journal, 192, 193.
—— Sound, 193.
Scott, Robert, death of, 59, 60.
——, Inlet, supposed to be a strait, 97.
Scurvy, cases of, 197, 268.
Seals, how to kill, 32, 33, 275.
——, the liver, flesh, and blubber of, 32, 50, 75, 81, 108, 275.
——, bearded, 158, 167.
——, of the species *Phoca hespida*, 72.
——, remarks upon, &c., 75.
Separation Island, name changed to Arcedeckne Island, 174, 217.
Shark, the arctic, remarks on, 40.
Ships, Franklin's, Esquimaux account of their fate, 206, 220, 227, 301.
Sledges of the Boothian Esquimaux, 205, 206, 224.
—— seen at Ponds Inlet, 127, 135.
Smith Sound, the natives of, 192.
Snow bunting, 81.
—— crystals, 44.
—— huts, our, 62, 68, 202, 295.
—— huts, Esquimaux, 204, 219, 224-5, 230, 238, 242, 261, 263.
—— porches, 63, 187.
—— shoes, 178.
Snowy peak, near Melville Bay, 39.
Soup, Loom, 128.

INDEX. 335

SPITZBERGEN.

Spitzbergen, incidental notices of, ice, &c. &c., 11, 12, 100, 184.
Stanley, the late Dr. S. S., R.N., *Introduction*, xl.
Stilwell Bay, 161.
Sugar, a supply of, obtained from Fury Beach, 211, 212.
—— beer, 181, 199.
Sun, departure of the, 49, 186.
——, return of the, 68, 196.
Swinburne, Cape, 292.

T.

TABLET to the memory of Franklin, and his companions, 145, 146.
—— to the memory of Lieutenant Bellot, 145.
Tallard Bank, the, 12.
Tasmania Islands, group of the, 220, 264, 265.
Temperature, the mean, throughout early spring journey, 207.
——, the, observations on, at Port Kennedy; see 'Meteorology,' *Appendix No. II.*
——, sudden changes of, 53, 194.
——, effects of extremely low, 191, 201.
Tents, Esquimaux, 17, 114, 131, 193, 242.
——, our travelling, 195, 208, 217, 222-3, 291.
Thomas, the late Lieutenant Robert, R.N., 253.
Thunder, two claps of, 280.
Tides, at Bellot Strait, 157; *Appendix No. II.*, 326.
Traces found of Franklin's expedition at eight places, *Appendix No. I.*
—— left about Port Kennedy of the 'Fox' expedition, 286.
Traps for foxes and ermines, 177, 181, 210.
Travelling, preparations for, costume, equipment, 195, 201, 217.
—— routine, 202.
Travels of the Esquimaux, 141.
Trout, 20, 274, 277.

WOLF.

'Truelove,' the whaleship, 302, and *foot-note*.

U.

UPERNIVIK, settlement, 22, 53, 101, 102.
—— Bay, 98.
Umingmak Island (musk-ox), 192.
Uria Brunnichii (*foot-note*), 120.

V.

VICTORIA, Cape, 200, 204, 222, 263.
—— Strait, 265, 299.
Victory, Point, the record found at, 244.
——, Point, 254, 256-9; *foot-note*, 260; 261, 301.
——, the, Sir John Ross's discovery ship, 205.
Village, Esquimaux, 131, 226.

W.

WALKER, Dr. D., of the 'Fox,' 6, 46, 64, 158, 210, 273, 276.
——, Mount, 162, 279.
Waigat Strait, the, sail through it, 21, 99.
Walrus, the, 115.
Warrender, Cape, 122, 124.
Washington, Capt. J., R.N., a bay named after him, 257.
Waterspace, in Bellot Strait, 190, 196-7, 274.
Whale-bone, 98, 139.
Whale-fish Islands, 94.
Whale-ships communicated with, 95, 101, 106, 126.
Whales, the bones of, at Port Kennedy, 285.
—— at Ponds Bay, 142.
—— skin, pickled, 99, 272, 287.
White whales, 41, 286.
Willocks, *foot-note*, 120.
Willow-grouse, 187, 233, 248, 264.
Winter quarters, take up our, 175.
Wintering, in the pack, prospect of, 34.
Wolf, the arctic, 175, 183-4, 273.

WOLSTENHOLME SOUND.

Wolstenholme Sound, 34, 119.
Wolverine, the, 175.
Women Islands, 102.
Wood, Sir Charles, declines to renew the Government search, 3.
Wrecks, 129–30, 135, 137 ; *foot-note*, 138; 141, 227.
Wrottesley, the late Lord, *foot-note*, 49 ; *foot-note*, 183.
—— Inlet, 183, 203.
Wylie, Fiord, 93.

ZOOLOGY.

Y.

YACHT FLAG, the Royal Harwich, 68, 214.
York, Cape, 37, 110, 114.
Young, Captain Allen, 5, 52, 200, 208–9, 211, 269–72, 292–6.

Z.

ZOOLOGY of the voyage, notes, &c. on, *Appendix No. II.*, 321.

THE END.

LONDON: PRINTED BY WILLIAM CLOWES AND SONS, STAMFORD STREET, AND CHARING CROSS.

www.ingramcontent.com/pod-product-compliance
Lightning Source LLC
Chambersburg PA
CBHW032021220426
43664CB00006B/324